ASKHAM BRY.
YORK

This book is due for return on or before the last date shown below

To renew please telephone (01904) 772234
with your library card number.

Blackstone's

Emergency Planning, Crisis and Disaster Management

Brian Dillon

Consultant Editors

Ian Dickinson
Professor Keith Still
John Williamson

Second edition

OXFORD
UNIVERSITY PRESS

OXFORD

UNIVERSITY PRESS

Great Clarendon Street, Oxford, OX2 6DP,
United Kingdom

Oxford University Press is a department of the University of Oxford.
It furthers the University's objective of excellence in research, scholarship,
and education by publishing worldwide. Oxford is a registered trade mark of
Oxford University Press in the UK and in certain other countries

Published in the United States of America by Oxford University Press
198 Madison Avenue, New York, NY 10016, United States of America

British Library Cataloguing in Publication Data
Data available

Library of Congress Control Number: 2014934942

ISBN 978–0–19–871290–9

Printed and bound by
CPI Group (UK) Ltd, Croydon, CR0 4YY

To all the emergency services and front line responders across all sectors for their dedication, commitment and bravery both physical and emotional, in particular those who are prepared to make those life-changing decisions without the benefit of hindsight.

Foreword by Ian Dickinson

Emergency Planning, as a dedicated and identified role in public and private organisations, has grown considerably in the last ten years and become established as a vital element of civil resilience. The role has been professionalised as an activity and the body of knowledge on which it relies has expanded greatly, particularly following the Civil Contingencies Act.

During my years as a police officer a well thumbed and often updated edition of *Blackstone's Police Law* was a permanent feature of my office library. It provided practical and ready access to the most relevant and necessary elements of police law that I needed without researching volumes of other texts.

Brian Dillon's *Blackstone's Emergency Planning, Crisis and Disaster Management* is likely to fulfil much the same role for Emergency Planners and be a reliable and often used source for those both new and experienced in the field.

It is a detailed but broad brush Emergency Planning reference which accurately brings together the essential elements of resilience and civil risk for those in this growing profession. Of course the activity of Emergency Planning in the UK relies much more on non-statutory guidance and established good practice than on clearly codified and established law. This book provides the statutory detail where necessary but also supports that with a clear summary of the broader doctrine base in each area of reference together with an outline of a straightforward route to self-learning of the most important or most relevant information. As a practitioner (and this book is written for practitioners) Brian has included a great deal of personal and practical advice throughout the text—the sort of 'critical friend' suggestions that are invaluable between professionals.

The style which Brian Dillon has adopted is also practical and direct: he uses straightforward, uncomplicated language and readily understood explanation that is familiar to those who are active in this field. He has not written the book as an academic text but rather a source of easy understanding of the breadth of Emergency Planning doctrine with more than adequate 'signposts' towards more detailed information if required.

Brian himself is a seasoned professional in his field and also spends time supporting postgraduate study of UK Resilience. He understands both the knowledge base detail as well as the way it may be applied. He brings both together in this book; a copy will become a permanent feature of my briefcase and I commend it to colleagues and students in the rapidly developing field of Emergency Planning.

Ian Dickinson
Associate lecturer, Cabinet Office
Emergency Planning College

Foreword by Professor Keith Still

'If history repeats itself, and the unexpected always happens, how incapable must Man be of learning from experience.'

George Bernard Shaw

I have had the pleasure of working with Brian, both as expert witness on a major safety case and as a fellow lecturer at the UK Cabinet Office Emergency Planning College for almost a decade. Brian is the emergency planning specialist with over 30 years experience and he has produced emergency plans for the police, prepared and delivered bespoke multi-agency training packages at all levels of the emergency management process, directed large-scale exercises and managed the implementation of the Civil Contingencies Act 2004.

Emergency planning requires a thorough understanding of all aspects of the process, from the initial risk and threat analysis to the development and testing of robust emergency plans. However, as Brian highlights throughout this book, it is not enough to develop a minimum or standard approach to the problems of emergency management. All too often we find pockets of isolated wisdom in key areas of emergency management that are known only to a few working in specific areas. What is required is both the vision and the imagination to encompass the wide spectrum of emergency management, to collate and disseminate best practices, outline the process and to provide a comprehensive guide for both novice and experienced professional alike. This book covers all of the above and to the appropriate depth required for a thorough appreciation of all aspects of emergency planning.

Keith Still
Institute of Civil Protection and
Emergency Management (FICPEM)

Foreword by John Williamson

Major emergency incidents occur very often without any warning and even those that do provide some warning (occasional natural disasters, for instance) frequently surprise us with their ferocity and destruction. The impact of terrorism has left us feeling vulnerable right across the world. There is very often a feeling of disbelief during the first phase of the incident. The only way to be prepared for these occurrences is to plan for their eventuality. Emergency planning has evolved from experiences of previous disasters and very often from the mistakes and omissions encountered along the way.

Major incidents and disasters bring all of the emergency services together and very often it will be the first time that these people will have worked together. Each organisation is used to working with its own people as a team, but very often the 'team' can experience difficulties when organisations come together. The problem can often be complicated because people do not understand or appreciate each other's role. They only really get together on the job and this is really not the place to learn.

The only way to achieve successful outcomes is to plan for them. Brian Dillon has provided us with a one stop shop for this planning. *Blackstone's Emergency Planning, Crisis and Disaster Management* provides everyone who might be involved in a major incident or disaster at any level with a complete guide. This guidance comes from someone who has been involved at the sharp end for many years. He uses his experience and vision to bring the emergency services together so that they can plan a cohesive strategy to deal with whatever might face them.

John Williamson
Institute of Fire Safety Managers

Preface

This edition of the Blackstone's Emergency Planning, Crisis and Disaster Management builds on the concepts and ideas contained in the first edition. It reflects changes in organisational structures and procedures, with some updates but maintains its original purpose and goal; to provide practical advice and guidance for those involved in emergency response and preparedness both within the public and private sectors. This is not theory, nor does it claim to follow an academic path, but rather it is a companion reference for the practitioner. Feedback has been incorporated from readers of the first edition and includes much new material relating to the role of the EPO operating in the private sector or acting as a consultant. This is as relevant to those in the emergency services and first responders as it is to those in the private sector, as it gives insights across a range occupational areas to enhance understanding and aid better collaboration and effectiveness. It also includes significant guidance on setting up a control room. Again, this is included not only to assist the private sector develop resilient arrangements but to offer a benchmark or assessment model for those reviewing or giving advice—this may be from the emergency services or local authority to a private operator. There is also additional material for those who may have to give evidence as an 'expert' witness around civil contingencies and the attributes required in that situation. This edition also focuses more upon the qualities of the EPO in articulating and communicating information as this forms an increasingly important role of the EPO as a skilled communicator.

The world of emergency preparedness is constantly changing and evolving and I have tried to reflect some insight into the areas that may prove a challenge in the years to come for the EPO and for those charged with taking command of emergency situations. I am grateful to those who have supported me in the completion of this edition, in particular my consultant editors for their knowledge, insight and their undoubted expertise. I would also like to thank both Peter Daniell and Lucy Alexander from Oxford University Press for their incredible patience and support.

Contents

Author

Brian Dillon MSc SBCI MIFSM is a former UK Police Inspector and was a Local Resilience Forum Secretary and Strategic Command Centre Manager for over 10 years. He was a police instructor responsible for both internal and external training in all aspects of risk crisis and disaster management. He has worked in the private sector as an emergency planning consultant and trainer. Brian is a specialist in exercise planning and management responsible for directing and umpiring major live play exercises, in particular civil nuclear emergencies where he represented the police service at Government level. His plans have been used to manage a wide range of emergencies including the Morecombe Bay cockling disaster of 2004.

Consultant Editors

Ian Dickinson BEd QPM is former Assistant Chief Constable of Lothian & Borders Police, where he served at the rank of chief officer for more than 20 years. He is an experienced Gold Commander, having led the Scottish response to terrorist incidents and many major events, incidents and civil emergencies in the Lothian and Borders Area. Since 2002 he has had responsibility for Specialist Operations, including the planning of the G8 summit, the Edinburgh Tattoo, Hogmanay, the Golf Open and civil nuclear resilience issues. He is an associate lecturer at the Cabinet Office Emergency Planning College.

Professor Keith Still FIMA FICPEM has 25 years of experience of crowd risk analysis, crowd modelling and simulations and both advising and planning for crowd safety in places of public assembly. Keith works around the world on projects such as the UK Royal Wedding crowd management planning, Olympic events, the annual pilgrimage to Makkah (Haj). Keith has lectured at Easingwold, the UK Cabinet Office Emergency Planning College, on human factors and safety considerations to the events industry for 15 years. He is a fellow of the Institute of Mathematics and its Applications (FIMA) and a fellow of the Institute of Civil Protection and Emergency Management (FICPEM)

John Williamson Dip FM, MSc, FIFSM is Chairman of the Institute of Fire Safety Managers. He is a former Assistant Chief Fire Officer and has commanded many major incidents, such as the Piper Alpha platform disaster. John is a Fellow of the Institution of Fire Engineers and provides expert evidence for the Courts. He also lectures on fire risk assessment and fire safety.

List of Abbreviations

ACPO	Association of Chief Police Officers
ARCC	Aeronautical Rescue Co-ordination Centre
BCM	Business Continuity Manager/Management
CBRN	Chemical, Biological, Radiological and Nuclear
CCA	Civil Contingencies Act 2004
CC	Control Centre
CCF	Core Competencies Framework
CCG	Clinical Commissioning Group
CCS	Civil Contingencies Secretariat
CCTV	Closed Circuit Television
CEO	Chief Executive Officer
CNC	Civil Nuclear Constabulary
COMAH	Control of Major Accident Hazard Regulations
COBR	Cabinet Office Briefing Room
CPD	Continuing Professional Development
CPS	Crown Prosecution Service
CRR	Community Risk Register
DECC	Department of Energy and Climate Change
Defra	Department of Environment Food and Rural Affairs
DoH	Department of Health
DoT	Department of Transport
DTI	Department of Trade and Industry
ECC	Emergency Control Centre
EP	Emergency Procedures
EPO	Emergency Planning Officer
EPS	Emergency Planning Society (UK)
FCP	Forward Control Point
FLO	Family Liaison Officer
FMB	Forward Media Briefing
FRC	Family Reception Centre
FSA	Food Standards Agency
GO	Government Office (Regional)
GPMS	Government Protective Marking Scheme
GSB	Gold, Silver and Bronze
HAC	Humanitarian Assistance Centre
HRA	Human Rights Act
HSE	Health and Safety Executive
ICP	Incident Control Post

IEM	Integrated Emergency Management
LA	Local Authority
LGD	Lead Government Department
LRF	Local Resilience Forum
MA	Marshalling Area
MACA	Military Aid to the Civil Authority
MACC	Military Aid to the Civil Community
MACP	Military Aid to the Civil Power
MBP	Media Briefing Point
MCC	Media Co-ordination Centre
MDP	Ministry of Defence Police
MI	Major Incident
MOU	Memorandum of Understanding
NAIR	National Arrangements for Incidents Involving Radioactivity
NARO	Nuclear Accident Response Organisation (MOD)
NCC	National Co-ordination Centre (Media)
NHS	National Health Service
NOSCC	National Occupational Standards for Civil Contingencies
NPIA	National Police Improvement Agency
NRE	National Resilience Extranet
PA	Public Address
PCT	Primary Care Trust
PIO	Police Incident Officer
PNICC	Police National Information and Co-ordinating Centre
QA	Quality Assured
RADSAFE	Radiation Safety (Transport)
RAWG	Risk Assessment Working Group
RC	Rest Centre
RCCC	Regional Civil Contingencies Co-ordinating Committee
REPPIR	Radiation Emergency Preparedness and Public Information Regulations
RNLI	Royal National Lifeboat Institution
RPD	Radiation Protection Division of Health Protection Agency
RVP	Rendezvous Point
RWG	Recovery Working Group
SAR	Search and Rescue
SCG	Strategic Co-ordinating Group
SCC	Strategic Co-ordination Centre
SIM	Senior Identification Manager
SIO	Senior Investigating Officer
SRC	Survivor Reception Centre
STO	Strategic, Tactical and Operational
STAC	Scientific and Technical Advice Cell
TCC	Tactical Coordination Centre (multi-agency)
TOR	Terms of Reference

List of Useful Websites

www.england.nhs.uk

www.nhs.uk

www.police.uk

www.fireservice.co.uk

www.thebci.org

www.epcollege.com

www.the-eps.org

www.environment-agency.gov.uk

www.gov.uk

www.dft.gov.uk/mca

www.local.gov.uk

www.gov.uk/government/organisations/ministry-of-defence

www.ifsm.org.uk

www.readyscotland.org

www.scotland.gov.uk

www.wales.gov.uk

www.dhsspsni.gov.uk

An Introduction to Emergency Planning

Overview
In this Chapter we will cover the following topics:
- Introduction to 'Risk'
- The Emergency Planning Officer
- Personal qualities and attributes
- The EPO image
- Personal kit
- Who's who in the emergency planning world?
- The Independent Emergency Planning Officer
- The 'Expert' witness
- Overview—the Civil Contingencies Act 2004
- The resilient organisation

Introduction to 'Risk'

What is emergency planning? It is quite simply an activity, which is intended to prevent and reduce harm to society from hazards produced by both man and the environment. The profile of emergency planning has certainly increased and gained prominence in recent years. Emergency planning has also expanded into other areas of risk management and become more aligned with other 'crisis' management activities such as Business Continuity Management (BCM), the threats to which also have the potential to have a serious impact on society, from a number of perspectives, from financial supply to commercial infrastructure.

The terrorist attacks in America in September 2001 presented scenarios that were in effect 'off the scale' in terms of risk management in relation to events that had gone before. To many, the attacks were beyond comprehension and expectation. The capacity, ingenuity and sheer ruthlessness of the terrorists had reached new levels and was a wake up call to the world. On a natural environmental level here in the UK widespread flooding in 2007 and 2014 heightened awareness of the devastating effects these events can have on society as a whole, and local communities in particular; again, this resulted in major changes and preparedness planning for similar events in the future. On both the environmental and industrial level the Japanese nuclear emergency in Fukushima in 2011 following the tsunami demonstrated that even a technologically advanced nation such as Japan can face a national crisis, despite the best engineering and planning activities. There is no doubt that confidence in nuclear power generation has been affected by this event which demonstrates that even with the best risk assessment modelling calculations and predictions accidents can and will happen, the terrorist will continue to attack with new and imaginative ways of killing people, and nature will catch everyone by surprise with the scale and ferocity of its power. Perhaps we are living in a world where 'risk' is now a part of our lives; where compromises have to be made—to take advantage of new technologies, freedoms, and activities we all want and enjoy we have to learn to live with risk. More worryingly, perhaps, are we as a society creating and accepting risks that in reality we simply cannot control or predict with any degree of scientific consensus or agreement? Scientific discourse is becoming more polarised as we attempt to tackle climate change, create genetically modified foods, plan for pandemics, invest and build in nuclear power, or build larger and faster transport systems. Across all these areas not even the 'experts' can agree—what chance has the layperson of making sense of the arguments or feeling reassured? Combined with the terrorist threat and apparent determination to use weapons of mass destruction, is it any wonder people feel nervous and more conscious of risk?

But is this raised risk awareness and this apparent change in attitude to risk because society has generally become more risk conscious and risk averse? Or does society really have to face up to previously unforeseen new risk challenges? Some commentators take the view that society has moved from a relatively stable position in terms of feeling secure about itself, to a situation of living with more risk and feeling more uneasy. Is society as a whole turning a blind eye to the risks it creates, or is it simply ignorant of the consequences? Is society responsible for climate change by the continued production of harmful industrial emissions? Planes are getting bigger, trains get faster, and roads are getting more congested, all with the potential to produce more serious consequences if they go wrong. Global climate change and natural disasters, whether they be a 'normal' phenomenon, natural cycle, or man-made, can create unpredictable forces previously unseen which have to be managed.

Terrorism, too, holds new fears related to the use of chemical, biological, radioactive, and nuclear materials—all capable of mass destruction. Global stability is uncertain. Cultural, religious, and political differences can and do create conflict. Access to information to produce weapons of mass destruction is readily available through information posted on the internet. Notwithstanding the power and capability of terrorist organisations, sometimes state sponsored, to create large-scale and co-ordinated death and destruction, the 'lone wolf' or individual with extreme views cannot be monitored, infiltrated, or stopped entirely. The ability of an 'anonymous' individual to plan, prepare, and execute acts of mass death and destruction is evident, as was seen in Norway in July 2011 when Anders Behring Breivik openly confessed to killing 77 people using a vehicle bomb and shooting dead a group of young people at a political rally.

These are major issues of ideological, economic, political and cultural difference and change that are shaping attitudes to risk and our sense of well-being. It would therefore appear that the public are gradually becoming less passive and more aggressively reactive to risk—perhaps not surprisingly. The ability of the public to mobilise, communicate, and access information on a global scale is becoming a powerful vehicle to articulate their concern and distrust in the 'establishment'. 'Twitter' and 'Facebook' have played major parts in mobilising change in Middle Eastern cultures, both culturally and politically. Better and more rapid reporting of socio-technical and environmental events and disasters can alter public perception of risk. News reports have a strong influence on public and political perceptions and can result in people becoming aware of risks they have either ignored or not considered, or indeed seeing threats and hazards in a new way. The public reaction to the Fukushima incident demonstrated that point, in as much as 'anticipated' public behaviour and reaction was not catered for or underestimated. The 'design based' accident as planned for was insufficient to cater for a tsunami. Planning assumptions fell away.

It is clear that society has changed and is changing. This transition to a more risky society is one that has to be accepted. Perhaps the emergence of emergency planning is a product of that shift and a desire to control and moderate that risk which is causing such unease. Whatever theories prevail there is no doubt that emergency planning is here to stay and will continue to develop and emerge as a vital aspect of modern living.

On a commercial level there is now an accepted understanding that ensuring that the infrastructure and service delivery of commercial organisations is vital as it supports communities in crisis; from utilities and food supply to economic and financial support. Indeed, having effective business continuity plans also ensure that an organisation can survive commercially.

Successful emergency management is dependent on a number of factors, all of which will be examined and explained in more detail within this book.

However, it is suggested here from the outset that there are four factors in particular that will drive effective emergency preparedness, response, and recovery.

The first is the Emergency Planning Officer or EPO, someone who is responsible for ensuring that statutory regulation and associated guidance in emergency management is implemented where necessary; that their own organisation is alive and responsive to developing emergency preparedness which can be achieved by analysing organisational risk, preparing plans, training, and exercising those plans. The EPO should, if not already in the role, ensure and facilitate a BCM approach that supports and complements the overall emergency response. In addition, the EPO has an important role to play in promoting, contributing, collaborating in, and driving risk awareness and education—with partners and society generally—to be more resilient and better prepared for the inevitable emergencies to come.

For the UK, the second influential factor is a national emergency preparedness, response and recovery framework that provides a consistent, co-ordinated approach to address a range of hazards and threats in a holistic way. In England this framework was created by the Civil Contingences Act 2004. The Act, as we will see during this book, is the framework around which emergency management is based in England and Wales and to a large extent in Scotland and Northern Ireland, forming a consistent approach and delivering a unified national standard. Those living in any of the devolved administrations, however, should review their own localised structures with those of emergency co-ordination arrangements across the UK to get a deeper understanding of the variations and interaction that will occur in the event of a cross-border incident. That said, the principles contained within the Act transcend local variations which generally allude to differences in nomenclature. In support there is also national guidance in the form of the UK Concept of Operations (CONOPS)—setting out the UK Central Government response arrangements supported by the police in the form of the Association of Chief Police Officers' (ACPO) Emergency Procedures; the police being the primary emergency co-ordinators.

TASK 1.1

If you live within any of the UK devolved administrations ensure you have access to and are familiar with the comparable nomenclature whilst working through the book. Subtle variations are emerging as these processes and structures mature. Keeping up to date is important.

Thirdly, high levels of preparedness can be achieved by having and creating resilient organisations that have the capacity to respond to crisis and emergencies in a way that enables them to continue to operate and deliver services. This aspect falls into BCM; but not just ensuring the business continues to run, producing services or products, it means ensuring that an organisation can effectively manage a threat or attack where lives are put at risk. This is beyond BCM. This is 'corporate resilience'—a combination of BCM and Emergency Management. BCM looks inwards to ensure the organisation continues to operate, recognising vulnerabilities and dependencies that could compromise that operation, but also (and sometimes overlooked) is how an organisation engages and interacts with the organisations and agencies that form the front line responders. Ensuring that there is full integration, effective communication, and mutual support among all organisations and businesses concentrates and directs effort most effectively. Relying entirely on the emergency services and emergency responders is no longer a reasonable 'risk treatment'. Increasing self-reliance and capability is a prudent and sensible way for all organisations to move forward in being prepared for any crisis or emergency.

Fourthly, and perhaps the key factor in emergency preparedness, is about you and me—the public. How do we communicate risk to the public in a way that is measured, accurate, transparent, proportional, and informative? Why should we do that? After all, there are experts, commentators, and scientists who know better, who inform our planning activities. Do we engage the public as an equal partner recognising they have relevant and valid views, even if they seem irrational and 'ignorant' to the experts? The answer to this question is 'yes we should do'. Listening to public opinions, views, concerns, perceptions, and anxieties will inform better risk communication strategies that are relevant to the public and assist in preparing plans that really work. An informed (of the risks) public and educated (to the risks) public will behave more rationally in a crisis, make better decisions, and will be more likely to follow advice and information given to them. There is no doubt that many experts will say *'but we do that because legislation requires us to do that'*: this is a weak argument to engage the public which effectively is saying *'we only consult because we have to'*. In many cases this results in lip service to those intentions, ticking a box, where in reality little is done to achieve true consultation and engagement. That is where the Emergency Planning Officer can make a real difference as we will discover later.

Related to maintaining a good two-way communication with the public, is having a dynamic, fast means of communicating warnings to the public. Again, we will examine that later.

But first let us look more closely at the Emergency Planning Officer to gain a better understanding of the role.

The Emergency Planning Officer

Emergency planning is now a complex activity. It now requires considerable knowledge and skills. For many years it was a role bolted on to other responsibilities, if indeed it was recognised or acknowledged at all. The original role allocated to the EPO was in fact to prepare and train the emergency services and the local authority for nuclear war during the Cold War era. Funding for such posts came from central government. Following the diminishing threat of nuclear war it was inevitable that the role of the EPO would transform or perish. During the 1980s a series of disasters shook the emergency planning community in the UK. This led to a review of roles and responsibilities across the emergency planning community and to the publication of the seminal Government Home Office publication called 'Dealing with Disaster'—a document that laid the foundations for emergency response as we understand it today. The evolution of the EPO from the previous 'war duties' officers working for the emergency services and local authorities in the 1970s and 1980s was now developing into a specialist profession as a result. The role essentially moved from that of solely war preparation to that of civil protection generally. Issues relating to risk, both from industrial and environmental hazards as we know them today, were planned for, but in a very ad hoc and unco-ordinated way; this did, however, lead to a growing recognition of the increasingly important role of the EPO. In particular, many police forces established dedicated EPOs to manage their emergency planning obligations as emergency response co-ordinators within the emergency response phase of an emergency or major incident as outlined in 'Dealing with Disaster'. The role began to develop and evolve across the country but at different rates with differing priorities, confused financing, and different levels of commitment from senior managers and executive officers.

Although the emerging role of the EPO was already developing, the terrorist attacks in New York occurred in 2001 accelerated this change. Overnight the role of the EPO changed. This was followed by the creation of the Civil Contingencies Act 2004 a few years later. The EPO became a high-profile figure within organisations in the public sector, primarily charged with implementing the Civil Contingencies Act. The profession had come of age.

At about the same time BCM was emerging as a natural bedfellow to emergency management but had gained little foothold within public services and seemed confined to private sector businesses. These two complementary disciplines began to converge to create an holistic approach to general corporate resilience and many EPOs also hold the title of Business Continuity Manager in many organisations, particularly the public sector organisations.

The word 'profession' is used here because that is what emergency planning has become in its own right, requiring thorough training and qualification.

Although still a relatively 'new' role compared to long standing business professions, there is evidence of its growing stature within the public services and the commercial sector. The professional development and qualification element for the EPO is developing at a rapid rate and is now often seen on many university and college prospectuses. Qualifications such as MSc, Certificate, and Diploma levels of attainment in subject areas such as Civil Contingencies, Risk Management, and Risk Crisis and Disaster Management can be obtained at many UK universities. Many universities have significant numbers of overseas students studying for such qualifications which tend to make these courses non-specific in terms of local procedure, such as the UK, and are therefore quite generic. The prospective UK EPO candidate must ensure therefore that the course they are considering is relevant to their needs. Notwithstanding the fascinating subject area of risk management on an academic level, which provides valuable insights in many cases, the courses offered are at a very high academic level and therefore very theory based. On the other hand, more practically-based skill and knowledge attainment can be achieved by seeking out courses that specifically remain practitioner focused. In either case such training and courses are increasing, which is a reflection on the emerging role of the EPO.

To achieve a consistent level of skill and knowledge in the profession a set of National Occupational Standards in the UK for Civil Contingencies (NOSCC) now exists and are aligned with the Emergency Planning Society's (EPS) Core Competencies Framework (CCF), which can be accessed and viewed on the internet (<http://www.the-eps.org>). Allied to attaining and maintaining a competent skill level the EPS have developed a Continuing Professional Development (CPD) scheme to allow its members to maintain records of achievement and gain CPD points to ensure that they retain and improve their knowledge and skill levels. This is a significant development in creating a standard set of skills and knowledge against which training and personal development can be assessed and measured. Moreover, many employers are now seeking evidence of achievement in the NOSCC and CPD as a means of assessing job candidates.

It is interesting to note that many of those who undertake emergency planning duties as part of their occupational role, such as those in the police service, do not routinely measure civil contingencies performance against the NOS, rather they are subject of a Personal Development Review (PDR) based upon standards and behaviours which are not always a good 'fit' with the EPO role; many EPOs therefore choose to subscribe to the EPS to take advantage of the CPD opportunities to maintain their professional status.

Professional bodies such as the EPS and the Business Continuity Institute (<http://www.thebci.org>), together with many academic institutions and training establishments, such as the Cabinet Office Emergency Planning College (<http://www.epcollege.com>) are driving up standards and the profile of the profession. All offer services and support for the practising emergency planning and business continuity professional. But there is more to being an effective EPO than attaining paper qualifications as we will now go on to discuss.

> **TOP TIP**
>
> Checkout the websites just mentioned as they will be a constant source of references to you.

Personal Qualities and Attributes

What makes a good EPO? Many of the skill sets needed for the role are outlined in the NOS and EPS Core Competencies. Apart from gaining the essential knowledge, skills, and qualifications, being an EPO means being a good communicator too and having an analytical approach to problem solving.

The skilled communicator

The EPO role requires excellent communication skills which in many ways are more important than in most spheres of business. The EPO informs, educates, trains, facilitates, arbitrates, negotiates, and briefs—to mention but a few skills. The communication content, which makes the role so important and different, relates to managing potentially threatening or damaging situations as they affect people, business, or the environment.

Getting the message right and being understood is crucial. Issues to consider are:

1. Informing—creating risk messages and emergency procedures including public information.
2. Educating—raising awareness and increasing knowledge.
3. Training—assessing training needs. Preparing and delivering training across all areas of resilience.
4. Facilitating—promoting discussion and exploring issues.
5. Arbitrating—finding solutions and resolving conflict.
6. Negotiating—presenting unbiased, objective, and evidenced-based arguments.
7. Briefing—preparing and presenting key facts and information.

There are many others that can be cited but it is clear that good communication is a cornerstone to being an effective EPO.

So what are the key points to remember in formulating any piece of communication?

Know and understand your target audience. Understanding their knowledge needs, their biases, fears, assumptions, vulnerabilities, concerns, and agendas are all part of assessing and analysing your audience. Often 'generic' information is 'trotted out' to address a particular communication task—for example, giving an overview of the Civil Contingencies Act 2004 is a common request for an EPO. The tone and content will need to vary between audiences: on the one hand it could be to members of the public, in which case it should cover basic principles; in a case where the audience already have emergency planning knowledge the content should be given in more depth, but even then, the areas to be covered need to be tailored. If it is to emergency planners the content needs to planning-, response-, and recovery- focused. Whereas if it is to chief executives of a Category 1 responder it will be more focused upon support, buy in, and consequences of non-compliance or non-collaboration. Same subject—difference emphasis. This applies across all communication tasks, written, verbal, or visual.

Who are the audience—how much do they know? What do your audience need to know? What are your communication objectives? It is often a good idea to write out the 'specification' to clarify it in your own mind. 'Mind-maps' are useful if you can use them. Essentially, have a central theme then radiate and link secondary themes around that. Then radiate a third layer and so on building a picture of the issues and topics you want to cover. Then place in order as you want to deal with them in your communication. You can visualise your ideas using this method. Look at the example in Figure 1.1.

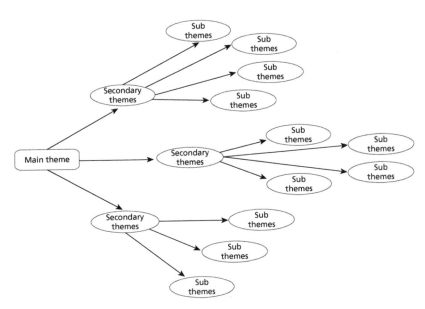

Figure 1.1 Visualising your ideas

Evidence your work

Consider what evidence you need or should support your communication type. In an argument or persuasive piece of work evidence is vital. Research that evidence and make sure you reference it in your communication. This will give your communication form and framework in a logical progression. It will also give your work credibility and objectivity. This adds weight to your work and demonstrates your ability to research, critically assess, extract relevant information and use it appropriately. Always reference anything you use from other sources and authors—in some cases you may need permission, in particular if your work is for sale.

It is not intended here to outline all the methods of effective writing or preparing effective (PowerPoint) presentations as there are many excellent publications and software packages to give you that information and those basic skills. PowerPoint has always been seen as 'boring'—you only need to remember the phrase 'death by PowerPoint'! It still remains the main type of effective communication. If it is boring—you are doing it wrong! Developing skills in this area will provide the tools to communicate most effectively, to hold an audience, express issues clearly with evidence and conviction to enhance the role of the EPO. There is no point in having all the information and knowledge without being able to express it.

In terms of written communication, again there are excellent publications and courses to develop those skills. Learning to prepare and present academic quality writing is not difficult and there are books to guide you in that process.

Poor or lazy communication skills will reduce the effectiveness of the EPO, inhibit the messages, portray the EPO as unprofessional, and reduce the uptake of vital information.

Being a good communicator, as we have seen, extends also to being able to negotiate and facilitate. Inevitably situations arise where there will be conflicts of interest. This is unavoidable in particular within a multi-agency environment where people have differing perspectives and priorities. Indeed this conflict may arise between the public and private sector where emergency arrangements for industry may demand considerable expenditure to comply. Issues will also occur where persuasion and negotiation are required, for example in securing funding or agreeing where responsibility for actions lie. All of these require an approach which is confident, robust, and authoritative whilst being sensitive and understanding to the other position.

As an EPO, being able to communicate at all levels in all situations—from protracted negotiation to dynamic crisis management, from training to umpiring—requires high levels of skill. One key factor for an effective communicator is 'know your stuff'. If the EPO is confident in their own knowledge and skills they will project and instil confidence in others. This is so important when giving presentations, training, and in briefings—which every EPO will have to do. Good communication skills also come into play when called upon to debrief an exercise or an incident; Again adopting the 'facilitator' approach as opposed to the 'crisis' management approach which we will discuss later.

In preparing plans a critical, analytical approach with attention to detail and a flair for logic and sequencing is vital. Being able to articulate complex ideas is vital. This will ensure ideas and thoughts are translated into a form that others will understand easily. It is too easy for an EPO to slip into 'emergency speak' or use acronyms in plans and presentations which are only meaningful to colleagues and partners. Creative thinking and innovation will attack problems and render solutions, which may sometimes be different or radical, where negotiating skills may be required to persuade people to change. Being prepared to be receptive to new ideas and accept change is also an important attribute.

The EPO is now without question a vital part of any organisation's management team, who will be a valuable adviser across a range of organisational activities, indeed corporate resilience will depend upon the EPO/BCM manager. To be able to fulfil that role that person must fully appreciate and understand their organisation. They should be familiar with the organisational structure, functional areas, processes, policies, systems, business continuity plans, crisis management plans, critical incident criteria, philosophy, strategic aims and objectives, goals, ambitions, and vulnerabilities—in short, know the organisation, its strengths and weaknesses. But beyond that they need to understand how their own organisation affects or is affected by other organisations, what can impact upon their organisation and where they fit in to the bigger resilience picture: looking outward as well and looking inward.

The EPO Image

This may seem a little out of place, or an unusual issue to discuss, within what is being proclaimed as a professional environment and to some may appear a little patronising, but impressions do count. Projecting the correct image will not only promote the standing of the profession but can make a big difference in how effective you are on a business or professional level. Firstly, the EPO must look the part. It is perhaps an area that seems to be perceived as less important in working environments today where casual wear seems to be more readily acceptable, in particular within the IT or more 'creative' workplaces or indeed a 'backroom' workplace where image and impressions don't count for much. However, in a business environment impressions and image are important, in particular when dealing with senior managers and members of the public. In many instances, those who we interact with form an opinion of us before we speak! Be mindful that communication is not all about what we say, but how we say it and the image we project. Imagine turning up at the airport and your pilots are wearing jeans and tee shirts—how would that affect your confidence?

In meetings the EPO should always contribute, they should have a personal introduction prepared in advance when they 'go around the table'. The EPO should make notes during the discussion; this shows involvement and being engaged. This will be noticed by others in the room. Mobile phones should *always* be switched off unless it is essential to remain in touch, then vibrate mode should be used. It is difficult to describe how off-putting it is and what a sign of indifference to the business in hand it conveys to be constantly looking at and playing with a mobile phone. Playing with mobile phones is becoming obsessive and misguidedly thought by some to indicate how 'busy' or 'important' I am. Others around the table will notice, as will the chairman. Leave them in your pocket or bag.

A good impression and reputation will affect business dealing. You will achieve more by remembering some basic principles as just outlined.

TASK 1.2

Using the website references provided together with your own personal research, familiarise yourself with the key emergency planning forums that will become your sources of reference. Consider membership where appropriate, if you think it will assist you.

Personal kit

To a large extent the 'kit' you carry will depend upon your role. As an emergency planning professional the EPO should be in possession of appropriate health and safety equipment (Personal Protective Equipment—PPE) as determined by the circumstances. At least a high visibility coat specified to highways standard, an industrial hard hat, reinforced rubber boots, and a good torch as a minimum. The high visibility coat should ideally have a logo on the back indicating 'Emergency Planning Officer' or similar with your organisation's name upon it. This is important for other people who are involved in an incident or exercise to recognise you as an EPO and your organisation.

Depending on the role, which may include being called out—being prepared is essential. Many EPOs attend scenes of major incidents to offer onsite operational and tactical dynamic advice and guidance. Visiting sites, exercise locations, and real incidents can be hazardous and an EPO should not rely on someone else to provide the necessary equipment and although there is some obligation on site owners to supply appropriate PPE the boots never fit nor the hats!

Many EPOs, senior officers, and managers carry hand-held computers and laptops which hold emergency plans. But it is essential that these are secure and not left in places where they will or could be stolen or lost. This may seem obvious, but it occurs regularly. For many in public and private service, the loss of sensitive data is a disciplinary issue, apart from the potential damage losing such data could have. In 2009/10 BBC staff lost or had stolen laptops and mobiles worth £241,019 (BBC FOI data reported on 9 August 2010). In July 2010 Lewis Communications (Lewis PR), reported, following an FOI request, that 340 Ministry of Defence laptops were either stolen or lost in the preceding two years. A further 593 CDs, DVDs and floppy discs, 215 memory sticks, 96 hard drives, and 13 mobile phones were also stolen or lost. Many of those computers probably contained sensitive information.[1] Also, bear in mind that public networks and wi-fi can be accessed and 'hacking' into voicemail can occur—beware when sending sensitive information. Personal integrity is vital as many areas of EP working are highly sensitive. In many cases EPOs—through their own organisation—have to be security cleared at high levels to work on sensitive plans. The following levels of security are typical:[2]
1. **BC** (Basic Check) Baseline Standard, 2. **CTC**—Counter Terrorist Check, 3. **SC**—Security Check, 4. **DV**—Developed Vetting—Long-term and uncontrolled access to Top Secret.

It is your responsibility to ensure that you have the correct level of clearance and understand the procedures for handling that information, including the document classifications of Official, Secret and Top Secret.[3]

Carrying a digital camera is also useful to record images that can be used in presentations, documents, to illustrate plans, as evidence, or to emphasise a point at debriefs. With any photograph obtained in the course of your duty or employment relating to your work there is an obligation to ensure that that material is kept secure and not disclosed or sold to a third party without due authority.

---

[1] <http://www.bbc.co.uk/news/uk-10910170> and <http://www.techweekeurope.co.uk/news/mod-loses-340-laptops-in-last-two-years-8588>.

[2] <https://www.sis.gov.uk/careers/working-for-us/security-vetting/what-is-security-clearance.html>.

[3] <https://www.gov.uk/government/uploads/system/uploads/attachment_data/file/251480/Government-Security-Classifications-April-2014.pdf>.

Communication is also vital, so a mobile phone is essential with a spare battery with charger options. Always ensure that mobile phones are keypad locked at all times. Many EPOs, in particular those in the emergency services and local authorities may have access to encrypted radio/telephone equipment on multi-agency channels. In addition, many emergency response organisations can apply for and use network preference mobile or landline schemes to allow priority use over the public network. Ensure you can access them if you have them.

The advice in this section may seem quite simplistic but it is given based upon observations and bitter experience of the author over many years' practical experience.

Who's Who in the Emergency Planning World?

Having looked at the EPO role we should now place the EPO into a wider context within the public and private sector emergency management community. Not only has the profile of the EPO increased, but the numbers too, and variations in the role (see Figure 1.2). Emergency planning offices and departments across all emergency responder organisations have grown incredibly to meet the ever increasing demands for organisational resilience and the requirements of regulatory guidance such as the Civil Contingencies Act in the UK. Private sector organisations also recognise the need to be resilient from a commercial perspective, the way they support the community and support the emergency services following an emergency or fulfilling obligations to their customers, for example in the transport industry. Many organisations have both emergency planning officers and business continuity managers or a combined role. This proliferation of disciplines and indeed job titles all related to planning can be confusing. References will be made to emergency, contingency, resilience, and continuity, so it may be useful also at this point to take a brief look at some job titles and descriptions that may be experienced within the wider profession. There are several titles describing the role of EPO-related work, for example, Emergency Planning Officer (or Manager), Contingency Planning Officer (or Manager) or the Civil Contingencies Officer are examples and all currently in use. They broadly describe the same role but there are subtle differences to be noted. Essentially, the Emergency Planning Officer and Contingency Planning (or Civil Contingencies) Officer all perform a similar role.

To put the Business Continuity Manager into context, they will be focused more on the risk evaluation, mitigation, and the 'cost' of risk which is business-orientated in a commercial sense; whereas the Emergency Planning or Contingency Planning Officer to a large extent are more aligned with preventing injury and loss of life or damage to public property and the environment. The Resilience Officer (or Manager) tends to indicate a more holistic

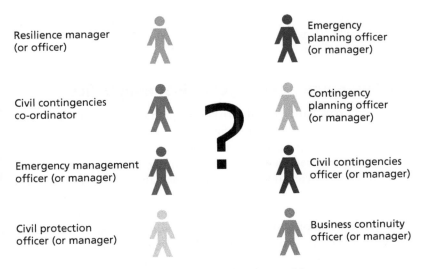

Resilience manager (or officer)

Emergency planning officer (or manager)

Civil contingencies co-ordinator

Contingency planning officer (or manager)

Emergency management officer (or manager)

Civil contingencies officer (or manager)

Civil protection officer (or manager)

Business continuity officer (or manager)

Figure 1.2 Who is who in the emergency planning world

approach to both BCM and Emergency Management and is becoming more popular as a job description, but each discipline is complementary. Indeed, many emergency responder organisations require business continuity planning as part of their 'resilience' capability needed to respond to an emergency. It is perhaps indicative of the profession's current lack of maturity that there is such variation and interpretation of terms. Emergency is a term that sits well with the layperson and is used as the primary term to describe an adverse event within the Civil Contingencies Act and so is probably the most common term.

To that extent and to further clarify these terms: emergency is described as 'an unexpected and potentially dangerous situation requiring immediate action'. We will look later at the official definition of 'emergency' for planning purposes, but within the ordinary meaning there is a sense of urgency in the description of emergency which will later determine how to prepare plans and tends to relate to life-saving situations. Contingency on the other hand describes a future event or circumstance which is possible but cannot be predicted with certainty. This title is broader in context and caters for a whole range of events which may not be considered 'urgent' but nevertheless present critical situations. For clarity and to avoid repetition Emergency Planning Officer and Emergency Plans will be used in this book, but recognising a read across to 'contingency', 'resilience,' and 'business continuity' as they are dependent and integral parts of the overall function of emergency preparedness.

There is also a growing sector of independent emergency planning trainers and consultants. Usually they are drawn from those who have retired or have had previous experience in the emergency services or Local Authorities as established EPOs.

The Independent Emergency Planning Officer

Is the word 'consultant' viewed with contempt in your office? Undoubtedly, consultants can be seen as lightweight, ill-informed, and a facilitator that simply steals and regurgitates others' ideas and charges a fortune! There is, however, another view. If used effectively, properly engaged, vetted, and managed consultants can offer a real alternative to sustaining a full-time member of staff or trying to achieve something you simply don't have the time, skills, or knowledge to do—which can result in you being made to look unprofessional, as if you are time wasting, or risk damaging your reputation as an organisation. An independent EPO can have vast experience, achieved over many years with high status or rank in their previous organisation, that can be utilised for a fraction of the cost of trying to achieve that in-house. Independent EPOs usually emerge as retired EPOs from the Local Authority, emergency services, the armed forces, or those moving over to the private sector simply to set up a business offering training and/or consultancy services. They may also seek work with established emergency management or BCM consulting companies on a permanent or contractual basis.

In any case, proper vetting and interviews are essential to engaging a consultant that is right for you. There are those, it has to be conceded, that have little experience or in extreme cases have no experience and rely on their skill as a facilitator to impress or persuade you to engage them. As a general guide you need to ensure that they have significant experience, at least 5 years within one of the Category 1 responder groups, to be reasonably reassured that they will deliver the information and advice you need. Proof of their qualifications and experience, with up-to-date CVs, and possibly testimonials from trusted organisations will assist you to assess their ability prior to engagement. A factor often overlooked is 'credibility' and the ability to speak from experience. There is no doubt that credibility has impact and can affect the learning process for many. Those who can literally speak from experience have a great advantage over others.

It is also important to agree terms and conditions in writing at an early stage of negotiations—which applies to both sides. This will save any misunderstanding in terms of delivery of training or the extent of consultation, and in particular the use and copyright of material. The consultant may place restrictions on the use and general circulation of their material. In particular many 'trainer' consultants will supply course material on computer disk with copyright symbols attached. Although much of the core material will be in the public domain already, the presentation, interpretation, application, and usage may be the original additional material of the consultant. In many cases the consultant may develop new material for a client for which they are paid. In that case the material becomes the property of the client, in much the same way that when an employee creates material for their employers during their employment it belongs to the employer.

Let us look at some issues relating to using consultants. First, those acting wholly independently can offer specialist tailored services which can be very cost effective, delivered at a time and place to suit the client. This holds great advantages for the client. The independent EPO can also be more objective in their judgements and assessments as they are not tied into corporate policy or restricted by regulations or 'toeing the company line'. The independent EPO can also be a force for change in an organisation that will be more inclined to take notice of an independent consultant rather than an employee. Choosing an independent EPO can also mean being able to choose a true 'specialist' in a particular area, for example nuclear, chemical, transport, etc., and not a general practitioner. As a general rule those who choose to be independent EPOs have a great incentive to do well and be the best they can as their business depends on it. In terms of cost the independent consultant can offer services at a fraction of large consulting companies, who have major overheads and their profit margin to secure. Cost is certainly not a measure of their ability!

A perceived disadvantage of using an independent EPO is their currency or 'shelf life' after leaving the mainstream workplace. This is in fact not the case in most situations and in fact can be the reverse. Access to information and guidance is now more readily available within the emergency planning community, within industry at both private and public sector level, than ever before. 'Freedom of Information Act' legislation makes withholding information difficult for public service organisations. In fact, the independent EPO is often better informed at all levels as they have the business incentive, usually have the time, and are pro-active in regular self-briefing and engage regularly with the most relevant societies and organisations to stay updated. It is vital that they remain up to date at all times to ensure that their advice is accurate and relevant. It will soon become obvious to a client if the consultant is out of date. However, all independent EPOs should hold professional indemnity insurance which is also an incentive for a client to engage an independent EPO as they can secure compensation should the need arise.

For the independent EPO selecting work and securing work can be a challenge. It is essentially creating and running a small business. Creating a website is essential to act as a source of information to prospective clients. There are numerous publications and courses on starting a small business offering valuable advice on start up, taxation issues, and marketing. The important issues for the independent EPO is maintaining good links, networking, maintaining visibility, and building a good reputation. Being a member of key organisations, societies, and professional bodies is vital and, where possible, self promotion through giving talks, writing articles, and giving presentations all contribute to acquiring new business, even if the remuneration is small or non-existent!

Secondly, look at the EPO employed by or contracted to an established consulting company. They can offer many of the advantages of an independent EPO but of course the work will be monitored, corporately badged, copyrighted, and supervised by the senior management of that company. In addition, they can be very expensive, as the overheads are that much higher resulting in rates up to five times that of an independent acting alone. Bear in mind also that an independent trainer/consultant may be sub-contracted to a consultancy company. The advantage of a consulting company is that work is found for the consultant and many companies support their consultants by assisting in their personal development or CPD. Working freelance for a company can, however, create conflicts of interest for the independent EPO which have to be assessed carefully. Again, contracts are vital to make a clear distinction of what defines 'conflict'.

In short, do not dismiss the independent consultant/trainer. They can have a great deal of experience and having moved around numerous companies in their consulting can often bring new ideas, perspectives, and ways of working that will be outside the experience of most practitioners. Indeed, selecting a consultant from a different background can add a whole new perspective on entrenched company or organisational views and policies, and can be a useful vehicle for change.

KEY POINT

Do not disregard the support of a consultant—they can be cost effective and add new perspectives. They are highly accountable too.

The Expert 'Witness'

Increasingly, litigation and prosecution are becoming a reality for individuals, public service organisations or companies alike, as likely outcomes following major incidents which have resulted in death, injury, or damage to property or loss of goods. Emergency planning issues can also have a direct effect on many aspects of public policy and consultation. On a specialist level there are, or can be, contentious or conflicting issues surrounding hazardous technologies, such as the transport, storage, manufacture, or use of hazardous goods or materials, such as at chemicals or nuclear sites. These are usually raised by special interest groups, from the environmental lobby or developers, for example, to those who just have a personal or community interest, in that they are uneasy at the prospect of something dangerous near them and want to object or state 'not in my back yard' (hence the term NIMBY).

In other cases, a plan may have failed or a procedure not been used correctly which leads to accusations, counter-accusations, and possible liability issues or even criminal culpability. This is particularly so where there was injury and death. Any of these events could lead to an EPO being asked to provide independent professional 'expert' opinion or defend a position on the relevant emergency planning issues to a range of inquiries or judicial bodies often at odds with established institutions or large companies. So what makes an expert?

This is a difficult question to offer a definitive answer to, but a common definition of an expert is 'a person who has extensive skill or knowledge in a particular field' (*Collins English Dictionary* (2009) Harpercollins: Glasgow). Extensive would mean being able to demonstrate considerable experience in terms of both years and application within that specialist area, including the following in support:

a) High level academic qualification in a specialist related topic—at least MSc.

b) Published author on the subject—a book.

c) Published academic papers and journal articles.

d) Associated with an academic institution relating to the subject—a speaker/ marker.

e) Member of relevant societies or associations—special status, e.g. Fellow.

f) An acknowledged teacher or lecturer in the subject.

g) Specialist knowledge of a subject, e.g. chemical or nuclear emergency arrangements.

h) Previous experience as an expert in similar proceedings.

The weight given to such evidence or advice, although in some cases very technical, will always be taken as subjective and ultimately a matter for the adjudicating person or panel (jury) to consider, no matter how expert the EPO. However, there are risks with offering yourself up to be an expert. The 'other' side will wheel out their 'experts' and attempt to demolish your credibility, attack your expertise, your relevance, your qualifications, and even your personality at times; the objective being to reduce your opinion to nothing less than useless and irrelevant. Apart from being unsettling and stressful, it may also have long-term implications for you as a professional, particularly if an independent consultant. An experienced and determined advocate will not spare your feelings—be prepared. Some areas for consideration with your client should include:

a) Insist on having all the information that could impact upon your assessment and professional view of the issues—read everything!

b) Meticulous research is required to cover every aspect of the issues in question including legislation, regulations, guidance, relevant books, research papers, previous inquiries, or cases (to cite evidence), other professional opinions (which you pay for).

c) Insist on witness meetings (if there are any) to review evidence and eliminate contradiction and any misunderstanding.

d) Have a 'devil's advocate' session to identify weak areas.

e) Understand and digest the opposing opinions and issues and prepare for them.

f) Agree your fees in advance, and terms.

g) Ensure you have professional indemnity insurance.

Although the list is not definitive, addressing all of the points will position you for what will come. Finally, a few pointers when offering opinion or giving evidence in public.

a) Have ready your material you intend to refer to—notes, maps, and relevant documents—have sufficient to hand out to panels/jury members etc.

b) Talk slowly and clearly—someone will be recording what you say.

c) Dress for the part—create a good impression.

d) Consider each question before answering even if you feel it is taking a long time.

e) Ask for the question to be repeated if you do not understand—be absolutely sure you understand the question—asking to repeat the question may allow more time to formulate your answer.

f) Do not be bullied—refer to the Chair or adjudicator politely if you are put under undue or unfair pressure—some Chairs or adjudicators have little legal or court experience, for example in a planning inquiry, and professional advocates such as barristers may push the boundaries a little to unsettle a witness which would not be allowed normally. In any case, getting to the facts is the goal, not intimidating a witness into making mistakes.

g) Do not expand on answers too much—be concise and to the point. You may be led into unfamiliar areas if you show hesitation or apparent lack of knowledge. If the topic or question is not in your area—say so.

The emergence of the EPO, in all forms, in recent years is only matched by the growing volume of guidance, legislation, policy, and procedure which now governs emergency preparedness. For the UK, one vital piece of guidance and regulation that unites all those within the planning world is the Civil Contingencies Act 2004, which we will now take a brief look at.

Overview—The Civil Contingencies Act 2004

It would be fair to say that multi-agency working across the emergency services in the UK is not new. Many examples of good practice existed going back to the 1980s where local police, fire, and ambulance services regularly met with their colleagues from the health sectors, local authorities, and the military to plan and prepare for civil emergencies. Indeed, some areas had highly developed 'major incident co-ordination groups' in recognition of the value of shared skills, knowledge, and developing better understanding. That picture was not reflected across the whole of the UK, however, where locally perhaps, and certainly at government level, the attitiude prevailed that catastrophic events happened to someone else in other countries subject to volatile climates, unstable governments, civil wars or unsafe technology in third world countries.

The terrorist attacks in New York on 11 September 2001 changed the way in which emergency response is perceived worldwide. The ability to respond effectively to and manage a catastrophic event was brought into question. It also raised the prospect of dealing with new threats involving mass casualties brought about by the use of chemical, biological, or radiological devices. Perhaps more disturbing was the realisation that existing benign technologies can be turned against society with catastrophic effects. Combined with the global threat posed by climate change and pandemic disease it is perhaps not surprising that emergency management is on everyone's agenda. Managing the consequences of such events is a real challenge and developing the necessary skills and knowledge is now a key priority for many organisations.

Notwithstanding examples of local good practice in the UK in multi-agency emergency planning and response and in recognition of the growing risks presented by manmade and natural threats, the UK Government introduced legislation in the form of the Civil Contingencies Act 2004 (CCA). For the first time this legislation put certain statutory duties on emergency responders and established a national framework to manage the risks through groups known as Local Resilience Forums (LRF) located across England and Wales and Local Resilience Partnerships in Scotland, and generally within police force boundaries.

Understanding this emergency planning structure created by the CCA is essential for the EPO and for the development of emergency plans. It is not intended to replicate the whole of the Act here as there are ample references available from other sources. The Act and associated guidance is constantly changing, under review, or being developed or enhanced, but the key points are worth emphasising here. Bearing in mind our earlier discussion relating to risk, it is perhaps logical that the CCA is founded on a robust risk assessment process to inform and prioritise planning.

Through the LRFs the CCA aimed to:

- Provide a single framework for civil protection.
- Improve resilience at local, regional, and national levels.
- Deal effectively with emergencies.
- Prevent disruption to essential services.

To do that the CCA established new responsibilities and definitions:

- It created a statutory duty for the first time. Prior to the CCA commitment to emergency planning was largely unregulated and very ad hoc.
- It defined what an 'emergency' was. To that point 'emergency' was subjective and therefore open to a very wide interpretation which led to anomalies in levels of response. However, we will see that the term 'Major Incident' is still in use for good reason.
- It required risk assessment activities as a basis for planning. This process gave some degree of rationale and quantification to risk.
- It created a framework for preparing and responding to emergencies outlined in two volumes of guidance. This set of guidelines ensured a consistent and integrated approach to emergency planning. Up to that point the only reference was the Home Office publication 'Dealing with Disaster', which was a very useful and productive document but lacked detail and authority to enforce standards.
- It promoted effective warning and informing the public. This followed recognition that communities, indeed informed and educated communities, in terms of emergency response, would be safer communities because informed people clearly make better decisions. It required warning and informing obligations to have ownership. It also promoted effective two-way dialogue with 'at risk' communities and the wider public concerning responding to emergencies.
- It encouraged business continuity planning and hence BCM. Building resilient businesses and organisations created a better chance for them to survive a crisis or emergency. It also allowed for less reliance on the emergency services and other support agencies, so leaving them with more resources to concentrate on the 'at risk' and vulnerable communities.
- It redefined 'State of Emergency'. This allowed the Government to make special temporary powers and this could apply to one area or region as opposed to the whole country.
- It incorporated performance measures and sanctions for those who do not fulfil their responsibilities under the CCA. This is a critical element as it 'enforces' the regulations. Many emergency responders now have their requirements

under the CCA embedded into their performance measures. This allows objective comparisons and evaluation of effectiveness in emergency planning.

Quite a list! As can be seen, these are fundamental changes, indeed, that had a profound effect and impact on the emergency planning community nationally.

The legislation also created two categories of responder known as Category 1 and Category 2 responders. Essentially Category 1 responders are those whom we think of as the emergency services, hospitals and ambulance services, local authorities, and the Environment Agency—the front line. Category 2 responders are those key support utilities, transport infrastructure, Health and Safety Executive, and other health support services.

TASK 1.3

- Find your Local Resilience Forum website (or equivalent) and familiarise yourself with the members and their organisations.
- Who are your Category 1 and Category 2 Responders?

The CCA continues to be revised and updated—or enhanced—based upon feedback and lessons learned since its inception in 2005. An extensive 'Enhancement Programme' now drives a wide consultation process.

TOP TIP

Find out the names of your Category 1 Responders (perhaps from LRF minutes) or get hold of an Emergency Planning Directory—get to know your stakeholders and partners.

The latest updates can be found by referring to the UK Government website <https://www.gov.uk/government/organisations/cabinet-office/about>. The CCA guidance also continues to mature and evolve—for example, with documents such as 'Expectations and Indicators of Good Practice Set for Category 1 and 2 Responders' and 'The Role of Local Resilience Forums: A Reference Document'. Keeping abreast of changes and develops in guidance and regulation is a key responsibility and function of the EPO.

The CCA enabled two sets of guidance documents to be produced; these are accessible to you for reference:

1. *Emergency Preparedness*.

2. *Emergency Response and Recovery*.

Emergency Preparedness together with the accompanying *Emergency Response and Recovery* sets out the generic framework for civil protection.

Every EPO must read and understand the latest versions of these documents as they form the basis upon which all emergency planning is driven in the UK. They are also invaluable reference documents and form an integral accompaniment to this book and should be available to be read in conjunction with it.

Although this book is not solely concerned with the Civil Contingencies Act 2004 it would be fair to say that the CCA resulted in a massive shift in attitude and approach to emergency management. It created a benchmark in standards, a uniformity and accountability within the emergency planning community. The CCA also embraced the business continuity as a vital component in the drive for effective emergency planning. Business continuity and emergency response are now more closely linked than ever before.

The CCA drives a principle that organisations who are well prepared for managing a crisis or emergency will not only be more likely to survive from a business perspective, but will take some pressure off the emergency services. They can do this by being more self-sufficient and in many ways they can shape how the emergency is managed themselves by early intervention—the 'Golden Hour' will be discussed in a later chapter but endorses the principle that remedial action within the first hour of an incident will have the most impact.

In addition, any organisation, including the commercial sector for that matter, should not take for granted that the emergency services have all the answers to managing an emergency. Indeed, long held assumptions about what the emergency services will or can do need to be dispelled or moderated. Although well trained and practised through daily routine, a crisis or emergency will stretch everyone, blue lights included. The message is that a resilient organisation is a smart organisation.

The following introductions to emergency response arrangements in the UK devolved administrations is intended to illustrate the variations that exist. It is important, however, that the reader relies on the latest information presented by the relevant government offices.

The Scottish emergency arrangements

Emergency response in Scotland is very similar in overall structure to the CCA, i.e. that it is dealt with at the local level and lead UK Government departments will liaise with the Scottish Government Resilience Room (SGoRR) and Scottish Ministers to ensure national co-ordination that affect cross-border issues. However, on issues of terrorism, this is a 'reserved' responsibility in which the UK lead department of the Home Office will lead. The SGoRR will maintain contact with the Cabinet Office Briefing Room (COBR) and the Scottish Office in such cases. More detail about these national structures will appear later.

In Scotland, in 2013, three regional resilience partnerships were created supported by 10 Local Resilience Partnerships equivalent in function to the Local Resilience Forums. In addition, if required, the Resilience Advisory Board for Scotland (RABS) and the Scottish Police Information and Co-ordination Centre (S-PICC) will support the Scottish emergency response. The Scottish Government Press Office will provide public information and co-ordinate the media response at Scottish level. In cases where emergency powers are considered for Scotland the UK Government may appoint a Scottish Emergency Co-ordinator with terms of reference as agreed by the UK Government.

A useful reference document called *Preparing Scotland* (<http://www.scotland.gov.uk>) will provide more information relating to the Scottish emergency response. Also, the CCA Guidance Emergency Response and Recovery has more information.

The Welsh emergency arrangements

In terms of devolved administrations, civil contingencies is largely a non-devolved matter in Wales. However, The Welsh Government (WG) has functional responsibility for a number of important issues. The Wales Resilience Forum (WRF) is a body made up of senior Category 1 and 2 responders and senior Welsh Government representatives who promote good communication and emergency planning across Wales. They are supported by the Welsh Resilience Partnership Team (WRPT) who monitor issues affecting resilience in Wales and report to the WRF. They address a range of resilience issues, for example Chemical, Biological, Radiological and Nuclear (CBRN) and flu pandemic. WRPT has several functional sub-groups to assist in providing advice and guidance to the WRF.

In the event of an emergency in Wales the initial response will be managed as per the CCA guidance and overall co-ordination via a Strategic Co-ordinating Group at a Strategic Co-ordination Centre (SCC). There are four covering Wales based upon the police force areas of North Wales, South Wales, Dyfed Powys, and Gwent. There is a Pan-Wales Response Plan which will only be activated by the Welsh Government (WG) depending on the nature and scale of the emergency. This decision is taken by the Civil Contingencies Group (CCG) or Welsh Civil Contingencies Committee (WCCC). The establishment of the Emergency Co-ordination Centre Wales (ECC[W]) will act as a central conduit for information with UK Government and Welsh national co-ordination. As in Scotland, a terrorism incident will be led by the Home Office and where necessary activating COBR.

The Welsh Pan-Wales Response Plan can be viewed at <http://wales.gov.uk/docs> for more information. Also, the CCA Guidance Emergency Response and Recovery has more information.

The Northern Ireland emergency arrangements

In Northern Ireland (NI) civil protection is largely devolved. Northern Ireland emergency response is based upon the CCA principles and is managed through the NI Executive. NI have their own unique administrative arrangements and emergency response differs in terms of inter-agency co-ordination. Perhaps that is not surprising considering the unique situation and historical context in that province. At strategic level the response is provided by the police, the NI Office (NIO), and the NI departments by triggering the NI Central Crisis Management Arrangements (NICCMA). Strategic Co-ordination is through the Crisis Management Group (CMG). The CMG is supported by the Civil Contingencies Group, Northern Ireland (CCG(NI)).

The CMG is supported by the Office of First and Deputy First Minister which will establish the NI Central Operations Room (NICOR). In large-scale emergencies the NICCMA will link into UK arrangements. Terrorist incidents are managed through the NIO which would activate the NI Office Briefing Room arrangements (NIOBR) (note the similarity with the UK COBR).

More information can be found in *The Northern Ireland Civil Contingencies Framework* and *A Guide to Emergency Planning Arrangements in Northern Ireland*. Also, the CCA Guidance Emergency Response and Recovery has more information.

Historically NI has close alliances with the remainder of the UK. In recent years the NI administrations have developed some stronger ties with their neighbours in the south—the Irish Republic—on cross-border collaboration relating to emergency procedures. Indeed there is an Emergency Planning Society branch in the Republic of Ireland.

More information in relation to emergency response co-ordination for NI can be found in the 'Refreshed' NI emergency planning guidance of September 2011. This document contains information about relevant NI government departments <http://www.ofmdfmni.gov.uk/nicivilcontingenciesframework.pdf>.

Although differences exist in emergency arrangements across the UK—which one could argue is not conducive to smooth interoperability, in particular where cross-border incidents occur so frequently—there is sufficient synergy. The understanding, cultural similarities, and joint exercising together create an emergency response that is flexible and resilient but modelled on a standard set of structures and processes set down by the CCA. As such, a solid platform is established to respond to any emergency.

However, how can that response be more effective? How can organisations assist themselves?

The Resilient Organisation

Resilience is a term used extensively within the Civil Contingencies Act 2004. Resilience is defined as the ability to withstand, recover quickly from or spring back into shape having been bent![4] This definition is extended within the context of the CCA to refer to the 'ability of the community, service providers, an affected area or infrastructure to withstand the consequences of an incident'.[5] Resilience is the overall aim that supports effective emergency preparedness. To build in resilience for Category 1 responders the CCA placed a statutory duty on them to maintain plans to ensure that they can continue to deliver their core services in the face of an emergency to which they may have to respond. This concept also embraced the idea not only of looking closely into internal organisational dependencies but reliance on external services that may be contracted to that organisation or the 'supply chain'. Although the BCM requirement within the CCA is quite narrow, only applying to 'emergencies' defined within the CCA, the process and exercise driving that requirement will and does inevitably address a much wider range of threats and crises. In effect the CCA is creating more resilient organisations. The implications of a Category 1 organisation not being able to deliver core services because they are suffering from an internal crisis or not having foreseen a threat that could compromise public safety should be avoided at all costs and planned for.

However, the resilient organisation should not only be concerned with internal BCM issues to keep the business running or provide services, but must also be able to develop emergency response procedures that fully integrate with the guidance created by the CCA. In other words, are emergency response arrangements in place that are sympathetic, compliant, and supportive? Do they integrate with the response of Category 1 responders' expectations and demands? Do non-emergency response organisations understand what is required of them? For example, would a large university be able to manage effectively the initial response to an onsite terrorist incident? Do they exercise with Category 1 responders? Do they ensure their emergency plans (if they have them) are compliant with expectations and fit for purpose? For many organisations, BCM is simply not enough, in particular where the 'business' involves large numbers of staff or providing services to members of the public. Combining BCM and emergency response arrangements complete the resilience picture.

---

[4] *Oxford English Dictionary* (2008).

[5] Civil Contingencies Act 2004 Guidance—*Emergency Preparedness.*

The resilient organisation is also important in terms of developing national infrastructure, in particular those businesses that supply key services and utilities. They in fact support our critical national infrastructure as we shall see later.

But the concept of the resilient organisation does not only extend to emergency preparedness but can make good business sense and increase the chances of commercial survival. We will see in a later Chapter how exercising can in fact help build resilience into an organisation.

An informed community

Finally, let us consider engagement with the public, or community resilience, as a critical factor in emergency preparedness. An essential part of risk management is risk communication. Communicating in a way that should be open, honest, transparent, two-way (inclusive), and appropriate for the audience. Academics have long understood through research the narrowness and exclusive nature of risk communication. Research has shown that many well-intentioned 'experts' consider the issues of quantification of risk as too complex for the layperson to understand or that explaining the risk may alarm or frighten the public. Others may argue that this reticence to be more open about risk is contrived to confuse and hide the risk or smooth the way in key public 'policy decision making' relating to potentially 'risky' technologies, for example nuclear power. Indeed, confidence in science as the objective source of reassurance no longer holds true when one considers the nuclear crisis at Fukushima, Japan, in March 2011, in which risk assessments actually failed to identify the potential impact of a tsunami. Today other scientific 'certainties' are now called into question regularly in the media. It is fair to say, from a policy making perspective, that the exclusion of public opinion, views, or concerns in risk communication is no longer sustainable. In fact, it is argued here that effective public engagement is a cornerstone of good emergency planning. This is endorsed by the UK Cabinet Office in a public information document called *Communicating Risk Guidance*.

TOP TIP

Understanding the principles of risk communication and perception will pay great dividends for the EPO in framing risk messages in real events or preparing plans.

Indeed, in recognition of the importance of effective risk communication the CCA directs 'Warning and Informing' the public as a key activity in emergency preparedness. It is, however, too easy to pay lip-service to this vital part of emergency planning without attracting too much adverse attention—until the emergency occurs. Recent national efforts by the Government have tried to engage the public with leaflets like *Preparing for Emergencies* and many Local Resilience Forums have published more localised documents, but for specific 'at risk' communities that may not be enough.

It should be standard practice for identified 'at risk' communities, such as those near chemical (*Control of Major Accident Hazards* [COMAH]) or nuclear sites (subject to the *Radiation Emergency Preparedness and Public Information Regulations* [REPPIR]) to be the subject of regular 'community profile' surveys seeking views, concerns, analysing population make-up and vulnerabilities, seeking potential behavioural intentions in the event of an emergency, and testing understanding of warning arrangements. In this way informed planning can proceed with more accurate and realistic planning assumptions, an informed risk communication strategy, informed ways of moderating unrealistic perceptions of the actual risk, and perhaps most importantly, creating trust. By identifying where trust lies will enable emergency messages to be framed correctly and communicated by the most appropriate agency or person. If you don't trust the messenger, you won't trust the message!

In conclusion, the key factors in effective emergency management rest with the EPO, the Civil Contingencies Act 2004, the resilient organisation and an informed confident public (see Figure 1.3).

KEY POINT

Community profile surveys are an essential tool in developing localised plans.

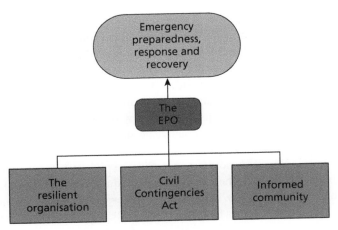

Figure 1.3 Effective emergency management

These four factors form the foundation for emergency preparedness, response, and recovery.

TASK 1.4

- Explain why organisational resilience is important to emergency planning.
- How would you rate your organisation's resilience?
- What performance measures under the Act, if any, affect your organisation?

Summary

You should now understand:

- How 'risk' is shaping our attitudes and approach to planning for emergencies.
- The diverse and vital role of the 'Emergency Planning Officer' in organisations.
- The personal qualities, attributes, and image of the effective EPO.
- An overview of essential personal EPO kit.
- Who's who in the emergency planning world?
- The Independent 'Emergency Planning Officer' as a consultant.
- The EPO as an 'Expert' witness.
- Introduction to the Civil Contingencies Act 2004.
- The resilient organisation and community.

Conclusion

The role of the Emergency Planning Officer has become a vital management tool for both the public and private sector over the last 10 years to ensure emergency management is developed and maintained. Emergency planning itself has transformed in the last 10 years, brought about by the Civil Contingencies Act 2004. The ability to withstand and recover from a crisis or emergency is a primary objective for many organisations today, from a commercial, reputational, and legislative perspective. There is a stark global recognition that we are living in a 'risky' society. Planning to respond to the many threats and hazards now facing society is a priority for everyone.

This book will prepare the foundations to acquire the necessary skills to begin that planning process. In the next Chapter we will examine the need to plan and the part exercising has in building resilience into an organisation.

Plans and Exercising—
An Introduction

Overview
In this Chapter we will cover the following topics:

- Types of plan
- The emergency planning cycle
- Integrated emergency planning
- Guidance
- Measuring and managing risk for planning purposes
- Over planning
- Who creates plans?
- LRF planning
- Regional and national planning
- Local Authority planning
- Multi-Agency plans in perspective
- Individual organisational plans
- Making planning decisions
- Business Continuity Plans
- Do we need to exercise?

What is an emergency plan? One dictionary definition states that a plan is 'a detailed proposal to achieve something.'[1] If we add 'emergency' the nature and context of a plan becomes more specific. An emergency can be defined as 'an unforeseen or sudden occurrence, *esp.* of danger demanding immediate action' (*Collins English Dictionary* (2009) Harpercollins: Glasgow). Therefore

---

[1] *Oxford English Dictionary* (2008) OUP: Oxford.

our emergency plan could be further described as a set of proposed actions designed to manage a dangerous unforeseen sudden situation. This concept will become more relevant when we consider the preparation of a plan later; the concept of an emergency plan is well understood and accepted but the nature of a 'plan' and what it means is perhaps less well understood, or indeed, taken for granted. Emergency plans are never finished. When a plan is written it enters a cycle, the emergency planning cycle, for the duration of its life (see Figure 2.1). It begins degrading immediately. An emergency plan needs constant maintenance and attention because it is dynamic. It describes activity, gives instruction, directs policy and crucially is only effective when implemented by people trained in its use. A plan that is not used, reviewed, updated and tested will in a short time become redundant and will ultimately fail to deliver what it was designed to achieve. In fact such a plan can become a hindrance and counterproductive.

Having a plan brings with it responsibility and accountability. Deciding to have a plan is a big commitment and should be the result of a detailed logical assessment process based upon risk analysis, which we will examine later. Once a plan is 'live' it creates duties and obligations on the participants which could later form the basis for rigorous scrutiny or even litigation and prosecution. The more detail that is included in a plan the more scope there is for criticism. We will discuss 'over planning' later but the key in effective plan preparation, if one is required, is to include only the essential information.

Plans are obviously central to effective emergency management and they can vary in style, format, content and medium (how they are accessed, sorted and used) but they fall into broad categories.

Trying to envisage the multitude of plan types could be bewildering and trying to choose the right type for your circumstances can also be confusing. Where to start making those choices often leads to questions such as:

- Why produce plans anyway?
- Do we really need a plan?
- What or who tells us we have to have plans?
- Who is required to produce plans?
- What has to go into a plan?
- What is the best format?
- Who needs to be aware of the plan?
- Do we have to test plans, how and how often?

In fact the list of questions could go on and on. This Chapter is intended to answer those questions and many more to assist the EPO in making that choice. The first consideration is the type of plans that are in general use today, which will be a starting point for consideration.

Types of Plan

It is interesting how people refer to plans, often very loosely, causing confusion, for example:

- an Emergency Plan;
- a Contingency Plan;
- a Business Continuity Plan;
- a Multi-agency Plan;
- A Major Incident Plan.

All the plans just mentioned are generic in nature describing general principles and procedures of specific aspects of a response to different situations. They do not refer to a specific hazard or threat but are designed to create a management framework for that given circumstance. All are in fact 'resilience' plans, an overaching descriptor of their function. All plans exist to create, improve or establish that state of 'resilience'. Resilience planning for an organisation may include many plans, including Emergency Plans, Contingency Plans and a Business Continuity Plan depending on the nature of the organisation. It is important to understand what the plan is for and ensure the correct title is used.

Beneath those generic plans live the very specific plans such as the flu pandemic plan, flood plan, smallpox plan, CBRN plan, heatwave plan, etc. Depending on the nature and purpose of the plan it could attract another label, with potential to confuse matters again, such as 'Emergency Flooding Response Plan' or 'Heat Wave Contingency Plan' or 'Multi-agency Contingency CBRN Plan' or a 'CBRN Emergency Response Plan'. Choosing the right plan title is important. 'Emergency' suggests fast response, with actions to mitigate or prevent an imminent or ongoing or potential threat to human welfare or prevent serious environmental damage. 'Contingency' on the other hand describes a future event or circumstance which is possible but cannot be predicted with certainty. This latter description is broader in context and caters for a whole range of events which may not be considered 'urgent' but nevertheless present critical situations. This discussion may seem rather convoluted and full of semantics but there is merit in making these distinctions to add clarity in production of plans. They are important descriptors in terms of the hierarchy of plans.

For example, the police: they may have a series of emergency plans to cater for 'emergencies' of all shapes and sizes which require a fast response set with a list of actions. Then they may have a series of contingency plans to cater for non-emergency situations such as VIP visits, planned public demonstrations, football matches, etc., and finally they will have (as required by the CCA as a Category 1 responder) a business continuity plan to ensure the organisation can function. So, all three sets of plans go to create a resilient organisation.

For our purposes we are looking at the characteristics of plan type. In general plans will fall into six main categories:

1) Generic

This type of plan can be viewed as the organisational default procedures that can be applied to any incident or emergency but will not contain incident-specific detail. They will spell out general principles and prompts on management roles and responsibilities within the organisation, organisational procedures and policy containing definitions, general actions and checklists. They are used to deal with incidents and events that are not specifically planned for in detail. These are often formatted in an *aide mémoire* style on a few pages of laminated card. They are often used as an operational reference for first line responders to assist initial decision making. For example, it may contain general health and safety advice based upon likely scenarios that may be faced. The procedures within generic plans are applicable across all emergencies.

2) Site-specific

A site specific plan refers to a known location—e.g. industrial plant, football stadium, airport, port, industrial unit, warehouse, office block, etc.— where known hazards could occur and require planning for. For example, known flood risk areas would fall into this category. Therefore more detail is known about potential hazards, resource requirements, population profile and geography. These plans contain more specific information such as maps, floor plans, photographs, evacuation routes, assembly points, hazard inventories and descriptions. They also can contain more specific health and safety advice and information as the potential hazards are known. They can be a statutory requirement for certain industries from one or more regulatory bodies.

3) Incident-specific

These plans refer to incidents which could occur at any location, usually transport- or movement-related, e.g. aeroplane, train or coach crash, including the spillage or discharge of dangerous chemicals, plumes or radiation into the environment. They could also include 'flash flooding' outside known river or coastal flood risk areas. They are heavily focused upon health and safety advice and warning and informing procedures for the public. Into this category would also fall the terrorist-type activities such as explosions or chemical, biological, radiological or nuclear (CBRN) attacks. Included in this category would be system failures on large computer or communications networks or cyber attacks. They would also include issues related to disease.

The plans listed so far are designed to address various types of hazards and threats, known and unknown. The next group of plans are configured to ensure that the response to those events is the most effective possible, involving the right people and organisations in terms of integration and co-ordination.

4) Individual (Ind) or single agency

These plans are produced within a single agency or organisation and are intended for internal use. They will describe how the organisation will respond to an incident within the organisation which includes business continuity and emergency management arrangements. Essentially they are management tools which are only relevant to that organisation. They describe internal specific procedures and processes which are unique to that organisation, without which the organisation cannot respond effectively. In effect they are the most important plans of all. If the organisation's response forms part of a larger multi-agency plan the single agency plan will also describe how it will respond, react or support a multi-agency plan to which it subscribes. These are really the driving force of organisations' response and therefore the building block behind all multi-agency and multi-level plans. This type of plan will be used as the example in Chapter 3.

5) Multi-agency

Multi-agency plans, in effect, are a composite of individual or single agency plans drawn together under a single narrative. They describe the planning arrangements of many organisations and are brought together and amalgamated into one set of arrangements by a lead organisation. They are plans to co-ordinate a response. They tend to be very comprehensive but designed for reference and slow-time activation compared to single agency or individual plans which can be applied rapidly and dynamically with actions. They have that co-ordinating function to ensure the combined response operates in harmony. Many of these plans are required by legislation and regulatory guidance—such as that concerning chemical sites, nuclear sites, flooding, etc, It is also this type of plan that is more likely to undergo radical and frequent change in as much as there are so many organisations involved that inevitably they are changing constantly in terms of their procedures. There are also changes at a political level in which public service organisations can change as a result of political change where established organisations are amalgamated, subsumed into other organisations, re-organised or abolished entirely—for example the abolition of regional government offices. These changes can have profound impact on emergency procedures in which everyone has to relearn who is who and who does what. This can be very confusing—not only for the planners but also the public. Examples include new geographic boundaries, new responsibilities and titles, new groups or new regulatory frameworks and so on.

6) Multi-level

These plans are produced to address more than one level of the civil protection framework. They can be international, national or regional and then local but all dealing with a single issue for example, foot and mouth disease, coastal pollution, pandemic influenza, radiation emergency, etc. Each layer or level will describe a part of the response but they will fully integrate. This multi-level arrangement works well where there may be slight differences in structure between localities, regions or devolved governments. These plans are always multi-agency and are without doubt the most complex to prepare and maintain. For example, a serious civil nuclear emergency occurs in the UK, plans will exist on the site, locally off-site, sub-nationally, nationally and internationally—all have to dovetail.

Although there appears to be quite a number of plans, each has a specific role to fulfil. Too generic and the specific detail and information is lost. Too specific and there is a danger of duplication and overlap, leading to potential confusion. The key is getting the balance right, but it is important to be able to distinguish between types and how they influence each other. What they all have in common is that they are all living, dynamic and changing. They all also form part of the emergency planning cycle.

TASK 2.1

List 10 site specific plans

List 10 incident specific plan

List 3 multi-agency plans

TIP: Check out your Local Resilience Forum web site.

The Emergency Planning Cycle

Producing plans and exercising those plans lies at the heart of emergency planning. It is a skill that is essential for every EPO. Creating plans and exercising forms part of a cycle of emergency planning (see Figure 2.1) activity that ensures that plans are up to date, viable and efficient. The example in Figure 2.1 is a simple illustration to show a plan as a living dynamic document. Once the plan is complete the people in the plan need to be trained. The plan is then exercised or tested, which will inevitably indicate where lessons can be learned. This is then fed back into the plan—leading to more training and the cycle continues throughout the life cycle of the plan.

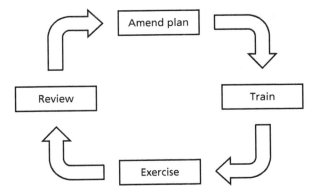

Figure 2.1 Emergency Planning Cycle

This activity also supports the principle of building a resilient organisation, with properly trained staff working with effective emergency plans. In this Chapter we will examine the issues that drive the planning and exercise processes. What directs the production of plans? And, having produced the plans, how we can ensure they will work?

Integrated Emergency Planning

The CCA supports and endorses the principle of Integrated Emergency Management (IEM) which is based upon six activities:

1. Anticipation—Identifying threats and hazards.
2. Assessment—Quantifying and analysing those threats and hazards into risk.
3. Prevention—Putting in place measures to reduce the risk or stop the event happening.
4. Preparation—Making a plan, this includes training and exercising staff.
5. Response—How to deal with the event when it happens.
6. Recovery management—How to return to near normality.

IEM as described within the CCA guidance is the definitive usage of the term. However, the term IEM can also be used to describe the process of engaging other partners and stakeholders in the emergency planning and response processes. This is by way of ensuring each organisation's set of processes, procedures and structures are compatible, complementary and 'fit' one another to produce a joined-up approach—and are therefore integrated. This is particularly important in developing multi-agency plans where different approaches need to be developed into a single coherent set of arrangements. This approach can also be seen in individual organisations where they develop their internal emergency planning or BCM procedures as a seamless progression from their day-to-day activities and so 'integrate' their arrangements into a coherent whole.

We will now look at each IEM activity in turn as described in the CCA guidance (see Figure 2.2).

Anticipation

The whole emergency planning process is underpinned by the IEM activities. Each activity has to be considered in turn to ensure that all aspects of the planning process are fully addressed. The key planning areas centre initially on anticipation and assessment—establishing a need to plan and risk assessing the potential hazards: what should be planned for? Anticipation means trying to identify what new hazards and threats could arise, sometimes referred to 'horizon scanning' or risk identification. The hazards and threats may result from many factors such as environmental issues, industrial issues, legislation, terrorism, economic issues or disease. Having identified potential hazards and threats their impact has to be assessed to inform the level of planning needed to mitigate or eliminate the risk.

Measuring risk for planning purposes—assessment

How can risk be measured? As there is no 'ideal' plan to suit all events for all organisations nor is there a totally reliable risk model to inform the decision to produce plans. Risk is an ethereal concept which can, to a degree, be measured and the risks most of us face are quite obvious and the decision to make plans is clear. Nevertheless a risk assessment process is needed to ensure all aspects of risk have been addressed. Working through a 'process' will ensure

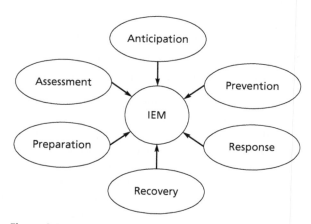

Figure 2.2 Integrated Emergency Management

a level of consistency and objectivity in making those risk assessments and ultimately whether to plan for them or not.

Before beginning the process of attempting to measure risk with a view to producing a plan, it is important to establish a 'position' on plans. The implications of having a plan as opposed to not having one is a risk judgement in itself even before the risk assessment related to the threat and hazards itself is considered. Unless driven by regulation or directives the decision to have a plan or not can in fact require a risk assessment process within an organisation before that decision is taken; alternatively they can simply turn a blind eye. But why would anyone want to do this? Some might argue that not having a plan eliminates the consequences of it going wrong, having to write it, maintain it and exercise it and all the associated costs—which can be considerable. Producing a plan has consequences, and not just the time spent in creating one and maintaining it. On a positive note a plan will be tangible proof of an organisation's commitment to prepare for and mitigate a threat or hazard that has been deemed to be a significant risk. However, the plan could be examined and analysed by a third party such as a court, inquest or inquiry to establish any shortcomings and deficiencies. A plan written by a public service organisation will be open to public scrutiny and criticism and indeed private organisations and companies that share their plans with public organisations may have them exposed to public scrutiny. In addition, a plan will have an effect on someone, and the mere existence of the plan can create a 'duty of care' at some level towards those affected by the plan, in particular, employees. In addition, if people have been informed that there is a plan, and they will be affected by it, the plan cannot simply be discontinued or modified without involving those affected. So it is quite a responsibility and the plans must be robust, tested and fit for purpose. But not having or even considering a plan in the face of a potential hazard is a high risk strategy in itself and one which could have very serious consequences if the incident in question occurs. The position of not having a plan is short-sighted and a potentially dangerous view, but one that does exist.

Every organisation, both public and private of whatever size, should undergo a risk assessment process to identify internal vulnerabilities, threats and hazards—from a business continuity perspective at least. This should also include any potential external threats and hazards that may have an adverse impact. This process should also include how they would interact with external partners and agencies.

KEY POINT

Every organisation should complete an organisational risk assessment covering areas of BCM and emergency management. This should be documented.

Planning has many undisputed benefits in terms of managing crisis and emergency events but getting the right planning balance is crucial. Over planning can occur as we see later, and indeed, inadequate planning is often the cause of response failure—as the old saying goes 'failing to plan is planning to fail'. In addition, not engaging with partners and stakeholders sufficiently can result in another saying from one partner or stakeholder to another—'lack of planning on your part does not constitute an emergency on my part'. Assessing the risk is therefore vital as it will inform your decision to plan or not.

So how can risk be quantified or measured? Risk measurement and quantification can be a highly complex activity. There is an enormous body of literature on the subject and it is not intended to go into great detail here save to illustrate a process that the EPO will find useful and complies with the CCA guidance. Trying to create a set of criteria which justify the creation of a plan can be problematic. An event that is potentially catastrophic but extremely unlikely may be worth writing a plan for because of the serious consequences, whereas a moderate event which happens relatively frequently may also lead to creating a plan because although the consequences may be less serious the event has regular adverse impact on the community, albeit low level. How is moderate or frequently defined?

Risk is subjective. Trying to measure risk accurately can be and is often unreliable. There is no doubt that the Japanese nuclear site in Fukushima had undergone very complex and extensive risk assessments and a sound safety case agreed with regulators and the operators. However, the events in March 2011 following an earthquake and tsunami off the coast of Japan showed how vulnerable the process is to the unforeseen or unexpected. In highly complex industries containing thousands of processes and interactions with the possibility of unknown variables (such as a tsunami or terrorists in jet airliners) combined with the vagaries of human behaviours and weaknesses, there is little wonder that risk assessment can be only be judged as an educated guess. Organisations can and do get it wrong; but not all is doom and gloom! The actual risk assessment process can be very difficult, despite very clever calculations of probability, failure and impact, in many cases it is beyond most EPOs to understand. For our purposes, however, we need to be able to quantify the risk to be able to inform our decision as to whether to write a plan or not against a set of reproducible criteria. To focus our thoughts, the use of the traditional risk assessment matrix such as the one in Figure 2.3 may help to categorise the risk. There are numerous forms and formats for this chart but essentially they do the same job. Essentially you are measuring severity against probability and hopefully assigning a 'value'.

It must be remembered that the trigger point, or criteria at which one decides to create a plan, can be determined in a number of ways. Within the context of a national framework created by the CCA there has to be a degree of consistency across the country. For example, it would be unacceptable for

Likelihood →

Impact ↓

RISK	IMPROBABLE	POSSIBLE	PROBABLE	HIGHLY PROBABLE
MINIMAL	Low	Medium	Medium	Medium
MODERATE	Low	Medium	High	High
SEVERE	Medium	Medium	High	High
CATASTROPHIC	High	High	High	High

Figure 2.3 A typical risk assessment model matrix

one Local Resilience Forum (LRF) to agree to have a certain plan in place and a neighbouring LRF not to. Therefore risk criteria can be 'a given' as directed by legislation (for example, in relation to chemical and nuclear sites), advice from Government Departments (such as the National Risk Register) or professional advice such as insurance companies or internal company policy. Where this direction is not so explicit the ultimate decision rests with the individual, organisation or appointed committee or group (either public or private sector) by having a detailed impact analysis about how that risk can be managed—planning being only one element of this. But whatever criteria or risk level is agreed, the risk matrix is a very simple way of creating a process in quantifying risk and the process also demonstrates that the risk has at least been addressed or considered and can provide a rationale for writing or, more importantly, not writing a plan.

The risk matrix has inherent flaws, probably the most obvious being the assigning of values to the descriptors. For example, what does 'probable' mean in our example of a matrix at Figure 2.3? A useful and potentially entertaining exercise to demonstrate this is to ask an audience to rate 'probable' in terms of percentage certainty. Is probable 70% of the event happening or is it 50%? You will get many interpretations! To make the matrix more accurate it is best to define your descriptors. 'Probable' may lie between 60% and 70%. But how do we know we can rate that event as 'probable' or falling between 60% and 70% probability? The only way is to seek advice from those who know the most about the hazards. This can be from experts who can calculate potential failure probability, refer to historical data or review similar past events and extrapolate the calculation by scaling up or down.

Again, what is 'moderate' impact? How many lives lost or properties damaged?

So the most accurate means of quantifying those hazards and threats is to engage with the experts and rely on their opinion and advice. If this can be achieved it adds a factor of reliability into the assessment. This is often the reason that many risk assessments are directed to LRFs to ensure a consistency across all LRFs.

In short, if reliable numerical data can be obtained and applied with a degree of confidence it should be used. This is known as 'quantitative' risk assessment, where measurement is applied, whereas a more subjective approach is understanding and appreciating the 'qualitative' characteristics of risk.

Qualitative aspects could include the non-measurable issues, such as fear of the hazard or threat, and lack of understanding of the risks. It could be argued that it is the qualitative aspects of risk and risk perception that will have more planning implications than quantitative measurement alone. It is individual risk perceptions that will influence behaviour, and so understanding those qualitative elements of risk perception will inform the EPO how to address the risk on a practical level. Listening to community concerns, fears and understanding can add value to the risk assessment process. But the qualitative nature of the data can complicate assigning an objective value, so it is not surprising that many risk practitioners favour a more measurable entity. The message for the EPO is: use a more quantitative risk assessment approach to inform planning decisions but be very alive to the flaws that approach holds, also seek out and embrace the qualitative information and use that in developing the plans themselves. In other words, engage the affected community and understand the risk through their eyes and plan accordingly.

Risk treatments

Writing a plan is a risk treatment in itself as a means of managing that risk. Other accepted risk treatments exist which may include:

1. Avoid the risk—it is too dangerous or 'risky' so eliminate the activity or proposal.
2. Accepting the risk—the adverse impact is such that we can cope with it—no planning.
3. Minimising or managing the risk—plan for it.
4. Share the risk—reduce its potential impact by spreading the risk by contracting out or using partners to accept some of the risk.

Therefore, once a risk is identified there are options for managing that risk open to the risk manager or EPO. In basic form, they can avoid the risk entirely and cancel the activity or adopt a totally different way of approaching the risk. They can totally accept the risk as tolerable or where possible reduce one of the factors such as probability or impact and so reduce the risk to a more acceptable level and in this case they do not expend time, effort and money. They can keep or retain the risk as it stands and put in place arrangements to mitigate and reduce the impact, for example writing a plan. They can transfer the risk by insurance, contracting out to another or sharing the risk by engaging multi-agency approaches. These are basic risk management options. For planning purposes we will assume that the risk treatment against agreed criteria will be to create a plan.

Referring to the matrix (see Figure 2.3), assume that all 'high' risk hazards will be planned for, that is the chosen criteria. If the hazard is judged to be 'possible' and 'catastrophic' a HIGH rating would result. This would require a plan. If however, the judgement or analysis for another hazard came out as 'highly probable' but 'minimal' impact that would result in a MEDIUM risk and therefore no plan is required or can be accommodated in a more general generic procedure.

This trigger level must be agreed and supported. In an individual organisation their trigger level for internal planning purposes is their choice alone. But remember if they are part of a larger multi-agency plan that decision may not be negotiable. If the risk management/assessment process is committee led, such as with an LRF Risk Assessment Working Group (RAWG) there has to be an agreed trigger level that is consistent with national guidance to ensure that no hazards slip through the net.

But let us differentiate the kind of risk we may encounter in emergency planning. As we now understand, the first 'risk' relates to planning—shall we or shall we not create a plan? The second 'risk' is associated with the hazards and threats associated with responding to the hazard or threat on both the responders and those affected, e.g. the public or staff. The second risk factors we will discuss in our response Chapter later.

TASK 2.2

What is the six-step risk assessment process? Refer to the CCA Guidance notes.

Over planning

One of the important advantages of using a risk assessment methodology is to prevent 'over planning'. Setting a risk threshold too low or not using an assessment tool at all can result in producing plans unnecessarily with all the attendant problems that may incur. An informal or casual approach to planning can lead to a situation where every conceivable potential adverse event seems to result in a plan. This is an exponential activity in which a final conclusion is never reached because many incidents can be the combination of a series of unforeseen unconnected events that are completely random. It is impossible to plan for everything and producing a plan should not be seen as a 'comfort blanket' or 'ticking a box' exercise. There has to be rational purpose behind a plan. The over planning approach could be classed as paralysis by analysis! What is reasonably foreseeable is the key and the applied test.

Preparation, response and recovery

Having managed and understood the risks the next stage is to consider preparing for and responding to the event if it happens. These activities will focus on creating the plans and everything which supports that process, such as training and exercising. Preparation, response and recovery within the IEM are the three activities that produce the main area of planning activity and indeed, form the basis for the two CCA guidance documents. They can be viewed as almost a continuum and are interdependent, each leading into the other as issues emerge and are taken up by putting arrangements in place to address them.

Recovery management is often seen as a post incident activity but effective post incident management begins at the response phase and is usually managed by established groups (like the Recovery Co-ordinating Group (RCG) followed by the Strategic Recovery Co-ordinating Group (SRCG) we shall discuss in Chapter 5) set up for the purpose of restoring and rebuilding the community in the aftermath of an incident when the emergency phase of the incident is over. Recovery management is without doubt the most challenging aspect of emergency management and can far exceed the level of support and resourcing associated with or needed in managing the incident itself. It will also be demonstrated later that the RCG has a role to play in the emergency phase of an incident to ensure that issues under consideration and decisions made are taken in the light of their potential impact on longer term recovery.

Prevention

The remaining activity within IEM is 'prevention'. Prevention is mainly addressed through legislation and regulation, generally on health and safety and environmental protection grounds and putting in place the physical barriers and procedures to reduce the likelihood of the event happening in the first place. For example, this is seen in the very high safety standards within the aviation and nuclear industries. This area is often the focus for Health and Safety legislation monitored by the Health and Safety Executive (HSE) and other legislation that governs safety on industrial sites and transport. In terms of the CCA, prevention does have a place in response in that activating a plan can avert an emergency occurring and so prevent it happening.

IEM is the framework around which the emergency management and response is built and articulates principles that every EPO should understand and be able to apply.

Plans and the rationale behind creating plans, as we have seen, is central to managing risk and dealing with crises and emergencies. In understanding the types of plan in use we will now examine, within the context of the UK emergency planning community which creates plans and how they are integrated and used to manage incidents from simple low level events right up to widespread catastrophic events.

Planning Guidance

Emergency preparedness, response and recovery within the UK is influenced, if not governed, by three sets of guidance—one of which is the CCA and its Guidance. The CCA offers guidance as to what must appear in each plan and how plans are treated; these stipulations can be read in the CCA guidance documents.

In addition, every EPO should have ready access to the two sets of documents about to be mentioned. If the EPO operates within one of the devolved administrations they should also be familiar with all of the amendments the devolved administrations subscribe to.

The UK Concept of Operations (CONOPS)

This document sets out the UK Central Government Response under the following headings:

1. Emergency management in the UK.
2. The Central Response Framework.
3. The Role and Organisation of the Cabinet Office Briefing Rooms (COBR).
4. Planning assumptions for the UK central response.
5. Local response and recovery to an emergency in the UK.
6. Sub-national response (please note that at the time of writing this was under review).
7. Devolved Administrations.

The Association of Chief Police Officers (ACPO)

The following important documents[2] set out the police approach to co-ordinating the emergency phase of an emergency where public safety is at immediate risk:

1. Emergency procedures.
2. Command and control.
3. Multi-agency interoperability.

The content and guidance within all of these documents will be reflected in the text of this and other Chapters but are required reading for the EPO.

Who Creates Plans?

Before looking in detail at how the plans are put together or used in a real time response, it will be useful at this stage to consider the main planning groups that may be encountered and identify how they integrate plans. Plans should never be seen in isolation. Every plan will have impact and dependency at some level on others. This may be to assist in the implementation or at least to notify and inform others. It may simply be a case of quality assuring the plan or raising awareness of its existence to others to ensure it does not create conflict with other responders. For example, a business may consult outside organisations about their internal BCM plans to ensure that their emergency contact numbers are correct or their assumptions about external support are correct.

The CCA also encourages information sharing and collaboration in many areas of emergency management but particularly in plan preparation. Plans written in isolation have limited use. Having an understanding of the different planning levels and types will assist the EPO to develop an appreciation of how plans produced by different organisations can, and should, build into a coherent meaningful response.

Organisational/business planning

Historically plans seemed to have been the reserve of the traditional emergency responders or 'dangerous' industries. Both areas are well versed in preparing plans, but there is a growing recognition that every organisation must consider its own vulnerabilities and requirements to respond to an unforeseen adverse event happening, even if they are not part of the multi-agency response themselves. This category can range from small manufacturing businesses, service industries, to schools and colleges to mention a few. Not only does it make good business sense to plan for emergencies but it addresses obligations to take all reasonable steps to ensure the welfare and well-being of those within their care or responsibility. At the very least the Health and

---

[2] <http://www.acpo.police.uk/documents/crime/2009/200907CRICCG01.pdf>.

Safety at Work Act 1974 requires the business owner to carry out actions that are reasonable and practical in order to protect the workforce. The Act effectively covers everyone on the premises at any given time. The Management of Health and Safety at Work Regulations 1999 also require employers to risk assess any dangers that could arise in that workplace and implement procedures to cater for that event to safeguard those on the premises. Can an organisation anticipate what incident or event could compromise the organisation? Should it plan to avoid one or more of the following?

- possible injury to employees or the public;
- damage to the environment;
- legal action;
- financial loss through litigation;
- adverse publicity;
- loss of reputation;
- causing corporate manslaughter;
- casuing criminal negligence.

If the answer to any one of the points just listed is yes—they need a plan. The first consideration is clearly a business one. Business continuity is essential for all organisations at some level—the size, complexity and type of business will determine the scale and nature of BCM planning needed. Although BCM has grown into an industry in its own right, it is weighted in favour of ensuring the running of a good business or good business governance. Although emergency procedures do feature within some BCM plans, BCM for non-emergency responder organisations tends to be more inward looking about preserving the running of the business; often overlooked is the impact external events and agencies can have on their business, or indeed the impact they can have on those outside their company. All those involved in BCM should understand that a business can be affected by a range of external events, from supply chain issues, external contractors, utility and IT disruption, weather, terrorism, crime and sickness. Where they often fail is by planning in isolation and not engaging with external agencies, assessing external risk and integrating their plans to the emergency response. Many commercial organisations and learning institutions, even of modest size, fail to appreciate the importance of engagement and sharing information with their external stakeholders and partners. In practice, few business organisations have understanding of the role of the LRF or external emergency responder organisations. The following key points are often overlooked:

- To what extent have external agencies contributed to your plans?
- What experience does the senior management team have in working with external partners?

- What emergency management training is offered involving external partners?
- How compatible and integrated are our processes with those externally?
- What external support is out there to help us?
- Can our emergency facilities 'Incident Room' accommodate external partners if required?

Preparing plans is not just for the large organisations, emergency services or those required to do so by law. It is an activity that all commercial organisations should consider; however small, they should seek advice, support and guidance. Where necessary they should prepare plans and test them. This is the first building block in building community resilience; it makes good business sense too and demonstrates a competent resilient organisation. Engagement with the LRF will assist many organisations to make those decisions and obtain that information they need to plan effectively.

Look at Figure 2.4—only when there is complete inter-organisational interoperability operating in harmony using the same terminology, emergency management compatibility, mutual understanding and communication will a truly joined up emergency response be achieved.

KEY POINT

All commercial organisations should engage with their LRF as a matter of routine to discuss issues of general resilience.

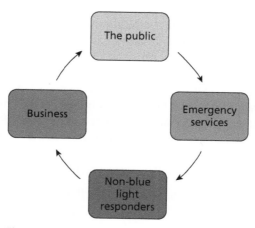

Figure 2.4 Interoperability

Note in the idealistic illustration in Figure 2.4 how interconnected these groups are, or should be: all groups working in harmony and all part of the emergency response, building total resilience.

Local Resilience Forum planning (or Local Resilience Partnerships in the case of Scotland)

The LRF is not only a source of information and guidance for all those involved in plan preparation but is the primary planning forum at local level. Within an LRF the risk assessment process is usually carried out by a Risk Assessment Working Group or RAWG, a sub-group of the LRF. Based upon the risk assessment outcome plan preparation is recommended or not, with the ultimate objective to reduce, control and mitigate the effects of an emergency created by that risk on their community. The issue for the LRF is to agree what criteria should apply to trigger the creation of a plan. Some planning is obligatory following direction from government or legislation but other hazards, often localised, are not subject to that direction and rely wholly on a risk assessment process to inform that decision. That decision has to be based upon a level of risk that is acceptable or unacceptable to the LRF and that will direct them to declare that a plan must be created. Therefore, each LRF should have set criteria that trigger the production of a plan together with a process to identify who the lead organisation(s) will be to produce that plan. The risk assessment process must have a 'product' or 'outcome' otherwise the risk assessment can become meaningless and diluted.

In terms of identifying a lead organisation, it is difficult to see how LRFs can achieve this effectively as they have no authority to direct any agency to carry out work. If it cannot be agreed it is incumbent upon each organisation with a stake in the response to create their own plans (individual or single agency). This option will be discussed under multi-agency plans later. The tendency is to mitigate the risk identified by the LRF by listing and producing existing emergency arrangements prepared by individual Category 1 and 2 responders and using them in a generalised way. This is really not ideal but a well run LRF should resolve those issues.

Multi-agency planning units

Although not common practice at the moment the establishment of multi-agency planning teams is a more focused and efficient means of fulfilling completely integrated emergency management and should be a consideration for all LRFs. Essentially it is a means of bringing together lead Category 1 responders who can work more closely together, co-located to apply their individual expertise in creating multi-agency plans on behalf of the LRF and developing their own plans in closer liaison with partners.

At least two pilot schemes in England have seen the police, fire and rescue service, the ambulance service and the local authority co-locating to be able to work more effectively together. The advantages of such an arrangement are numerous:

- Better and easier communication between participants.
- Enhanced use of resources, deliver Best Value principles.
- Better co-ordination in joint training and exercising.
- Co-ordinated and centralised cost recovery regime where used.
- More effective and rapid updating and amending of plans.
- One stop shop for advice and information outside agencies, business and the public.
- Better 'problem solving', 'think tank' capability.
- Centre of excellence—collective and in-depth experience.
- Quicker response capability and dynamic incident management.
- Reduced formal meetings—less time and energy wasted.
- More cost-effective administration.

The LRF, however, remains the focal point of local planning and response and supports the underlying principle that in the UK response is locally driven in most cases. An important product of the LRF risk assessment process is the Community Risk Register.

Community Risk Register

Notwithstanding who contributes to the planning process, all local hazards and risk assessments are contained in a public document called a 'Community Risk Register' or CRR, produced by each LRF. In it can be seen how each identified hazard is assessed and treated and what plans are in place. These important documents can be examined by approaching the local LRF and/or by viewing the document on their local websites. The CCA makes this process a statutory duty for Category 1 responders which is usually discharged through the LRFs.

TASK 2.3

- Find your LRF CRR.
- Where can it be found apart from the web site?
- Examine the risk treatments—what kind of plans are in place?

Sub-national and national planning

Sub-national support and involvement in emergency management forms a bridge between the local response, and the central or national response. Sub-national involvement also facilitates co-ordination of the local response and the preparation of wide area plans. Historically, the regional or wide area involvement was not very well developed and indeed was not mentioned in the seminal publication 'Dealing with Disaster' 1992. In fact it was recognised and assumed that a large-scale emergency would be notified to the Cabinet Office as co-ordinator to alert the relevant lead Government Departments, specifically the Secretary of State to the Civil Contingencies Committee (CCC). Day-to-day executive, policy and representational work was carried out by officials from the Emergency Planning Division in the Home Office.

However, in Spring 2001 the UK suffered a major national outbreak of foot and mouth disease. This lasted many months and communication flow between central government and local strategic co-ordination centres proved less than efficient and showed gaps in the role of regional co-ordination, as it was then. As a result, the regional role was enhanced dramatically over a short period of time with large regional offices established and large numbers of staff. This created Regional Resilience Teams (RRT) and introduced the concept of the Regional Civil Contingencies Committee (RCCC) to co-ordinate resources and information flow to central government. These processes were ultimately reflected into the drafting of the Civil Contingencies Bill about that time and then into the Act of 2004.

The regional tier of emergency support and resource co-ordination did in effect dramatically increase, but at the same time it generated extra workloads for emergency planning local offices and EPO managers across all UK regions. However, RRTs did create opportunities to put in place co-ordinated regional plans to assist the local response. Communication with central government was improved as regional government staff would quickly attend local multi-agency co-ordination centres to begin that communication link with central government. However, the underlying proposition of having high level regional involvement created other potential conflicts in terms of blurring command and control and was in danger of diluting the autonomy exercised by Chief Constables to direct and co-ordinate the local response.

In March 2011, the Government announced the abolition of Government Offices of the regions and with that the demise of the regional resilience structure as it was. As part of the new restructuring arrangements the Government Department of Communities and Local Government (DCLG) created the Resilience and Emergencies Division (RED) to support all LRFs using the Resilience Direct (RD)[3] to support information sharing,

---

[3] Resilience Direct (RD)—A secure web-based facility created (sponsored) by the Cabinet Office which can be accessed by Category 1 and 2 responders to share information, receive updates, share

collaboration and communication. In addition, to provide local support, rather than having nine government offices of the regions, each with an RRT and RCCC, England has been divided into three areas, with London standing alone and with the devolved administrations of Scotland, Wales and Northern Ireland remaining the same. These 'sub-national' areas in England are described as North, Central and South. Each area has a dedicated point of contact for all LRFs to access and there is a commitment to deploy a Government Liaison Officer (GLO) to any Strategic Co-ordination Centre (SCC) as required 24/7 to act as that conduit of communication for government and provide 'situation reports' (also known as 'sit-reps') as required. The area office emergency planning advisors would attend LRF meetings to offer advice and information together with providing support to facilitate better collaboration and information sharing on a wider area basis. This new position would reflect the 'localism' agenda being promoted by the government to place more control into local hands.

At a response level, what is emerging, with regard to regional resilience, is a bringing together, as required, of a number of LRFs affected by the emergency. In other words, a collaborative multi-LRF resilience structure based on variable geography, to create that co-ordination role previously provided by the RCCC. These are called multi-LRF Response Co-ordinating Groups (RCGs) (not to be confused with Recovery Co-ordinating Groups). It is intended that these groups may meet virtually by teleconference.

Where does this leave regional planning? Essentially, collaborative arrangements will exist whereby clustered LRFs, with a lead LRF, will address regional planning programmes. Specific planning forums overseen by DCLG/CCS will ensure adequate planning arrangements, risk assessments and that collective work proceeds accordingly. For example, working on recovery issues with multi-agency Recovery Co-ordinating Groups with and across government departments in developing guidance. It would perhaps be more accurate to describe this new approach to 'regional' planning as area planning since 'areas' may not be coterminus with previous regional boundaries.

Local authority planning

At a local level, depending upon the local authority (LA) structure—District, Unitary, County Council or Metropolitan—the planning function and who within the authority carries that out may differ although the generic term 'local authority' remains. But local authorities do have certain emergency planning responsibilities and obligations. In fact it could be argued that the LA bears the brunt of civil emergencies in terms of support and long-term

---

real time incident management information and use as a real time message management system in local Strategic Co-ordination Centres (SCC). To be replaced by 'Resilience Direct' in 2014.

recovery. As such, LAs have developed expertise and capability which is vital in emergency response.

As a lead Category 1 responder their planning obligations are considerable but they also facilitate and prepare the creation of multi-agency plans related to planning requirements, for example under the Control of Major Accident Hazards (COMAH) Regulations 1999 including the Pipeline Safety Regulations 1996 and the Radiation Emergency and Public Information Regulations 2001 (REPPIR). These pieces of legislation were initially set aside from the CCA on the premise that the regulations already fulfilled the principles underpinning the CCA. Therefore the LA have a requirement to prepare multi-agency plans for fixed chemical sites as required by COMAH and fixed nuclear sites as required by REPPIR. Many LAs also prepare other multi-agency plans and link in closely with the LRF to ensure a fully integrated and co-ordinated approach. These plans would include those to assist managing the voluntary services and their role in caring for the community, for example plans for rest centres, call handling facilities, faith community plans, emergency mortuaries, etc.

A major shift in LA planning responsibilities occurred in April 2013. The local authorities assumed new responsibility for public health provision for the community following the restructing of the UK National Health Service (NHS). This will require the local authority to take a prominent role along with Public Health England (previously the Health Protection Agency) with additional planning responsibilites for managing disease outbreaks and general health of the population.

Multi-Agency Plans in Perspective

As we have seen the LRF, multi-LRFs, local authority and central government subscribe to and support multi-agency plans. There is a duty on Category 1 responders to consider the production of multi-agency plans where each organisation has a role to play in dealing with a particular emergency. The CCA also stipulates that each organisation should agree who will take the lead.

But having agreed to create a multi-agency plan—what is it and how useful is it? A multi-agency plan is just that—it co-ordinates the combined response, or each individual response is included based upon their own individual plans. Multi-agency plans will 'outline' the roles and responsibilities of each participating organisation and describe an agreed set of arrangements. But if an organisation contributes to that plan they will need to set up their own internal arrangementsin support of that plan, an individual or single agency plan. In fact many organisations do hold their own plans which direct and reflect their own emergency arrangements. These are not multi-agency plans per se but could be viewed as internal management tools for that organisation alone as we have seen earlier. The police, for example, will probably have numerous internal plans because they have to co-ordinate the overall emergency response to so many incidents and have additional responsibilities to support many multi-agency plans. The lead organisation is often the local authority for multi-agency plans or a group formed from the LRF. Where multi-LRFs are operating at sub-national level on planning issues the lead could be a single LRF.

TASK 2.4

- Describe the difference between a single agency plan and a multi-agency plan.
- What is the relationship between the CCA planning requirements and existing civil protection legislation?
- Outline how communication is established between local and central government in a large-scale emergency.

Plan format

Whatever motivates or requires plans to be prepared—be it producing plans under legislation, producing plans simply as good business practice, or contributing to a multi-agency plan—requires a decision as to what type of plan is needed. What type of plan meets the requirement? Individual plans can range in content from merely call out lists to highly complex notifications, activations, actions and multiple appendices. It is a matter of experience, judgement and consultation among stakeholders, internally and externally in making that decision as to the scale and complexity of the plan required to deal with the risk. Beware of over planning! The plan is designed to address the risk—the risk is not configured to fit the plan.

An important factor to remember is that emergency arrangements in the UK are designed to put in place as quickly as possible the necessary multi-agency management structures to take control of an incident. Once those structures are in place and operating a plan becomes less important as real time dynamic decisions are being made directly with the circumstances presented by the incident. Therefore, the critical time for a plan is the period from the incident beginning to the management structures being in place. The plan, depending on its format and purpose, will become a reference only.

TOP TIP

When preparing a plan remember that the main aim of the plan is getting from the start of the incident to a management structure being in place and operating. At that point people are talking and working together.

Plan formats will vary from organisation to organisation but the plan format described in Chapter 3 is flexible enough to cater for arrangements that are simple as well as complex. The described format may also act as a checklist to ensure every important issue is covered. The key point to remember with individual plans or single agency plans is that they are prepared to meet the need for an organisation, to slot into existing organisational practice and policy; they are unique to that organisation. They will be and should be configured to support and be compatible with other plans produced by other stakeholders, but the emphasis is that they are there to support that individual organisation. Within the major planning framework individual plans are vital for organisational and business resilience.

Making Planning Decisions

Whatever process is put in place to consider risk and produce plans, a planning group will need to be assembled to address the issues. For example, the LRF considers the production plans by using the RAWG to inform their planning process. In the same way organisations who potentially require plans will also need to identify a core planning team to assess risk and create the plans, in effect, their own RAWG. This can be centred on a specific department, as large organisations may have a dedicated unit whereas a smaller company or organisation may only have a business continuity manager or emergency planning officer, or combined role, who can co-ordinate the activity. It may be more cost effective to hire a consultant to address and co-ordinate the process as they will progress more quickly and be able to apply specialist experience.

The benefits of having a core planning team are illustrated and endorsed by BCM requirements.

Emergency Plans Versus Business Continuity Plans

Is there a difference? It is not intended here to cover all the BCM processes and the theory of risk management in detail; rather, the intention is to raise awareness for the EPO to appreciate the interconnection between the disciplines and to recognise the holistic approach needed to address both areas in building complete 'resilience'. Risk management is a required skill that affects both emergency planning and BCM as it underpins the decision making processes relating to the preparation of plans.

It is hoped by now that the reader can see a close relationship emerging between both sets of arrangements. It has been said that emergency planning and business continuity are different faces of the same coin. There is no doubt that there is crossover, similarity and common ground between the two (see Figure 2.5). We have already made a case for all organisations to review both their internal and external vulnerabilities, risk assess those issues and if necessary create plans to manage them. There is a strong case for an approach that sees both plans being fully integrated or, if separated, being merged together.

Established BCM planners perhaps need to look beyond BCM and conversely EPOs need to look more closely at BCM issues as each will impact the other. The inclusion of BCM references in emergency plans created by Category 1 responders is now essential; to be explicit about how the emergency response will impact upon the organisation and including BCM issues, such as managing the disruption to daily activities, loss of facilities or fewer staff. Perhaps this could be covered in a section of the plan under 'administration' as we see later in creating plans (see Chapter 3).

Typically in terms of rationale and priority, BCM plans set out a whole menu of contingencies (business critical) to address issues that can threaten a business or organisational operation, whereas emergency plans address the issues that could be considered as a threat to human health and well-being: Computer failure, loss of heating, loss of supplier or a critical contractor going out of business can create a business crisis but is not threatening to life and limb. But a critical part of a BCM plan is the emergency planning element where those life threatening issues can arise. The emergency plan will sit alongside the BCM plan and should be cross-referenced. BCM is concerned with looking inward to an organisation's resilience and emergency planning is more outward looking—both activities are indeed two sides of the same coin, but they overlap and share features in terms of management.

The emergency plan element is therefore absolutely critical as it affects lives. Failure to address the risks presented in the risk assessment or not to have in place an effective plan to address those life threatening risks could have serious implications for any organisation, including potential prosecution.

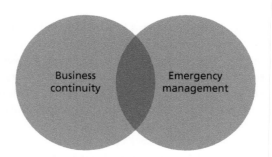

Figure 2.5 BCM and EM share common features

This book is principally focused on the emergency planning elements. However, the EPO needs to have an appreciation of BCM and where possible they should work closely with the Business Continuity Manager. True resilience is based upon a combination of BCM and emergency management. Business continuity is so closely linked now to emergency planning by the CCA that it needs consideration. In terms of business continuity planning, it is a good example of an internal plan that builds and supports resilience. It is a sobering thought that '80% of businesses affected by a major incident fail within 18 months'.[4] It is probably no surprise therefore that the CCA requires that all Category 1 responders have effective internal BCM plans in place and that the LA are charged with providing advice and assistance to businesses and voluntary organisations on BCM issues in general.

This requirement is designed to ensure that the key responders can respond effectively even if they themselves are affected by the emergency. It means they can continue to deliver their daily function and still respond to an emergency. But in addition there is a view that a strong resilient business will be more able to look after itself and not rely on the emergency services or other statutory agencies to help them. This can only occur if that organisation has effective and robust plans themselves. As already alluded to, this takes the pressure off the emergency services but also it makes good business sense and will give a business the best possible chance of survival following an emergency.

In many organisations the merging of roles is not uncommon. The BCM and the EPO are joining forces so the EPO must have some insight into the discipline. In terms of business continuity generally, which includes emergency responders who have to plan for BCM within their own organisations under the CCA, they need to understand the basics of building BCM. It is not very difficult to get an overview of BCM issues. In essence it is identifying the critical factors that are needed to enable the organisation to function, albeit at a reduced level of efficiency. Issues to consider are: what activities absolutely have to be done without any change; what could be reduced or downsized; and what can be left out until the organisation recovers? Identifying what could threaten the organisation is key on a business level, for example using a recognised risk measurement model (matrix) as already described and considering the risk treatments (see Figure 2.3). In a large organisation this may require looking at each department, branch or office individually to assess the combined effect of each or all being compromised and the effect on the overall organisation. The following common process will illustrate the basic procedures to addressing BCM. This is known as the 'Business Continuity Lifecycle' and can be generally summarised in five steps as follows:

Step 1. Analyse your business

Step 2. Hazard/Threat Identification List (Business Impact Analysis—BIA)

---

[4] <https://www.manchesterfire.gov.uk/fire_safety_advice/business_continuity.aspx> 2013.

Step 3. Risk assessment

Step 4. Develop response and recovery plans

Step 5. Testing and exercising plans

The similarity can be seen to plan development and to the IEM described within the CCA. The process is quite similar and straightforward. On a practical level, as opposed to gathering LRF members together to assess community risk through the RAWG the Business Continuity Manager supported by the EPO should gather the key people in the organisation, for example managers or department heads, and in some cases this would extend to talking to suppliers and external agencies if they have an effect on your organisation. Together create a list of the threats or hazards that could adversely affect business activity—your risk identification. In the context of a business this could be very diverse and wide ranging. At this point those risks could be divided into BCM risks, common risks and emergency management risks. Looking at Figure 2.5 the overlap is made up of the common risks.

As before, the risk measurement process is the same as we have seen. Rate these risks in order of severity as previously described: which would have the most impact on the organisation's ability to continue production or offer services and which would have the least? Preparing an 'Organisational Risk Register' to capture this information forms an excellent audit trail and dynamic document to assist in identifying risks and implementing measures to address them. This is also a simple way of identifying trigger points at which the organisation needs to implement special measures as a precaution or in response to specific threats. A very similar process to the CRR we looked at previously.

Consider the use of contractors and supply chain—are they as resilient as they should be? They should be able to demonstrate that they have BCM plans too and can support the organisation in the event of a crisis or emergency. These requirements should be incorporated into any contract. Again this reinforces the earlier view that *all* organisations need to assess their risk—not being able to rely on support or contracted services is one.

Day to day risk or what could be described as 'routine' risk can be addressed in normal daily operations and will not need a specific plan; indeed, most organisations will have an in-house health and safety policy document covering daily activity such as office, workshop or operational activity, within which full risk assessments have already been completed. This risk assessment process relates to activity, not to business critical threats and not whether to have a plan itself. In cases of this type of 'routine' disruptive risk, a simple procedure to bring together key managers to deal with the problem (perhaps a first level crisis management team) may be all that is required without having to prepare structured procedures and processes within a BCM plan—be aware of 'over planning'.

In general, the hazard and threat impact analysis will inform the basis of the plan. Remember too that business continuity advice can now be obtained from the local authority. The key message here is to be prepared, have sound BCM plans in place to ensure the organisation is resilient and flexible.

TOP TIP

Engage with the local authority to get business continuity advice and support. If they cannot help they will know how to find the right advice.

Having discussed the many different plans it will be useful at this point to place the various plans in context—known as the 'planning network'. This looks at how plans relate to one another, integrate and support each other.

The diagram illustrated in Figure 2.6 shows an overview of a planning network. It shows how individual plans produced by a variety of organisations and private companies support the individual plans produced by both Category 1 and 2 responders under their statutory obligations. It also shows how organisations communicate or should communicate with their local LRF even if they do not support a multi-agency plan. This demonstrates that the LRF is the focal point of planning locally. It also illustrates the relationship with BCM as an integral part of planning for resilience. It also shows the influence of the multi-LRF sub-national planning, national guidance and planning directives in informing the production of multi-agency plans and the separate requirements of the local authority to create specialist multi-agency plans.

As an example—all Category 1 and 2 organisations will have BCM and specific emergency plans in place to cater for emergencies they manage and BCM plans to ensure their continued functionality. Notice too that businesses have access to both the LA for BCM advice and the LRF for general advice and support.

It can be seen that planning and building resilience is not just an issue for the emergency services or a designated group of emergency responders, but it affects the wider community and local businesses. Working together, all the planning processes will join up and produce a seamless and robust response to any crisis or emergency.

TASK 2.5

- List five reasons why an organisation should consider a risk management approach to planning.
- Explain the relationship between emergency planning and business continuity planning.

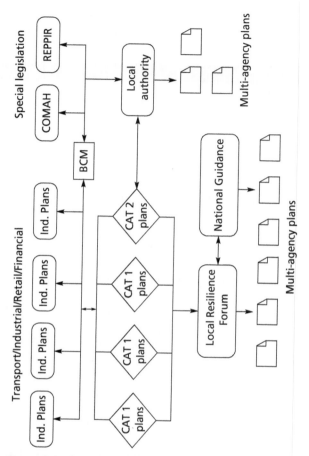

Figure 2.6 Planning Network

Having decided on the need to plan, whether it is driven by the CCA, legislation or a need to produce individual plans to direct organisational emergency activities, the next consideration is exercising. Is there really a need to exercise?

Do We Need to Exercise?

The obvious and predictable answer is yes, but it is probably the area which is not fully appreciated in the context of building to that resilient goal. Having a plan is not enough. Exercising is the fuel that feeds the plan; without fuel the plan will die.

The CCA under section 2(1)(c) or (d) requires certain categories of organisation to carry out exercises to ensure that the plans are effective *and* to train those people who would be charged with carrying out that plan. What this means in real terms is that there is a recognition of the importance of exercising and for some organisations it is now a statutory obligation. However, the message for everyone involved in preparing emergency plans or BCM plans is that exercising must form part of the emergency planning cycle, see Figure 2.1. It is suggested that those who fail to exercise their plans could become vulnerable to severe criticism or even litigation and prosecution.

Having comprehensive and robust plans is not sufficient for organisational resilience. Not using or exercising a plan can have dire consequences and can mean the difference between organisational survival and failure. A study showed that 38% of companies surveyed had actually invoked their BCM plans[5] and 43% of companies experiencing disaster never recovered. With as many as 30% of those *not reviewing their plans* it is hardly surprising that companies and organisations fail to respond effectively to a crisis or emergency. Being infected with complacency with regard to emergency preparedness is a fatal flaw in any company or organisation, a major symptom of this malaise is a failure to exercise. Many companies and organisations take the view that in terms of priority exercising is not crucial, especially when weighed against more pressing commercial or operational needs. This is understandable but is a false economy and short sighted. Losing the business entirely, a degree of performance or more importantly a member of staff or a member of the public owing to poor preparation and exercising will always be more expensive financially. Potentially being exposed to charges of corporate manslaughter is a real possibility also.

Assuming then that plans are produced for all the rational reasons outlined can it really be assumed that those plans will work? How will those who play a key role in the plan react or perform—are they trained sufficiently? Are there sufficient resources? How will other organisations impact upon the plan, such as contractors or the emergency services? How can an organisation know they will survive the inevitable post-incident scrutiny? Have any changes occurred that could affect the plan? There are many questions—the only way to find the answers to these and numerous other questions is to test or exercise the plans—but how often does it need to happen? This is a difficult question to answer and is really down to what is reasonable. A general guide, assuming no obvious significant changes have been identified, is probably annually. The exact exercising schedule will be worked out by the planning team and adjusted and amended as the plan matures. We will look in more detail later about exercise options to make exercising more achievable and manageable. It is perhaps more beneficial at this point for an EPO to consider the benefits of exercising as a means of persuading senior managers of advantages which may not be that obvious at first.

---

[5] Source: *London Chamber of Commerce* May 2003 and *Compass* January 2004.

> ### TASK 2.6
>
> Consider what the CCA guidance directs relating to exercising and training—summarise.

Benefits for the organisation—why exercise?

Perhaps the question should be why not exercise? Having a plan creates a 'comfort blanket' as we know and in fact in some cases a false sense of security. Having seen that there may be a reluctance to exercise plans, why do some organisations seem to avoid it or only exercise as a last resort? There is in many cases a fear that exercising will expose weakness or the plan when tested will fail, coupled with that is the potential 'finger pointing' and blame. In addition many organisations believe that exercising is expensive and takes away from valuable 'productive' staff time. All very understandable fears and concerns, but exercising plans can have major benefits for organisations in their day-to-day activities too and building a stronger business.

> ### KEY POINT
>
> Exercising and training builds strong organisations—**FACT**.

Testing plans brings people together to share in problem solving, facing unusual threats together and coping in a crisis. Working with all levels of management promotes team building, fosters understanding and builds confidence. Exercising can bring together disparate departments, branches and other stakeholders, both internal and external who would never meet during 'normal' business. Opportunities for networking develop and key partnerships can be forged or consolidated. Following many major incidents a comment often heard amongst responders relates to how useful it was 'knowing' the people involved, seeing a friendly face, how easy it made communication, especially in that chaotic phase when a rapport already existed. This can only be created and nurtured during exercises.

As long as exercising is seen as an enjoyable activity which does not create confrontation, frustration, embarrassment, belittle or confuse it will be become a valuable management asset.

Perhaps one of the key benefits of exercising is the part it plays in 'active' learning generally. This can extend to understanding the organisation better and not just in terms of emergency response. Active learning is a means of letting the learner learn for themselves. Teams can work in small groups, explore scenarios, act out roles, analyse case studies, share experiences and openly discuss. In doing so they embed the learning by involvement and being immersed in the activity. This is the essence of exercising. Getting involved, giving advice, assisting others are all effective learning methods.

Simply telling staff to read plans and memorise procedures is 'passive' learning and not very effective for embedding behaviour and knowledge. Active learning involves engaging staff through exercising on what they know or should know. It consolidates knowledge and highlights training needs.

In short, exercising can seem to many a complex, expensive or a risky activity. In fact it is not, neither is it arduous or time consuming. This book will provide the information and knowledge to explain the processes and administration that will help prepare exercises that are organisationally effective, fun and cost effective. But there has to be the will and practical support too.

Senior management 'buy-in'

It is important that the benefits of exercising are recognised and supported by senior management. Without high level support and backing it is difficult, if not impossible to achieve real progress in organisational resilience. Having a sound exercise programme supported by a written organisational 'policy' on exercising will create an organisation that is strong and resilient against crises and emergencies. Create an exercise policy—an exercise policy will demonstrate a commitment to continued improvement and development within an organisation in terms of building that resilience.

A senior management team will support that view.

TOP TIP

Create an exercise policy for your organisation, signed off at senior level. It will help drive exercising as a management tool.

Having a policy will provide the 'ammunition' or the organisational weight to drive exercising in an organisation. It can also mean minimising financial loss to a business, litigation or paying out compensation. It can also prevent loss of *reputation* and *goodwill* earned over many years. This is particularly important where public confidence and support is so important to overall effectiveness, as in a public service organisation such as the local authority or emergency services.

Perhaps even more relevant for senior managers is that exercising can actually help in mitigating or reducing the effects of criminal liability resulting from the crisis or emergency, in particular where lives are lost through accusations of manslaughter by negligence. The existence of plans and effective exercising can be used to demonstrate the extent to which an organisation has sought to prepare and reduce the risk of harm. How it has educated staff in procedure and trained them in emergency skills and driving a safety culture. Issues of corporate manslaughter are mentioned within the book to simply draw attention to the issue and direct the reader to further research. It is a complex subject area but one the EPO must be aware of and be able to offer advice on.

In brief, by definition corporate manslaughter is a crime committed by an organisation which results in the death of a person to which they had a duty of care. The Corporate Manslaughter and Corporate Homicide Act 2007 came into effect from April 2008. Critical factors for a jury deciding the guilt of an organisation is its attitude, policies and accepted practices with regard to health and safety. Extending that thought, what better way to demonstrate a commitment to health and safety than training and exercising? An organisation will be guilty if the way its activities are managed or organised causes a death and its activities are shown to be a gross breach of the organisation's duty of care to the person who died. The penalties for non-compliance include fines or even imprisonment. The Act focuses on organisations that ignore or are reckless with regard to health and safety.

How will an organisation know if its activities are fit for purpose and adequate without exercising? Having regular exercises as part of an active emergency planning cycle can demonstrate to others that an organisation has commitment to continuous improvement of risk management procedures and therefore an organisation that is responsible and caring.

Another feature of fatal incidents is that relatives of those involved and their legal teams will pursue corporate 'heads' relentlessly and will dissect plans, processes and procedures (which should include an auditable exercise programme). This is done in an effort to identify negligence and blame or simply to make sense of what happened, to find out every possible detail. It is worth mentioning here the 'school of thought' alluded to earlier that if a plan does not exist one cannot be criticised for it—it is suggested that not having a plan would have far more serious consequences. This may sound quite scary—but consider the situation in which there is no plan, an old plan, an untested plan and no record of exercises? The motivation of victims' relatives to obtain information is so intense because it is driven by the loss of a loved one or friend. One has only to consider the *Marchioness* Disaster on the River Thames in London on 20 August in 1989 in which 51 people died or the Hillsborough Football stadium disaster on 15 April 1989 in which 96 people died to see how relatives' action groups can mobilise and initiate change many years following the events.

In an era where corporate manslaughter is a real issue for officers of companies or organisations, getting it wrong could have serious consequences. Organisations must be prepared for intense scrutiny. This is a particular problem for the smaller company because it is far easier to attribute a causal link to the incident that resulted in death or injury to a 'controlling' officer of the company. The bigger and more diverse a company's structure, the more difficult it can be to attribute grossly negligent acts or omissions committed in the course of the company's operations to a controlling officer and, therefore, to the company itself. However, even if it is not possible to show that a company has been grossly negligent because there is no controlling mind, offences under other legislation may have been committed. But could the emergency responders be liable?

It is quite understandable and right that negligent companies and those acting with deliberate or reckless disregard for safety should be brought to account. Increasingly, however the role of the emergency responders is and will be brought under closer scrutiny in terms of their ability to deliver emergency response 'effectively' in saving life, preventing injury and reducing damage to property, more so in this growing litigious society. This is particularly so for those 'in-charge' or commanding. But how do we measure 'effectively'? We are all familiar with workplace health and safety protection legislation, indeed the emergency services and defence forces are subject to such legislation. In this case line managers and commanders may be liable, with their organisation, for injury and death to an employee or crown servant. As we 'professionalise' emergency planning by putting in place common national occupational standards in civil contingencies, training in those standards, specific legislation, and mandatory guidance the actions of those charged with delivering that emergency response will be subject to critical analysis as never before. Not just towards their employees but towards the wider public and in particular families and friends of those affected. This spectre raises many issues for those managers and commanders. No matter how well trained a person is in emergency response, can we truly measure a person's competency to deliver that response against a situation which is often unique, chaotic, imprecise, vague and often lacking in information? Can proof be established against a commander to demonstrate deliberate negligence or recklessness as opposed to simply trying to do their best in a difficult situation with good intent, or indeed, were they just incompetent or poorly trained? If so the latter may fall back on the organisation leaving it exposed to criticism and possible action. In this case 'commanders' brought to account may cite lack of training, exercising and qualification as a root cause of their lack of ability. Perhaps historically emergency responders have worked under the principle of the 'good Samaritan', in that 'we were only trying to help'; this may no longer be enough.

There is no doubt that the Hillsborough Football Stadium disaster in Sheffield in April 1989 where 96 football supporters died continues to focus on the effectiveness of the emergency response, as in April 2014 the event analysis continued with new inquests—25 years after the tragedy. It remains to be seen how this will play out as emergency response matures and new cases emerge for scrutiny, but for sure the only way to test and practice those responses is by exercising

The lessons must be to use exercising as a natural business process to build a strong resilient organisation.

TASK 2.7

- What are the possible implications of not testing contingency plans? List six.
- What are the benefits of exercising for an organisation? List eight.
- List three reasons why senior management should buy-in to exercising.

Summary

You should understand the following:

- The principles of planning
- Who creates plans and the processes that inform the decision to agree to produce a plan
- Risk assessments for planning purposes
- The different types of plan
- The need for BCM in an emergency planning context
- The rationale for exercising and the consequences of not doing so

Conclusion

Creating and maintaining plans are vital for BCM and emergency management. The CCA requires that plans be subject to update and revision by establishing a plan maintenance matrix to check that maintenance work is being done and plans revised in the light of a revised risk assessment or other factors, such as organisational restructuring or failings identified by exercises or an incident.

Crucially, the CCA requires that exercising and training be carried out. Plans must include within them provisions for carrying out exercises to validate plans and make them effective as possible. This must include adequate training of staff or other persons to ensure they are properly prepared. This is an issue too for the emergency responders as critical analysis of their response function becomes more prevalent.

The bottom line is an organisation cannot afford to not exercise and train their staff.

3

Creating Your Plans

Having now considered the type of plans in use and, who is involved in producing those plans the next task for the EPO is to look in greater detail at how a plan is put together.

Following the guidance in this Chapter will provide all the information needed to prepare comprehensive and effective plans. Expertise in plan writing comes with experience as knowledge is developed and the EPO is required to tackle a range of different plans addressing a whole range of risks. However, there are basic principles which form the core of a good plan and this includes a format that lends itself to being user friendly and therefore more efficient to use. This Chapter contains sufficient detail to demonstrate how a plan is made up and it will also assist in reviewing and in deciding if specialist support is needed to upgrade existing plans. The information within this Chapter will also assist those who regularly prepare plans by highlighting issues that may not have been considered before. The proposed plan format outlined in this Chapter exceeds the recommendations of the CAA guidance.

We have seen Chapter 2 the various types of plans from simple checklists to mutli-agency and multi-level plans; it is intended that the illustrated plan format described here can be adapted and modified to accommodate any type of plan requirement. Let us begin by looking at the underlying principles of plan building. This plan type is an 'Emergency Plan'. This plan format is perhaps the most difficult in that it has to display brevity, only relevant detail, extreme clarity, ease of use, specify actions and is probably going to be used to save life. The first general question is—what do you want your plan to do?

If it is a simple **generic plan** outlining general principles, procedures and policy based upon checklists as an aide memoire that is simple and straightforward. That plan is only intended to assist the first responders in the initial few minutes at operational level—these are often seen incorporating mneumonics and bullet points. This type of plan usually reflects the generic roles and responsibilities of an emergency response organisation such as the police or ambulance service. It can also form the basis for a general crisis management response across any organisation in the initial stages.

If the plan is an individual **single agency** emergency plan it needs to be just that—an emergency plan. It is operationally and tactically focused. It has to be capable of rapid implementation prioritised by 'actions' for specific post holders to carry out. Rapid notifications, alerts and warnings to the public if necessary are essential. The rapid notifications will initiate the necessary command and control arrangements. Once they are in place the plan takes a backseat as the incident is then being managed dynamically in real time by the assembled 'experts' in their respective command or management function. In reality these plans run for a short period—a matter of a few hours.

If the plan is not an emergency plan per se—for example, it is instead a contingency or BCM plan following a business critical event, such as a supply failure, utility failure, IT problem or staff shortage—more information can be included in the plan outlining in longer narrative covering more options, a scaled response or trigger levels in recognition that key management support may not be available immediately as key staff may not be on 24/7 cover, on annual leave or away from the site.

If many organisations need to be co-ordinated the plan is **multi-agency**— it is in effect a reference document supported by individual single agency plans and is used as a reference by managers and commanders once they are in role managing the incident. The same would apply to multi-level multi-agency plans and guidance. They are used as reference and can adopt a format that lends itself to more in-depth explanation, rational and strategic management.

Every plan must however, dovetail into organisational operational procedures and policies and planning guidance, for example that provided by the CCA guidance and any other relevant civil protection legislation such as COMAH and REPPIR. In other words it must be integrated.

The focus for the remainder of this Chapter will be around an emergency plan but the processes here are adaptable across many types of plan and the advice holds good for those too.

Integrated 'Internal' Planning

As we have seen the CCA refers to IEM as Anticipation, Assessment, Prevention, Preparation, Response and Recovery Management and is covered in great detail in the guidance documents that accompany the CCA. It must be emphasised that this IEM approach will ensure that there is compatibility, a synergy and interoperability across processes and procedures between organisations. Collaboration, liaison and consultation are key elements in developing plans, but 'internal' integration is also critical to creating an effective plan, in particular single agency or individual plans. What is meant by internal integration?

Having decided to produce a plan to offset an assessed risk it is also important that the new internal emergency procedures are aligned or 'integrated' into day to day activity. If that happens it means there will be a seamless move from normal activity into emergency response mode (see Figure 3.1). This will be examined in more detail in Chapter 5 on co-ordinating the emergency response, but in essence, the emergency response should be built upon normal procedures enabling an escalation of those procedures proportionally, either gradually or immediately to manage the incident presented— right up to disaster level.

Generally, common errors in plans include:

- Designating key roles in the plan to individuals who are never or rarely on site or available, or not trained for their role in the plan.

- Relying on facilities you assume will be available and are usually not.

Figure 3.1 Seamless transition

- Relying on equipment that is never used or tested, it usually does not work when you want it or it has been moved or scrapped.
- Relying on contractors and suppliers (unless they are contracted to provide the additional resources in a fixed time frame and can cope).
- Relying on emergency procedures and policies that are totally alien to staff through lack of training and familiarisation.

The emergency response should, where possible use the personnel and resources available on a day to day basis, so ensuring there are key trained staff on duty at the time of the incident. This is an important issue for the plan. There will of course be requirements to have use of special equipment, facilities or to require a change of roles but these should fall into place incrementally and in a triggered sequence, which starts from the daily routine. Therefore integrate emergency procedures into daily activity. It will save time and be more efficient.

TASK 3.1

Explain why it is important to integrate emergency procedures into day to day activity.

Electronic or Hard Copy Plan?

This is an important issue when considering the production and use of plans. Surely everything should be electronic in this day and age! Making the best and most efficient use of technology is a must, especially where accessing information and data is concerned—which is the case with plans. Electronic plans are useful in that many people can view them simultaneously from distant locations and they can be quickly and easily updated. They can also be integrated into IT communication or command systems. One would think that hard copy plans must be considered redundant and obsolete by now—so the software developers would tell you!

Perhaps not: the very nature of an emergency situation may prevent access to the relevant IT systems, for example in the event of a power failure, a system crash or virus. Accessing electronic versions of plans may also be problematic if the level of authority is restrictive, bearing in mind that maintaining security of electronic versions can be difficult within a large organisation. Computer viruses, hacking and deliberate electronic terrorism and sabotage are real issues that can affect not only law enforcement and government organisations but large corporate companies too. Portable computers moving in the public domain are susceptible to theft and are targeted by computer thieves (see Chapter 1). Another issue with electronic plans relates to their ownership and accountability, in particular where they are 'absorbed' into other electronic systems and begin to have dependent links into other databases which are managed and created by other people. Can a computer plan be audited when it becomes so amorphous? There is a danger that the electronic plan loses structure and direction. Electronic plans do have drawbacks which can be significant. In any case, in terms of electronic plans a hard copy must be viewed at least as a vital backup and should exist if only for that reason. Being completely helpless because the computer breaks down is no excuse and is bad planning!

It must also be remembered that those who are charged with implementing the plans will in fact be relatively few in number and having a hard copy version is a preferred option for many managers from the author's experience. There is something reassuring in having a hard copy plan to hand and being able to use the plan to keep notes in, using it as a working document for later reference. Highly sophisticated and technically advanced organisations still use and prefer hard copy plans and documents in many situations, such as the aviation, chemical, nuclear and space industries.

However, the hard copy plans also have drawbacks. They will be in various locations, will always need constant updating and checking to ensure the right version is being used and the amendments have been added. A significant contributing factor in the Chernobyl nuclear disaster was an emergency plan in the control room that had sections crossed out leading to confusion amongst staff when they tried to use it. Hard copy plans need a robust auditable system which is essential, set against numbered copies with regular physical checks to make sure the plans are where they should be. This checking process should be logged and kept on file. If plans are not being updated this must be brought to the attention of the plan holder immediately.

However, there is no reason why both electronic and hard copy plans cannot co-exist and complement each other. The hard copy has ownership, accountability, authority, portability, reliability and has a 'usability' and companionship as an effective working tool. Electronic plans are versatile, quick to use, updated easily and can be integrated into other systems opening a vast array of support data at will, with appropriate links. Utilising both systems has a place in modern emergency management and for the EPO being able to produce a hard copy plan is an essential basic skill. Without that skill it is impossible to create another form of plan.

With hard copy plans there should only be one 'master' copy which is kept by the 'owner' who should also keep a working file containing all relevant papers that support the plan. This forms an audit trail and will contain information relating to distribution, amendments, training sessions and exercising. In addition where updates and amendments come to light which fall between regular updates these can be kept on file until the review or update takes place. This is assuming of course that they can wait for that process! This is a judgement for the plan owner to make.

The same should apply to electronic plans in that one person should have ultimate responsibility for their ownership, again with a means of demonstrating an update, review process and exercising, which essentially will be in hard copy.

KEY POINT

All plans should have ownership, this ensures accountability.

We will look at the title/ownership page shortly.

What Should be in the Plan?

Six types of plan have been listed and it is intended now to describe the preparation of just one type—the single agency emergency or individual emergency plan. This plan has been chosen as it is the one which will feature most often in an emergency situation although the format to be described, with some modification, can be applied across all types of plan including BCM plans and contingency plans. This plan will concentrate on providing sufficient information to enable an effective response to the incident in the crucial initial stages, 'the golden hour' and provide enough detail to provide the reader with a basic understanding of the threat and the necessary response. The 'Golden Hour' principle refers to the period within which most lives will be saved and injuries reduced. It is a medical term in fact but is used to describe generally the period immediately following an emergency when escalation can be reduced significantly and response arrangements are most effective. As the incident consolidates and settles down and the response becomes more structured there will be more time to consider options and longer term strategies. The characteristic of the single agency or individual plan is that it is not overwhelmed with information, which in the early stages is not required, and would only inhibit its use and confuse the reader.

But whatever plan is produced the plan must satisfy a number of criteria:

- The plan must have ownership or title—there must be accountability.
- The plan layout must be clear and easy to use.
- The plan must be concise.
- Roles and responsibilities must be clearly defined.
- The plan must be revised and tested regularly.
- Those who have a role within the plan must be trained and regularly briefed.

- Where several plans exist within an organisation they all must follow the same format or 'house style'.
- Plans must be 'launched'—introduced to the organisation.

It may sound pedantic but in terms of hardcopy plans its ease of use is so important. That will include consideration of such issues as:

1. Plan cover—is it easy to see in a bookcase?
2. Folder type—how easy to turn pages and keep it open? Separate pages in a ring binder will lend itself to easier updating too.
3. Font type and line spacing (double spaced and at least font 12)—is it clear and easy to read?
4. Using colour pages—it adds emphasis to functions and tasks or actions.
5. Use of photographs, flow charts, floor plans and diagrams for clarity and understanding—we understand better and see more clearly in shapes and colours.
6. Using numbered paragraphs and sub-paragraphs is essential as it will assist in communicating information about the plan between people who may be using the telephone or e-mail.

The plan must be instantly recognisable—bright and obvious. Developing a 'corporate format', whichever format is chosen is very important. The format should remain consistent in terms of look and content. It makes training and exercising the plan more effective because only one plan type is being used. No matter what the size or geographic location of various parts of the organisation are the emergency plans it uses it will always look the same wherever the user is. Everyone within the organisation should know what an emergency plan looks like and be able to use them. Over time it will become embedded into the corporate memory.

TASK 3.2

Thinking of the organisation you work for or just considering a plan cover generally how would you design a plan cover so that it would be recognisable? What information would go on the front?

Plan Format

In the following list is an emergency plan format which, with adaptation as mentioned earlier, can be applied to most organisational needs. It can be used for very simple single organisational plans or complex procedures covering major plans involving many organisations. This system is expressed as follows:

- Information or Background
- Intention or Objective
- Method or Management
- Administration or Support
- Risk Assessment
- Communication
- Human Rights

This system is known as the 'IIMARCH' system, pronounced 'aye aye march', which is extensively used by many public service organisations including the police. These headings form the core of the plan but the plan will consist of other components and in effect every plan is 'built' or 'constructed' in a uniform and consistent way.

Building the Plan

The hard copy plan should be 'assembled' in the following order or formatted electronically as follows.

1. Inner front cover—duplicate of the front cover
2. Contents page
3. Foreword/preface (Optional)
4. Introduction—page numbers start here
5. Title—ownership and signatures
6. Distribution—the plan holders
7. Amendments—changes and insertions
8. Exercises—dates and types of exercise including the exercise manager/ director details
9. Information/Background– 1st Section. Each Section will be divided by card
10. Intention/Objective—2nd Section
11. Method/Management—3rd Section
12. Administration/Support—4th Section
13. Risk assessment—5th Section
14. Communication—6th Section
15. Human Rights—7th Section
16. Tasks or actions—8th Section

Note. For each separate task or action a new section is used. For example:

17. Duty Manager—9th Section

18. Media Officer—10th Section

19. Chief Executive Officer—11th Section

20. Etc...

21. Appendices—Final Section

Note. For each appendix a letter is used; A, B, C. For example:

A. Essential Telephone/Fax Directory.

B. Maps/Diagrams/Illustrations.

C. Equipment Inventory.

D. Any other relevant information.

Having described the plan format each individual section will now be examined in more detail as to what should be included.

TASK 3.3

Why is a corporate plan format important for an organisation?

Contents

In an emergency situation the first page looked at will be the contents page! It is important to ensure that the contents list is very detailed and comprehensive. The reader should not have to trawl through the document looking or searching for a relevant point. Clarity is essential. This is achieved by clear simple headings. In particular the 'Tasks' or 'Actions'section, therefore under 'Tasks' or 'Actions', the role of each facility or individual must be listed, e.g. Duty Manager, Communications Operator, etc. everything else, although important, can be read in slow time once the 'Tasks' or 'Actions'are initiated. A task or action is a directive to an individual to perform a function or functions. To avoid repetition here the word 'Action' will be used but task is as relevant depending on the organsiation.

Each 'Section' in the plan should be divided by a numbered card divider, which relates to the contents page to make finding the relevant section easier. Ease of use is the key—remember!

Foreword/preface (optional)

It is useful if the Foreword or Preface is written by a senior manager. It not only adds weight to the document but is a good means of attracting senior management buy in, in particular when it comes to publishing and circulating the plan. This section can emphasise the corporate approach to plans, training and exercising and generally a motivational and supportive approach to instil the 'resilient organisation' message. The organisational 'exercise policy' can also be referred to here.

Introduction

This page will briefly state the aim and objective(s) of the plan, identifying its scope and any limitations. Reference to other generic source material will be made where appropriate and references to 'assumed' information will be specified. The Introduction should also include reference to any statutory obligation, whether direct or indirect to write the plan, together with the risk-assessed rationale of writing the plan in the first instance with reference to the Community Risk Register (CRR) if appropriate.

Copyright

Copyright for some is perceived to be a problem, in particular where commercial interests tend to plagiarise for profit. The difficulty is that so much information is freely in circulation and has been adopted and adapted that it can be difficult to pin down its source. But if information is used genuinely to promote and develop civil protection it would seem counterproductive to inhibit or hinder that effort. It is a matter of judgement. It is worthy of note that the two CCA guidance documents can be produced free of charge in the spirit for which they were intended—to promote civil protection.

However, a copyright warning can be attached. If being used it is suggested that a copyright warning be placed in the Introduction, for example:

> 'The policy and information contained in this document has been compiled and presented for emergency planning purposes and sole use of 'MegaBolts' and its staff. This is a corporate Policy document for which 'MegaBolts' retains the copyright. Except in accordance with the provisions of the Copyright Designs and Patents Act 1988, written permission signed by the Chief Executive Officer is required to replicate the document in any material form'.
> –MegaBolts 2011

This section should also contain a reference to the Equality, Diversity and Discrimination Audit. Remember—if a plan is written we assume responsibility for it and its effect on others. A plan must be responsive and alive to issues relating to individual rights and must not knowingly advocate and sanction breaches of those rights. Further information can be found at <http://www.gov.uk>.

Information security

It must also state in the wording of the Introduction if it is suitable for public disclosure or the document contains sensitive information and it must not be disclosed. If appropriate, it should be ascertained if the document requires a protective marking under the UK Cabinet Office policy entitled the Government Security Classification Policy (GSCP). This is a simplified system which came into effect in April 2014 and replaces the older Government Protective Marking Scheme (GPMS). The new classifications are now, Top Secret, Secret and Official. In effect Official now replaces the old Confidential, Restricted and Protect. There is also a sub-category of classification called Official-Sensitive. It is expected that most public service organisations will operate under the Official category but it may be prudent for emergency planners to consider using this sub-category. The plan author should check this within their own organisation. If it applies there will be a policy on the subject with explanations as to what each marking levels entails, which will include information on storage, security, handling, transmission and disclosure. If sensitive material does appear in the document it is easier to collect or collate that information into one section which can be extracted for disclosure without compromising the whole document. In this case it would be better in an appendix or appendices which are appropriately marked. The most obvious section would be personal contact details, locations of dangerous substances, times of deliveries, etc. Anything which could give information that would be useful for criminal or terrorist use or which is commercially sensitive. In most cases emergency plans will fall into sensitive categories. However, the overuse of the protective marking scheme should be avoided as it can lead to totally unnecessary administration and expense in document handling and usage—often to the frustration of key stakeholder planners. In some cases it can also be divisive in that it can alienate fellow planners who feel excluded and devalued by having such restrictive access.

> **KEY POINT**
>
> Careful consideration must be applied to allocating security marking. It can be unnecessarily bureaucratic and restrictive for stakeholders and partners alike.

Everyone has the right to request information held by public sector organisations under the Freedom of Information Act 2000, which came into force in January 2005. The classifications just discussed do not prevent information being asked for and disclosed. The Freedom of Information Act applies to all 'public authorities' including:

- government departments and local assemblies;
- local authorities and councils;
- health trusts and hospitals;
- schools, colleges and universities (public institutions);
- publicly funded museums;
- the emergency services;
- many other non-departmental public bodies, committees and advisory bodies.

Some privately owned companies that have an obligation to plan for emergencies under legislation may be reluctant to submit their plans to public authorities in case the information contained within them is disclosed. LRFs are often approached to disclose information relating to plans but the CCA guidance advocates publishing plans in any case unless there is a good and valid reason not to. Commercially sensitive material could be annexed in a plan to assist easy removal if that is required. The issue is the sensitivity of the information contained within each plan and each request would have to be assessed on a case by case basis.

Title—ownership and signatures

This page will contain the plan title and the signatures of those involved in its production. It is important to complete this page. First, it will give ownership and responsibility. It must be remembered that a signatory to the plan will be deemed to have a 'controlling' effect or influence on its application and usage. This is a sobering thought when a line manager is challenged about having knowledge of the plan if called to account. Getting a signature ensures that senior management have sight of the plan and they are aware of it. This will be useful to generate support and 'buy-in' when it is time to exercise the plan. The ownership page should be signed by the following:

- Plan author—prepared by
- Line Manager
- Departmental Head

It is worthy of note that under the Corporate Manslaughter and Corporate Homicide Act 2007, Crown bodies such as the police, army and other emergency services are absolved from liability of 'duty of care' except for their responsibilities towards their staff. This is an issue raised for information only and awareness of EPOs. Further detail can be obtained by researching the relevant legislation.

The layout of the page could look like Figure 3.2.

CONFIDENTIAL-TITLE AND SIGNATURES

Title: ....   Ref No...............

This plan is owned by: Department/Organization

Only the 'Owner' of the plan can authorise any alterations.

The 'Owner' will ensure that:

- The master document is retained together with relevant supporting documents.
- The level of circulation of the plan is determined and details are recorded of copy holders.
- It is updated and reviewed.
- It is tested and exercised.
- Health and safety issues are regularly risk assessed.
- Changes and amendments are circulated to plan holders promptly.
- Electronic versions are updated.

Further information and advice on any of the above elements can be obtained from:

Plan prepared by: ....Date: ....

Contact Tel..

Line Manager: ....Date: ....
Inspected

Department Head...Date: ....
Approved

Figure 3.2 Title page

TASK 3.4

Research the Corporate Manslaughter and Corporate Homicide Act 2007—how could it affect the role of an EPO?

Distribution

This page will contain a list identifying the locations and destinations of the plans. It should also include the relevant post holder(s) who have key actions for implementing the plan or parts of the plan. Getting a signature on a receipt for the plan is important in terms of accountability and personal possession (some people will 'forget' they have it). Over time plans will be put in drawers or 'lost' and all knowledge will be denied by the recipient—so get a numbered receipt!

TOP TIP

When distributing plans always get a dated, numbered signature on a receipt and keep it safe. This applies to all plans—not just controlled documents.

Amendments

Amendments will be recorded as follows:

- *UPDATE*—This requires simple administrative changes only, an update is as the name suggests. This includes a regular (at least an annual) check on telephone numbers; areas of responsibility, changes in post holders, land boundaries, etc.
- *REVIEWED*—a complete review taking in all aspects of the plan. This will involve asking the question, do we need this plan? Does the risk assessment still apply? Involve all those who have a role to play, revisit all parts of the plan. This should take place at least every two years or when the plan is used for real. This will involve having a meeting to go through the plan which should be minuted for the records and general plan file.

Exercises

This section should contain details of when the plan was last exercised and by what method, i.e. 'live' or 'table top', which we will discuss later. It should also contain the name of the exercise manager or director. This will allow future exercise planners to liaise with previous exercise managers and exchange ideas. In the master copy held by the owner it would be good practice to include a list of personnel taking part in the exercises. This should be affixed into this section. In the event of a real incident, these people would be used if available.

Many organisations also include exercise details relating to their employees on their personal HR files or an information database. This provides an ideal reference in the event of a real incident to quickly identify staff that may have the necessary skills and experience to assist.

> **TOP TIP**
>
> Following any exercise include the attendance list in the plan file. In this way you will have access to those who know the plan.

Information—section 1

This section, being the first, will contain general details of the circumstances giving rise to the formulation of the plan and the risk assessment process used to arrive at that decision. This may include external direction to complete the plan, for example from central government. Details will include information giving rise to the risk, for example flooding, a chemical fire or business continuity issues. It could involve information about a company, industrial processes, storage of hazardous substances, the threats involved, hazards to be expected, site location and general geographic location. It will also include information as to when the company or organisation will implement the emergency procedures.

What will trigger the plan? How is 'emergency' or 'crisis' defined for the company or organisation? There is a definition in the CCA of 'emergency' but there will need to be a more specific description as to what constitutes an emergency or crisis for them. All organisations will define what an emergency (or major incident—see later) is for them differently. That in itself will not create a problem as it identifies specific issues that are relevant for that organisation alone. It must however comply and fall within the definition of 'emergency' within the CCA guidance if it is to have any meaning to responding organisations, such as the emergency services.

It is also important to agree what will trigger an alert and who will be responsible for doing it—not by name but post holder. The emergency responders must have confidence that in a real emergency they will be alerted. A common problem is who will 'press' the button. There is often a tangible reluctance for some organisations to alert the emergency services or even their own organisation for fear of being criticised, incurring some liability, cost or damage to reputation. The implications for activating an alert can be serious but it would be far more serious not to and for injury, death or serious damage to property to result.

Emergency definitions or triggers leading to the activation of plans often have assigned alert levels to initiate a particular response or sometimes a traffic light code is used. In this section define the 'alert' levels or colour code as provided by the alerting organisation. For example:

- Emergency Level 1—Activate Level 1 procedures—Standby (prepare).
- Emergency Level 2—Activate Level 2 procedures—Mobilise (move to action).
- Emergency Level 3—Full Emergency.

or

- Alert Amber
- Alert Red

or—one for the police:

- Emergency Level 1—In-house police response only
- Emergency Level 2—All emergency services response
- Emergency Level 3—Full multi-agency response

There are many variations that will be unique to each organisation. These levels will be defined and detailed in the 'Action' sections and within the 'Method' section (see later) outlining exactly what will happen if and when each level or colour code is reached.

This section should also *briefly* list any respective roles and responsibilities involving outside agencies or other departments if it is an in house response. This is why it is crucial to involve these organisations and departments in the planning process. The implementation of any special procedure and/or policy should be briefly explained, bearing in mind that a full and detailed explanation of the subject matter may be contained in other documents. In other words, attention may be directed towards an issue for further reading or reference. For example, the organisation may have a generic health and safety policy document covering day to day activity, reference may be made to this. This section may refer to other emergency plans that complement and support the one being written and may be used in conjunction with it. Without this approach, the contents of each and every emergency plan would be overwhelming and defeat the object of the plan. If it is not needed in the plan, leave it out.

In short, this section outlines the background activity and essential information leading to the activation of that particular plan—only up to that point. If it is written to respond to an incident by an emergency responder the detail will relate to that threat, hazard or site. If it is written for in house BCM issues it will contain a summary of the likely scenarios giving rise to the plan activation and the triggers or stages that that response would initiate.

Intention—section 2

This section will contain statements of intent in relation to the plan. There will be an 'aim' and support 'objectives'. Aims should be short single sentence statements avoiding 'ands'. Remember that one cannot endorse or encourage personnel to recklessly put their personal safety at risk or fly in the face of policy. Health and safety legislation does not always sit easily with emergency response activity. Very careful consideration of the words used must be given as 'legal responsibility and accountability' could rest on the statements of intent made at any subsequent inquiries. This statement also demonstrates the desire and commitment within the plan to staff and those who may provide services to the response. Common plan objectives or intent may include:

- Save life and prevent injury to the public;
- Protect staff, contractors and persons on company property;
- Protect company property and assets;
- Assist the emergency services;
- Co-ordinate recovery.

The list of objectives is a matter for the organisation, but it is important as it creates initial strategic focus, prioritises and provides goals to give the response structure. However, too many objectives can be confusing and vague. Keeping the objectives short and few in number provides clarity.

When the incident is running and strategic command/management is in place these objectives may change, being shaped by the incident. In that case they can become more specific.

TASK 3.5

Explain any CCA stipulations regarding plan maintenance and updating of plans.

Method—section 3

This is simply the management approach—it is a chronological narrative giving a management overview of the whole response process and is the most comprehensive section. It begins where the 'Information' left off. 'Information' takes the reader up to activation—'Method' takes the reader into the response. The very nature of this section is one of description and explanation and is intended to be read in slow time.

If the plan is being activated the reader must be directed from 'Method' to the relevant 'ACTIONS' so as not to delay the implementation of the plan by reading this 'Method' section first.

A simple warning on the top of the page will ensure this happens:

'IF ACTIVATING THIS PLAN REFER TO YOUR ACTIONS—**NOW**'.

Anyone with a role within the plan will know this as they will have undergone training and familiarisation of the plan before.

This is the start of the immediate response. This section will declare in more detail, in the first instance, what is required at an 'operational' level, the hands on level to deal with the incident then moving up to the appropriate managerial level. It should take the reader through the arrangements, logically, step by step, building gradually in a seamless way. It is a summary of the planned objectives and 'Actions' that will occur as the incident unfolds. Remember—specific and very detailed 'Actions' and responsibilities of personnel involved in the response, although mentioned in brief in this section will be highlighted in separate 'Actions' section, therefore, within this section the reader will often be referred to 'Actions'. They will be contained in separate sections and appear at the back of the plan.

In preparing this section imagine how the information would be told to someone who has no prior knowledge. Imagine completing this method section as though it was a briefing—explaining to a group who are about to carry out the plan.

The management approach to an emergency or crisis will depend upon the type and nature of an organisation. Emergency response organisations subject to the CCA, with duties or obligations to respond to an emergency as defined by the Act will subscribe strictly to the multi-agency co-ordination arrangements as set out in the following documents, which we have already seen.

1. The United Kingdom Concept of Operations, or UK CONOPS;

2. The Civil Contingencies Act guidance—'Response';

3. The Association of Chief Police Officers (ACPO) Emergency Procedures and Command and Control.

We will look at the procedures and guidance in these documents later when we discuss the co-ordinated response.

In terms of other non-emergency response organisations, including commercial companies, the emergency response or crisis management procedures within those organisations will be set out in their BCM plans and organisational policy. However, what is imperative for these organisations is to ensure that whatever management arrangements they put in place they integrate, complement and support the arrangements set out in the key guidance just listed.

There are many issues that will appear in the method section. Precisely what appears depends upon the nature of the response but there are some critical key issues to consider which will now be specifically discussed, principally because they are so important within the method section. The following explanations have been written mainly for the benefit of non-emergency service responders to highlight some of the key issues and how they are addressed within a plan. Equally as important they are here to refresh and highlight issues that repeatedly present misunderstandings across many emergency responders. This approach has been chosen as it gives a better insight to those within the blue light services on the issues under consideration by non-blue light organisations which in turn may assist them in developing arrangements that are a better 'fit' for themselves and those of partner agencies. It also acts as a general introduction for more detailed discussion later about incident management. The specific issues dealt with here are:

1. Incident management principles.

2. Working with the police.

3. Making planning provision for the vulnerable.

4. Warning the public.

5. Evacuation.

1. Incident management/command and control

Within this part of the method section outline *exactly* the management structure that will be adopted and at what stages. What will inform the move to another management level? How and when it will be activated? Whichever organisation the plan is for, when preparing plans there will be a need to establish clear management or command and control, using terminology that is part of the organisational language. Be explicit as to how the plan will work for the organisation and how it will integrate into the organisational structure. Explain how it will be integrated into outside agencies or partner organisations if the need arises. This will lend itself to a seamless integration with blue light organisations and other emergency responders. Imagine it as a jigsaw piece that fits into a bigger picture. This is the heart of a good plan. Who does what, where, when and why!

'Commanders' or managers will be those people who have managerial responsibility and authority for a particular aspect of the response. For non-blue light organisations, as long as their role is well defined and designated a title is all that is required. They can be called anything which carries meaning within the organisation and within the plan. However, try to avoid using titles that could be confused with emergency responders such a Gold Commander for the 'company boss in London'. There is more on this issue later and in Chapter 4 but simply, their job description should include a descriptor which clearly recognises their function as either strategic, tactical or operational (see later) so if the need arises their role can be aligned with that of the emergency services multi-agency response. Therefore the Gold Commander for the company in London could be called 'Emergency Director (Strategic)'. Ensure that they are identified by post and they have an 'Action Sheet' within the plan that is *explicit* as to what action they need to take. Also include their responsibility to attend any multi-agency co-ordination centre(s) as and when required—this is often overlooked by non-emergency responders. At any given time those who have a role to play or are 'in charge' for the organisation must be easily identifiable too. At an emergency site or incident room environment using identification tabards or jackets is a useful way of ensuring everyone knows who is doing what and who is who.

TOP TIP

If any member of staff is required to attend a police multi-agency co-ordination centre it is always a good idea to have a tabard with the organisation's name and their role displayed upon it.

There will be more detailed information which will assist in understanding that distinction in Chapters 4 and 5 with more about co-ordination. Clearly these roles are more clearly defined and familiar within the emergency services but the overall objective is to create a synergy and compatibility across all response organisations, including the private sector, so avoiding confusion when they are required to support and contribute to a multi-agency response.

It is useful at this point to briefly mention and emphasise the correct use of the Strategic (Gold), Tactical (Silver) and Operational (Bronze) (STO) or (GSB) system of Command and Control. This is an introduction to the subject and detailed knowledge is not required at this stage, but it is relevant to this section to draw a clear distinction in the use of STO or GSB in the overall management framework. There is a growing tendency for emergency response organisations to favour the use the terms Strategic, Tactical and Operational to describe management levels as opposed to GSB. The reason seems to be one of an association with the hierarchy of precious metals to assign rank or expertise or that GSB is now being adopted more frequently by non-blue light organisations which in turn is leading to a degree of confusion. However, GSB are still widely used and there is a direct read across between the two; this book will use STO in preference but will include GSB as necessary to add clarity when required.

There has been an added complication also in that there has been a gradual shift over many years for STO or GSB to be taken and modified by individual organisations which again can add confusion to a process that was in fact designed to add clarity. This has to be monitored by the EPO in their day-to-day activities to ensure clarity remains and confusion reduced to a minimum. Alignment with the key UK national guidance (including devolved administrations) is crucial to maintain understanding. STO and GSB are primarily designed to describe a multi-agency approach to incident management in terms of co-ordination. STO and GSB are familiar to many, but often non-blue light organisations try emulate the GSB system within their own plans and procedures as a means of trying to ensure compatibility with external agencies. But often the reverse is true.

By choosing GSB specifically, it can be confusing not only to non-blue light organisations but to the blue light organisations themselves. Remember to use language that is familiar within your organisation and if necessary assign a 'tag' which ties that role into the main co-ordination management levels. Consider the prospect of having Gold being referred to if there are several Golds operating from different locations? Is it an individual or a facility? Where are they? There is a real danger of multiple un-coordinated Golds, Silvers and Bronzes proliferating and creating a barrier to good communication and co-ordination which is not aligned with the UK CONOPS, ACPO or the CCA. So the careless use of GSB should be avoided if possible by non-blue light organisations because it will clash and over complicate the overall management structure if and when the emergency services and responders become involved. In most cases it will also be unnecessary. When assigning a descriptor to a management role, for example, Company Director (Strategic), it is obvious reading this title in a plan that the CD is a strategic manager and not Gold as this would become confusing. In the same way by designating a non-blue light facility with a title of 'Gold' or 'Strategic'outside the core multi-agency co-ordination process is again confusing to blue light services and emergency responders alike, in particular the police who are usually trying to co-ordinate the emergency response.

In short, in a multi-agency emergency response situation those assigned the title of Strategic or Gold Commander or manager will be expected to have a role designated within a multi-agency strategic co-ordination centre (SCC) if called upon and those with a title of Tactical or Silver Commander within a plan will have a role at either an identifiable scene or at the multi-agency tactical co-ordination centre (TCC), if called upon.

In other words, keep it simple, if your plan, includes or potentially includes a multi-agency emergency response—references to STO/GSB should refer to the co-ordination arrangements supporting that response and not to internal management layers that may in fact be out of 'sync' leading to confusion and indeed frustration.

In the illustration in Figure 3.3 the central multi-agency emergency response and recovery goal is driven by national guidance produced in the ACPO, CCA

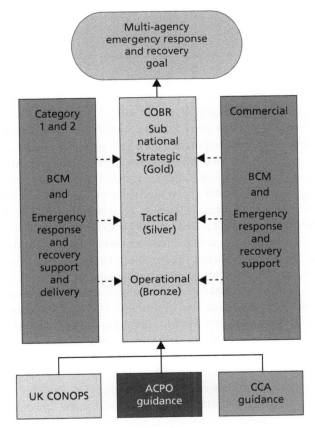

Figure 3.3 Supporting the multi-agency response

and UK CONOPS guidance documents (including devolved administration guidance). Running alongside to the left are the Category 1 and 2 organisations as defined by the CCA where they have to deliver an emergency response by supporting the national management emergency arrangements, and support of their own business continuity management plans.

In the case of commercial organisations or non-CCA designated organisations, to the right, their aim will be to survive as an organisation by managing their emergency or crisis led by their own BCM plans but at the same time being able to support and respond to the multi-agency response if needed. This is achieved by having mechanisms, processes and structures that complement, recognise and integrate fully with the central emergency response procedures while maintaining their own internal organisational integrity.

KEY POINT

Do not confuse the multi-agency emergency response by advocating the use of STO/GSB to internal management processes until they are in direct support of that co-ordinated response.

Closely related to the correct use of STO and GSB to describe management levels is the element of 'control'. This is the facility that offers administrative support to the operational response or activity.

Permanent or semi-permanent facilities to 'control' the response need to be identified in order to support the managers or commanders, even if the incident occurs 'off-site' such as a transport incident in any location where dynamic scene management is needed a temporary 'control' facility will be needed. The 'control' facilities for a multi-agency emergency response will initially be a Forward Command Post (FCP) at operational level, a Tactical Co-ordination Centre (TCC) and a Strategic Co-ordination Centre (SCC). However, any organisation responding to an emergency or crisis should have an identified facility or 'control'. The emergency services and emergency responders have tried and tested arrangements in place to achieve 'control' which we will discuss in detail later. For non-blue light organisations who do not have such arrangements as part of their organisational structure an emergency facility is essential to assist and support not only their own response and personnel but to support any interaction with the external emergency responders too. Setting up such a facility will be covered in detail later but the management issue here is where does this 'private' facility fit into the overall picture of emergency response management? Review Figure 3.3.

This facility can be called whatever is relevant within the organisation and is usually covered by policy within the BCM plan. It could be the 'Incident Room', 'Emergency Control Centre' (ECC), 'Emergency Room', 'Crisis Management Room' or any other name but it must not be confused with being part of the STO or GSB framework put in place by the emergency services. For non-blue light organisations the location can be anything from a full-blown communications centre to the staff canteen with extra phone lines and a few dry wipe boards, whatever meets the needs of the management arrangements within the plan. However, all non-blue light plans must be configured to expect to accommodate several other agencies should the incident escalate and expect to have at least a police liaison officer and possibly other emergency services attend their facility if the situation requires it. These arrangements must be discussed with the emergency services to ensure they are compliant and complement the emergency services response. Again this is where liaison with the LRF is vital. Many organisations that have emergency management in place or BCM plans often overlook the need to have their own facility in place. But having such a facility in place can ensure much greater control is exercised by the management or crisis team, dealing with both BCM and emergency issues, slotting seamlessly into external agency expectations. Guidance for setting up such a facility is covered in Chapter 5.

Activation of any 'control', (including the police co-ordination centres for example) will form an 'Action' and that must appear as an action for a post holder designated within the plan.

KEY POINT

Clarify the status and distinguish the difference between a 'co-ordination centre' and a 'control centre'; 'control centre' is a generic term used to describe any facility from which control is exercised. This can be used by the emergency services, utilities, private organisations, in fact any group. 'Co-ordination centre' is very specific as it is a facility which is designed to for multi-agency use only—hence the term multi-agency strategic *co-ordination* centre (SCC) or tactical *co-ordination* centre (TCC).

Until that dedicated control or co-ordination facility is functioning, there will be a need to ensure that plans allow for initial incident management of the situation through day to day arrangements and facilities; hence the need to have total integration with day to day activity as a precursor to building an emergency or crisis response. That may entail ensuring that staff such as switchboard or communications operators/supervisors/managers understand the initial response role—this is where internal integration comes in and a use of day to day facilities to form the initial and first stage of the bigger response. Again this is why training is so important. It will not be everyday that a member of staff will be exposed to the crisis or emergency situation so training is vital—if only to understand how the initial stages of the incident are managed. Their role may be further clarified in an action sheet within the plan or indeed pre-distributed generic emergency response procedures. The key here is ensuring that 'normal' daily staff are aware of the plans and can implement them. This is important because once the dedicated 'control' is running and managing the incident this allows 'normal' staff to resume their routine work and carry on the business, proceeding with as little disruption as possible to the organisation and is a demonstration of good business continuity management.

TASK 3.6

If you work within an organisation, what kind of emergency facilities are there in your organisation? Are they fit for purpose? Could they cater for multi-agency use?

---

2. Working with the police

This topic is discussed in greater detail in Chapter 5 but within the management section cognisance needs to be taken of the potential and absolute requirement to be able to work closely with the emergency services and the police in particular. The plan must support the police. It must be understood that the police usually co-ordinate the entire emergency response for all agencies. Companies, non-emergency services and other organisations must be prepared to support police multi-agency co-ordination if requested. That means the police will support or make available the facilities and locations to enable that co-ordination to take place. For an incident with an identifiable scene these will initially be (as alluded to earlier) at the Forward Command Post (FCP) which is operational management at or near a scene, a Tactical Co-ordination Centre (TCC) (Silver) and a Strategic Co-ordination Centre (SCC) (Gold) if warranted. It is vital that all responder organisations can attend and support these locations if needed and sustain that support perhaps over several days.

KEY POINT

The police are only 'in-charge' of their own staff—but usually co-ordinate the multi-agency response.

Police commanders are only in charge of their own staff and they have no authority over any other organisation with regard to management decisions. For clarity however, the police will still 'enforce' the law which is different from interfering in management decisions. But it is possible that they may request support at one of the co-ordination centres to offer advice, information and assist in decision making. It is absolutely vital that they are supported and those requested to attend police co-ordination centres are at the right managerial level as we have discussed by assigning the correct managerial function in the planning stage. Those requested to attend these centres should do so as a matter of absolute priority as it is within these co-ordination centres that decisions will be made that affect all organisations, including companies. Not being there means not having a say or input. Obtaining training in both strategic and tactical management for use in a police co-ordination centre is vital for those who may find themselves being asked to attend. This is a good investment for any organisation or company as the decisions made within one of these centres may be pivotal in the success or failure of a company from a BCM perspective.

But one important issue may become relevant or a concern for a company in this police environment—are they a suspect! This is an issue that can often be raised prior to arranging de-briefs as the full investigation into the incident may not be complete but can manifest itself at the emergency phase too. This will be discussed in more detail in Chapter 5 but being called into a police station/co-ordinationcentre at any level, Strategic/Gold, Tactical/Silver or Operational/Bronze should mean that those attending must be trained or at least have a good knowledge of the systems and processes that they will come across. *Failing to appreciate this will put them at a disadvantage.* They will or could be overwhelmed or mildly intimidated by the hustle and bustle of this environment. This knowledge and experience can be obtained by taking part in as many exercises as possible and ensuring that full collaboration and planning occurs in the plan preparation stage. Training is available for liaison officers/staff to ensure effective collaboration takes place. This is often an area where independent consultants can be beneficial.

3. The vulnerable

The management section of the plan must at all times cater for those who are less capable of caring for themselves for whatever reason, particular consideration must be given to those who may not be self reliant. This was alluded to in the 'Introduction' earlier and will be discussed in relation to Human Rights issues (see later). The term vulnerable may extend to those with disability or those who are confined or restricted in some way, for example in nursing homes or nursery schools. The scope is very wide. It can also extend to those within an organisation where provision may have to be made to assist or put in place special warnings for them. For example, the non-hearing or partially sighted. These are all issues and considerations outlined as a commitment at the beginning of the plan which include diversity and disability. For planning purposes a little thought and consideration combined with consultation between stakeholders should assist in identifying those vulnerable persons or sections of the community that will need special measures to be put in place to help them. Issues of communication are key to effective planning for the vulnerable and this issue of communication generally is important for communities and organisations as a whole. This leads onto developing effective and viable warning systems and procedures, which are termed 'warning the public'.

4. Warning and informing the public

A significant issue contained within the CCA guidance (see *Emergency Preparedness*) is the requirement to have in place public warning and public information arrangements within plans. This approach actually translates across into the workplace too. It really makes sense because people that are well informed will hopefully react in a more measured, calm and positive fashion to an emergency situation. The emergency services often witness inexplicable behaviours. People under conditions of stress created by situations they are unfamilar with tend to follow automatic reactions, for example returning to entrances or exits rather than following the nearest exits or ignoring obvious danger signs or conditions. However, they will be more likely to follow the advice of the emergency services or managers if they are properly aware and informed and it will reduce the likelihood of panic. It is about education and achieving a risk communication strategy that alerts but not alarms—a fine balance.

That will involve shaping risk perception so that the risk is viewed in a realistic way and not over exaggerated. The use of qualitative risk assessment data can assist in this area as we saw in Chapter 2. Another key issue for communicating warnings is trust in the message. People will take more notice of a message if they trust the messenger: 'Who will the public trust?'

Regarding the voracity of warning messages, research presented to the Lancashire Resilience Forum (formerly the Lancashire Major Incident Co-ordinating Group) by the author in July 2003 indicated that the police and the fire service were held in the highest position of trust amongst the immediate resident population living around the nuclear power stations at Heysham, Lancashire. The survey was conducted to establish the most efficient means of framing risk communication messages following a nuclear emergency at the site. Although this is not published research it informed the production and public warning information strategy.

This illustrates an important issue for the EPO that we have already alluded to in Chapter 1. In terms of developing risk communication strategies and on issues of warning and informing the public using small scale targeted surveys can yield valuable information to make plans more effective at a local level. Locally, population profile, attitude to risk and knowledge can vary a great deal. Surveys are a useful way of gauging and measuring public understanding and potential behavioural response which in turn will greatly assist in emergency management. EPOs should not be afraid to engage and listen to the public. This data can then be incorporated into the method section of the plan to inform the reader as to the preferred warning options.

How is risk communication achieved? This is achieved in broadly three ways. First, by raising awareness in the public mind of emergency response issues prior to any incident. Second, by communicating warnings and alerts and then third, followed by continued information on the situation.

Raising awareness has been approached at three levels. First, by requiring the publication of risk information (CRR) and plan information through requirements in the CCA, this is available to the public to view and increase their level of knowledge. Second, at national level, for example the Government's *Preparing for Emergencies* leaflet together with websites such as <https://www.gov.uk/local-planning-emergency-major-incident> Third, often supported by advice and information locally co-ordinated and financed through LRFs who circulate more emergency information, this may include postal drops, events, newsletters, media outputs, web-based information and so forth to raise awareness with the public generally.

There are also those 'at risk' communities, whether it is from a nuclear or a chemical site, where certain pieces of legislation such as the Control of Major Accident Hazard Regulations (COMAH) and Radiation Emergency Preparedness and Public Information Regulations (REPPIR) require a specific public warning and information strategy to be in place as a condition of the company's operating licence. In flood risk areas too, the Environment Agency lead on public warnings. Within an organisation prior warning and awareness regarding emergency response will be achieved through exercising, training and briefing.

Warning during an emergency and follow on information is a more critical factor as it is this action that really could save lives and prevent injury and damage to property. It should be made clear and agreed beforehand who is responsible for the warning—this is usually negotiated at the LRF. How will it be done and by whom? Making assumptions that certain agencies, such as the police, will always do 'that kind of thing' would be a mistake. If in doubt check this out. The police are bound by health and safety laws (as we will see later) like every other employer and some warning tasks may simply be too dangerous for the police to do—remember the risk assessment. In addition, the police and other emergency services do not have infinite resources and simply may not have the operational capability 24 hours per day.

What methods are used to alert and warn of an imminent or ongoing emergency will be a matter that best suits the situation and environment so that it is as effective as possible. A bespoke solution taking into account factors such a time of day, area to be warned, target population or group (including the vulnerable) and type of hazard should be considered. Always choose the most effective means of warning. Consider technological means first. Why? Because it frees up valuable resources and reduces the risks to those that may have to enter hazardous environments such as toxic smoke, flood water or radiation. Every warning task will have to be risk assessed and appear in the plan. Further and more detailed information about the legal requirements can be found at <https://www.gov.uk/government/policies/improving-the-uks-ability-to-absorb-respond-to-and-recover-from-emergencies> (2013). See also 'Dealing with the Media'—later.

In short, this section of the plan must address warning issues whether it is simple, as in a closed environment such as business premises, or a wide area such as a town. This must include pre-warning arrangements or prior information for at risk communities, to general public warning as the incident occurs and follow-up information as the incident plays out. Most importantly, who will do them?

TOP TIP

Always ensure that warning and informing responsibilities are assigned and documented and agreed in advance.

---

5. Evacuation—general

Finally, within this section we consider evacuation. Evacuation is one of the vital life saving issues when dealing with public safety and is often held up as the panacea to any emergency situation without sufficient thought. The decision to evacuate is a difficult one to make as the activity in itself can be dangerous, bearing in mind what was said about vulnerable people and warnings. With a fixed site and site specific plans including flooding, evacu-ation can be pre-planned to a degree. It is possible to designate areas and locations which are pre-identified to form evacuation assembly points and rendezvous points where the emergency services can assemble and where transport is provided (this is normally arranged by the LA) to remove peo-ple from an area. These evacuation collection points will be supported with safe routes (with alternatives) around and through the site or incident. Many fixed site plans will have sectored areas which make identifying affected areas easier to plot and designate (see Figure 3.4). This is achieved by means of scaled concentric circles on plastic overlays or software overlays used on a map or a specially printed map. Using post code areas or fixed boundaries such as main roads, railways or rivers is a way in which the public can relate to and understand an affected area more easily.

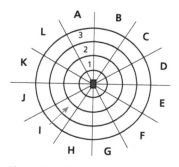

Figure 3.4 Sector overlay

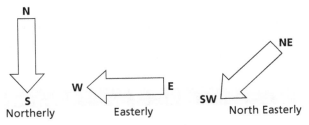

Figure 3.5 Understanding wind direction

Always bear in mind that an evacuation means removing people from an unsafe location to a safe one, usually caused by something harmful in the air, so taking into account wind shift is important for obvious reasons and allow for alternative routes if the wind changes. This includes considering the positioning of key resources and facilities near a site that could also be affected. Consider using, for example, red and blue routes as alternatives. Remember—wind direction is always given in terms of where it is coming from, e.g. a northerly wind is coming from that direction (see Figure 3.5).

The use of route maps and photographs, both aerial and ground level, are essential to illustrate this task for the plan.

Spontaneous and unknown threats or hazards present a more complex and dynamic approach to evacuation in which the safest options have to be assessed within an environment which will be unknown, such as topography and population profile. This requires considerable effort in an often fast moving situation. This is best co-ordinated by the police using mapping systems based in their control/communication centres. In a slower moving situation a more measured approach can be taken within a multi-agency co-ordination centre.

Communicating evacuation advice in these situations to the public can take many forms from using the media to utilising any pre-distributed information such as that provided under the COMAH and REPPIR requirements. These include calendars and leaflets with emergency information printed on them. There is no doubt that the police will assist using all resources available in a spontaneous incident to warn the public on foot and by vehicle if necessary following a dynamic risk assessment. However, wherever possible using any available warning technology should be considered first, for example, mobile phone technology, potentially social networking, cell broadcasting and the wider facilities available to inform the public generally like public address systems or public message boards.

KEY POINT

Using helicopter warnings can be counterproductive. Why?

But using public address (PA) systems, such as those on police helicopters or vehicles can have the opposite effect to that which is required. If the message is 'go in' and 'stay in' do not tell people by PA They will simply open windows, doors and go outside to hear the message!

TOP TIP

Utilise social media networks as a tool for warning and informing.

One important factor to which the emergency services have little control is spontaneous evacuation. This should never be underestimated or assume that the public will be totally compliant and co-operative. Reaction can be moderated to some extent by prior education and shaping the 'risk' message to avoid possible panic. This is very important around fixed hazardous sites. For example, for planning purposes assuming that those in the immediate vicinity of a site may evacuate because they reside within a specially designated 'danger' (Public Information Zone PIZ [COMAH] or Detailed Emergency Planning Zone DEPZ [REPPIR]) area is a realistic assumption but probably won't happen as assumed! However, extending that distance to perhaps twice or three times the distance from the site should also be considered and planned for because people will take 'precautionary' evacuation steps, perhaps even for only a few hours. Those effects will potentially gridlock

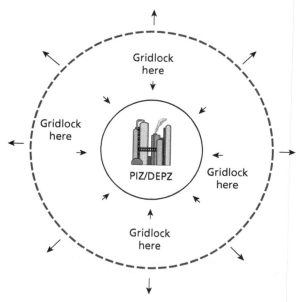

Figure 3.6 Creating 'Gridlock'

perimeter roads trapping those nearer the site who may actually need to, or are directed to, evacuate. This is known as the 'shadow' effect.

The illustration in Figure 3.6 demonstrates the gridlock effect with using wide area warnings. To 'shot blast' an area with warning messages via the media will lead to the shadow effect. In these situations targeted warnings are essential to control evacuation, in particular spontaneous wide area evacuation.

KEY POINT

Negotiate carefully with site specific warnings—using technical means as a priority. It will free up resources and safe guard responders avoiding unnecessary exposure to harmful environments.

This additional planning falls within an emergency principle of 'extendibility'. Plans must be capable of accommodating public reaction beyond the detailed planning that takes place near a site of an incident, both fixed and spontaneous. The safer planning option in these circumstances is to plan far beyond the immediate site vicinity. It is important that spontaneous evacuation be planned for, in particular in terms of traffic management arrangements. This may involve significant traffic diversions involving local agencies such as the police, local authority and the Highways Agency in particular if planning for wider scale spontaneous evacuation.

Evacuation—town centre

Town centre evacuation presents unique challenges for the EPO. Town centre environments are very dynamic places. They are changing all the time with diverse communities of residents, commuters, visitors and workers to mention a few. Town layout and geography, infrastructure and building type can vary as much as the population profile. Add to that the fluctuating population, time of day and weather conditions and it creates an environment which is very unpredictable.

Clearly town centres remain a target for the terrorist. It is quite obvious that the town centre environment presents large concentrations of people in relatively confined areas making them attractive targets. Planning for evacuation is now an important multi-agency activity involving the police, local authorities and shopping centre managers, to mention but three. 'Traditional' explosive devices are now only one of a menu of weapons that could be used which include the chemical, biological, radiological and nuclear (CBRN) devices. Responding to such events is now well planned, resourced and exercised.

Some town centre evacuation models will pre-designate evacuation assembly or muster points based upon identified zones combined with key evacuation routes with alternatives should some become unavailable. This is supported by a warning communication strategy to inform the public of what to do. In fact, this information is often freely available with road signs indicating the assembly points and evacuation routes. This model has the advantage in that facilities can be pre-positioned and arranged such as transport, medical support if needed, rendezvous points for emergency responders, mass decontamination sites and everyone knows what will happen and what to expect. However, so will the terrorist.

A dynamic capability will have to remain; in reality the location of the incident or threat, chemical attack or a bomb warning will be unknown. The wind drift if airborne substances are involved will be unknown or virtually impossible to predict in a built up area. The dynamic of the public reaction and behaviour will be unknown and many people will be unfamiliar with the town layout. Pre-planning is essential to identify all the features mentioned but keeping some of that information secure for the use of the emergency services through effective co-ordination by the police is essential. The key to having effective pre-planned and dynamic response capability is setting up effective means of communicating with the public in town centre environments.

Using a combination of strategically placed message screens, public address systems supported by trained and exercised emergency response personnel will ensure that the public are properly informed, quickly, with the best advice and reassurance, to indicate the most appropriate course of action for them to take. The benefits of CCTV in this situation cannot be over stated, not only from a detection and investigative point of view but assisting in co-ordinating an effective response and evacuation.

TASK 3.7

Consider the guidance contained within Emergency Preparedness concerning 'communicating with the public' and outline the advice relating to warning the public.

Administration—section 4

Aside from the core incident management response, which takes precedence, the plan should contain additional information, which although not crucial is nevertheless important. This will ensure the emergency response will run smoothly and is fully supported. Consider support as the processes that will underpin the initial response or 'oils the wheels'. These could include for example:

- **Business Continuity issues**—how the organisation will continue to operate by offsetting the effects of the emergency. For example, if a particular member of staff has duties to perform in managing the incident what alternative arrangements have been put in place to cover for them or if a room is being used what alternatives rooms can be used? Only brief outlines are needed within the plan. Longer working hours may need to be considered with extended hours of duty, alternative working arrangements will need consideration. What alternative arrangements will be put in place? An existing BCM plan may already be in place and simply require a reference to implement it.

- **Welfare Issues**—looking after staff in terms of both physical and mental well-being. Welfare, morale and stress are interrelated. People are at most risk of stress when confronting unfamiliar situations where uncertainty prevails. Stress can undermine confidence and performance too. Initial and regular briefing is therefore very important to remove uncertainty, by keeping people informed and setting clear tasks.

  Watching for symptoms of stress is important, as early intervention is vital to prevent longer term problems. Monitor hours of work carefully. Emergency response is not like working in an office. Burn out can occur quickly. Supervisors and managers must watch for stress. How can the organisation's personnel or human resources department assist? If the organisation has a medical or nursing section, how can they help? Consider the support of external agencies if necessary by seeking advice in the planning stage from local authority social services departments or the local health providers. Psychological de-briefing is an area of some controversy as individuals have many different ways of coping. But managing stress and post-incident trauma must be considered and arrangements should be put in place to accommodate this in due course to offer counselling and support, where requested.

- **Logging/Messages**—what methods will be used in control centres? In this section direct responders to the relevant 'user guide' for the police co-ordination facilities (see later). Reinforce the message to save and protect all information regarding the emergency including all messages, hard copy and down load computer information onto disc. This will be required later for de-briefs and inquiries. Ensure that this task or action is allocated to a person or team.

- **General Administration**—the necessary follow on for staffing arrangements, briefing arrangements and continuing that ongoing support. Preparing duty rosters and monitoring hours. Planning briefings and refreshments.

- **Logistics and equipment**—looking at arrangements to increase support, from whom and where if required. Looking at resource levels, trying to forecast what will be needed. Linking into other control centre(s) or co-ordination centres to ascertain what is needed. Positioning logistic support in the right locations at the right times. What mutual aid arrangements can support the response? Co-ordinating distribution and allocation of resources on advice from other centres. Each plan may require additional support structures that will have to be considered on a case-by-case basis. However, the constant to all plans is managing the media which we will now look at.

Dealing with the media

Most LRFs will have a multi-agency media plan in place. For planning purposes this can be referred to in the 'Introduction' section of the plan as an essential reference which means that little has to be repeated in this section. However, some essential basic details are contained here to assist the EPO in developing local in-house plans as required.

> **TOP TIP**
>
> Acquire a copy of your LRF multi-agency media response plan—it is *essential* reading for the EPO and BCM manager.

The general public, and therefore the media, in all its forms have an understandable curiosity in all unusual events resulting in loss of life, injuries and large scale damage. The power of the 24-hour media cannot be underestimated. The media carry a very heavy responsibility and bad reporting can exacerbate a situation creating difficulty for emergency response organisations. There will always be instances of bad, naive or even thoughtless reporting. Thankfully those cases are in general few and far between. The media must, however, be used as an ally, a communication link, a means to inform, to warn, to educate and to minimise risk. One of the biggest criticisms from the media is the lack of initial information. When an event occurs it is essential that an early press release is produced and this should be a priority, followed with regular updates, even if there is nothing to add.

> **KEY POINT**
>
> Early media engagement is vital to avoid speculation and rumour. Early means 'within minutes of the incident breaking'. Even just to confirm what they know.

The importanct of an early press release cannot be over stated. Even simple confirmation and saying that emergency response arrangements are in place will moderate media demand.

The vast majority of the press and media are responsible reporters. Being sympathetic to their needs and expectations will allow a mutually beneficial relationship to emerge. However, expect and anticipate some media coverage to be 'enhanced', in that certain reports, although accurate, may be taken out of context to increase the news worthiness. It is just the nature of the media and the culture we live in. There may be a separate media plan within an organisation, which is good practice, but the LRF will have special arrangements in place to manage the media. Viewing a copy would be of great benefit when considering producing an emergency plan.

It is important that there is a designated media spokesperson or persons within an organisation to address the media. Depending upon the size of the organisation this can range from a full department to perhaps one or two people. It is money well spent to have some form of media training for the spokesperson. Again the LRF can assist infinding suitable courses or someone who can assist in that area. The BBC has special responsibilities to promote and broadcast public safety information and again may assist with braodcasting emergency information locally. Contacting any local BBC broadcast television or radio editor is a useful communication tool in a crisis.

Being prepared, trained and confident to manage the media is an absolute must for any organisation. But close liaison with the police is essential to co-ordinate the information going out to the public if the multi-agency response is operating. It is a primary responsibility of the police service to co-ordinate a media response during an emergency. The co-ordination of the media response is covered in Chapter 5, but for the purposes of this Chapter, within this section of the plan, it is useful to include some essential basic information to assist those who may be called upon to address the media and this section can provide a valuable aide memoir.

In some circumstances an interview may be inevitable for one or more emergency responders or support organisations and that may include company representatives. This may be as a result of the rapid onset of the emergency or the need to quickly get essential messages out to the public, in particular warning messages. It may not always be possible to secure the attendance of the 'media professional' from within the organisation in time. Choosing the right person amongst those who are available may be the only option but can be the single most important decision in holding a successful media briefing. Remember issues of trust—who is the best or most appropriate organisation to confront the media? Is the person about to go in front of the media really the right person? If not, choose another person, be realistic and honest. It may be possible to get assistance from another organisation or the emergency services. Some people are very good and natural, their body language, facial expression, intonation, facial animation all contribute positively to the message. Being uncomfortable, ill at ease, angry or nervous can all detract from the message and as we have seen, trust in the messenger is vital to the public accepting and believing what they are being told. Appearance is also important in getting the right message across—dressing the part is also vital.

Being 'doorstepped' can be an intimidating experience, when a microphone is thrust at you to make a comment. Saying no comment can seem very evasive and shifty—a simple response can give you an opportunity to move through a media line relatively unscathed. For example:

1. Express deep concern and sympathy for those involved.
2. Commend the work of the emergency responders.
3. Express the determination to find the cause and learn lessons.

And then move on . . . .

Preparing for a more detailed interview requires more thought and is a key part to ensuring success and getting the message across. Here are some other issues to consider for inclusion in the plan under this section:

- Before any interview make sure the objective of the interview is understood with the reporter or interviewer. Is information being asked for—an appeal? Is it for creating a warning, giving information and advice or defending a position? This will inform the way answers are prepared and givesthe interviewee an opportunity to obtain further information or facts before the start.

- Establish the format of the interview, where the interviewer will take the interview or lead the interviewee. The reporter should be asked what their first question will be...the first answer can then be prepared and help building that initial confidence.

- Is it live? If it is recorded it can be stopped and started again.

- The interviewee should write down the key messages having analysed the interview objective—they must get those points across.

- Think of a way to emphasise the messages—a key phrase perhaps that will grip the viewer or listener.

- Try to anticipate the 'awkward' question. What would the interviewee least like to be asked—then prepare for it.

- If in front of a camera, dress correctly and avoid sunglasses.

Having prepared, what should then be considered whilst stood in front of the camera or microphone?

- Telling the truth at all times, this may seem obvious but there is a tendency to be over helpful or embellish which could colour the answers. If the interviewee does not know, they should say so and go and find the answer. They should never speculate.

- Remaining calm, composed and taking sufficient time is important.
- Never say 'No comment'.
- Try to be natural. Smiling when it is appropriate. Never be over sincere—it will appear false. Trying to be conversational and not talk in a series of statements is more natural.
- Avoiding jargon and acronyms or words where the meanings are unsure should assist understanding. Keep it simple.
- Do not be distracted onto side issues. Try to deflect the question and return to the message—a politician's skill—this is not easy.

If a prepared media statement is required, it should be prepared by taking time to write down the message objectives first and build the statement around that.

EXAMPLE

If it is a message to warn people about a toxic smoke plume, the key points will be based around the well established:

Go in—Stay in—Tune in—so address the following:

- Cover those who are residents, people in the open and car drivers
- Consider parents with children unaccounted for or pets outdoors
- What action they should take when indoors—close heating vents and close windows
- Those who may be affected by the smoke—medical action to take
- Reduce anxiety
- Stay tuned in
- Do not overload the emergency services with 999 calls
- 'All Clear' arrangements
- Any local issues such as traffic congestion.

TASK 3.8

Using the key points just discussed, prepare a warning message. Listing points in this way will ensure that all the key issues are covered and result in an effective message. Keeping the wording to about 100 words is a useful guide to have the entire message used by the media. If it is longer it will probably be edited.

Risk assessment—section 5

A plan is produced having identified the overall hazard and satisfied the criteria. There will now be a need to carry out a risk assessment to establish the level of risk associated with managing the hazard or hazards from a response point of view—in other words managing the 'Actions'. The 'Actions' required within the plan may require a risk assessment to establish how the actions will be accomplished safely

In Figure 3.7 the process begins with the hazard. That is risk assessed and if appropriate a plan is produced. Within the plan 'Actions' are identified to enable the plan to work. Those actions are risk assessed and if necessary modified to make them as safe as possible. From that analysis the 'Action' sheet

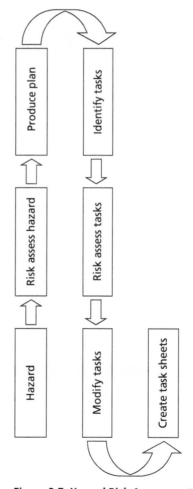

Figure 3.7 Hazard Risk Assessment

can be produced. Specialist advice may be required and guidance followed to do this, for example, if the hazards are outside general experience such as chemicals or radiation or infection. Those risks can be rated or assessed as already mentioned and then the EPO has to decide what action, if any, is needed to take to eliminate or reduce that risk to an acceptable level or apply risk treatments discussed earlier.

That may result in not carrying out the action associated with that hazard or using special training for the individual or providing personal protective equipment or PPE. Then and only then can the task appear in the Action sheet (Figure 3.8 below). It is important that the risk assessment process is documented and appears in the plan. There are many risk assessment forms on the market that can be used for this purpose.

We are all familiar with Health and Safety requirements and each organisation will, or should, have a Health and Safety policy covering all aspects of daily routine working—from office working to police patrolling. Emergency response may require consideration of other more 'risky' behaviours. Dynamic risk assessments are often required in a fast moving hazardous situation. Generally, in that situation the Fire and Rescue Service will provide the advice and information needed to make that judgement. There are many useful mnemonics which assist, for example:

CHECK SPRAIN

Care—be careful, stop and think before acting

Help—do I need help or advice—ask for it

Equipment—if provided use it (if trained to do so)

Clothing—personal protection—wear it if provided and trained to do so

Knowledge—have I been trained in this situation?

Situation—do I fully understand what is happening? What hazards?

Plan—is there a plan? Work out what you can do?

R isks—where do the dangers lie?

Alternatives—can I do this another way?

Increase safety—can I reduce the risks?

No—if in doubt

There are many others but overall the key message is always seek advice if unsure—putting yourself or others in danger only increases the workload on emergency responders.

However, within this section of the plan details can be included for use by dispatchers or communications operators in the initial stages of the incident if the potential hazards are known, that is for a fixed site, or generic health and safety advice can be given such as Steps 1-2-3 for

CBRN, upwind and uphill for toxic releases or liquid releases and so forth (see later).

It should be noted that the police service are subject to the Health and Safety at Work Act 1974 following the Police (Health and Safety) Act 1997—like all employees. However, there is recognition that the very nature of policing can be hazardous and operating dynamic risk assessments is now routine for police officers at all levels.

Communication—section 6

Communication here is defined in the broadest sense. It could be termed information management. It is about how information will pass, be shared, recorded and securing information. Communication is about using and sharing ways of exchanging that information. It could be by radio, telephone, e-mail, verbally, text and so on. No matter how good a plan may be, if people cannot talk to one another, it is useless. Include in this section:

- Reference to telephone numbers/directories—both internal and external.
- Radio call signs.
- Communication contingencies/backups.
- Reference to and encouragement to use information sharing and messaging systems in control centres including how to use them. All control centres should have a 'user guide' (see later) available to all who use them. This will outline how information is managed in that centre.
- Anticipated meetings such as Tactical Co-ordinating Group (TCG) and Strategic Co-ordinating Group (SCG).
- Glossary or lexicon of terms.
- Information and status boards.
- Briefing arrangements and timings.

At this stage it is sufficient to appreciate how to populate this section. We will consider in more detail the issues of information sharing in Chapter 5.

Human rights issues—section 7

Without doubt the human rights issues as outlined in the Human Rights Act 1998 (HRA) have an impact on all plans. It is now embedded into law in the UK. Although it may seem as though HRA can override all other legislation, it does not, but any conflict or breach of the HRA can be used as a basis to challenge. It is Section (1) of the HRA which states that it is 'unlawful for any public authority to act in a way which is incompatible with a Convention Right'.

It is not intended here to cover in detail each of the convention articles but in summary, those that may have relevance to emergency planning are:

- **Art 2—Right to life**. It must be assumed that the rationale within any plan, and often stated in the 'Intention' is to save life. Emergency planning is a manifestation of this right. Although not tested, situations literally requiring life saving actions must be weighed against this article.

- **Art 5—Right to liberty and security.** This really becomes an issue of restriction in cases which involve for example terrorism around issues of CBRN, perhaps the need to detain individuals in relation to contamination by chemical, biological or radiation.

- **Art 8—Right to respect for private and family life**. Again, it is difficult to envisage a situation where this article would need to be considered but issues around evacuation may produce circumstances which require consideration.

It is necessary to review every plan to ensure there are no obvious breaches of the convention and to include within the plan a suggested form of words for the Human Rights Act could be:

> **Human Right Audit** 'Consideration has been given to the compatibility of this plan and its related procedures, with the Human Rights Act 1988, particularly with reference to the legal basis of its precepts: the legitimacy of its aims: the justification and proportionality of the actions intended by it is the least intrusive and damaging option necessary to achieve the aims: and that it defines the need to document the relevant decision making process and outcomes of action.'

Action sheets—section 8 onwards as required

The Actions section will be the first reference point if activating the plan for those with a role—referred from section 3: Method. Actions are listed here for activating facilities and/or directly individuals to carry out functions. Actions should not be buried in the text where they will be hard to find especially when urgency is needed. Each separate Action sheet(s), i.e. for each individual or facility (Emergency Control Centre, etc.), should have a separate section.

If the plan contains distinct and separate emergency scenarios, such as for different buildings or hazards; for example, fire, bomb threat, chemical leak, etc. each one will have a separate Action Sheet.

The beginning of a typical Action Sheet may look like this:

PLAN: Title of plan included here.
**ACTION SHEET: COMMUNICATIONS OPERATOR/SWITCHBOARD MAIN
BUILDING**
1. Upon notification of declared emergency notify:
a) Duty Operations Manager
   Tel 23453   Completed Yes/No
b) Media Office/Duty media officer
   Tel 67856   Completed Yes/No
c) Human Resources Dept.
   Tel 65895   Completed Yes/No
2. Arrange for Emergency Control Centre to be **Opened.**
   Tel. Operations 65789   Completed Yes/No

3. **Notify Headquarters**   Tel 67890   Completed Yes/No

Etc...

Figure 3.8 Typical action or task sheet

Actions should be short, concise, clear and in numbered paragraphs. The user of the plan should use the action pages like a checklist, marking off each action as it is completed or adding notes on the progress of the action.

These action pages could be used as contemporaneous notes in a hard copy plan for use at a future inquiry or debrief. Similar action lists could appear in electronic versions of the plan and where possible including an audit trail or a failsafe means of recording completed actions.

Appendices

The final section of the plan. These pages are separated from the main body of the plan as they are likely to be changed more frequently, therefore making amendments easier to include during the 'update' process or indeed to exclude if containing sensitive information.

Appendices as a whole appear as one section and each appendix is given a letter. They will include such things as maps, telephone details, special arrangements, evacuation assembly points and maps, etc. The list can be extensive but an appendix is essentially a supplementary piece of information which would otherwise clog up the body of the text and make the plan difficult to use.

The plan building process may seem daunting but it is straightforward and having completed one the EPO or BCM manager will find subsequent plans easier to complete. Having produced the draft plan it now has to be finalised.

TOP TIP

Be careful of the use of the word 'draft'—a spelling error could lead to circulating a plan for information which reads...'please find enclosed our daft plan'!

Completing and Marketing the Plan

The plan must now be quality assured. It must be circulated to all those who contributed to it and feedback should be obtained. A final sign-off meeting can be held and minuted. A clear audit process must be recorded and retained in a file because this feedback may become relevant in the event of the plan being activated as part of the de-brief process or inquiry. Should any issues arise as to the content this feedback can be produced to demonstrate support or otherwise.

Once the plan is complete it must be introduced to those who may have to implement it. There is no point having a plan if nobody is aware of it. This is the point at which a seminar exercise will introduce the plan and indeed form the final quality assurance process before it is published. We will take a closer look at this type of exercise later—for those who have a role within the plan they must be *trained*.

Marketing

A marketing strategy is also required to publicise the plan. Depending upon the stakeholder profile during the sign-off meeting arrange for opportunities to engage with all those who may need to be aware of the plan. For example, use in-house newsletters, notice boards, magazines or e-mail messages. Attend in-house management meetings to promote the plan or at least have it placed as an information item on the agenda. Consider holding staff briefing sessions, attending meetings to give presentations or attending the LRF meetings or taking up invitations to visit other partner organisations or even businesses if they are the subject of *your* plan. This is a key role for the EPO. For example, for site specific plans:

1. Attending local community groups or liaison committees to outline the plan if it affects them.
2. Attending local business forums, for example Retail Parks or Industrial Estates if one site can affect others.
3. Place information in local papers.

Single agency plans need not be openly published as is required with plans produced by the LRF. Single agency plans need only be disclosed, or parts of them which are not subject to 'sensitivities', under the Freedom of Information Act and only if the organisation is a public body. They are essentially internal management tools.

The creation of plans is a specialised process. The guidance given here is intended to give enough information to produce a plan (in this case a single agency plan) and to give an insight and enough knowledge to critically review existing arrangements or to identify a need to produce a plan.

Summary

You will now be aware of:

- Integrating emergency procedures into day-to-day activity.
- Comparing the advantages and disadvantages of electronic or hard copy plans.
- Putting the plan together.
- What are the essential parts of a plan.
- Key plan components.
- Supporting the police.
- Evacuation.
- Dealing with the media.
- Completing and marketing the plan.

Conclusion

This Chapter has introduced the basic principles of preparing an emergency plan. There is a lot of information to take in and in many ways it is the core of the book. Real confidence and expertise will develop the more plans are produced. Having understood the basics of plan preparation we will now proceed to look at the role of the emergency services and how they respond to incidents—in effect, understanding the emergency response. This will provide an essential insight into the methods and expectations of the emergency services and how, by having that understanding, effective integrated plans and response procedures can be produced. We will also be able to begin comparing the emergency response and how that response is presented in a plan.

Understanding the Emergency Response

With the exception of a wholly internal organisational crisis—probably centred on a BCM issue, the likelihood is that at some point another external organisation will become involved and affect how an emergency or crisis is managed or responded to. The most obvious agencies that become involved are the emergency services such as the police, fire, ambulance services or the local authority. For many organisations, including those that work closely with the emergency services, the way in which they operate can be difficult to understand at times. Even the emergency services themselves can find it confusing!

Questions often relating to the emergency services include:

- What are their expectations?
- What powers do they have?
- Who is in charge?
- How do they organise themselves?
- What part can we play to assist them?
- What support can they give to an organisation in difficulty?
- How are they co-ordinated?
- Can non-emergency services influence what they do?

Understanding these crucial issues can have a direct effect upon how plans are prepared and how those plans are exercised. In addition, and perhaps more importantly, understanding how the emergency services work can also have a profound effect on how an organisation or business can survive a crisis or emergency in that many such organisations and businesses do not understand how they can influence and have a say in how the incident is managed when the emergency services are involved.

This Chapter will begin with consideration as to the planning foundation to enhance emergency response—in effect implementing emergency arrangements as soon as possible. An explanation will follow about the emergency services roles, their responsibilities, and their incident management procedures—expanding on the issues introduced in Chapter 3. For those already involved with the blue light services it will provide a much broader insight into the collective role the blue lights play and how they interact with each other and other agencies.

Within this Chapter there is a heavy emphasis on the role of the police. This is because it is the police who are so involved with the co-ordination and management of the incident which is key to planning. It is also the police who have primary investigative responsibility and therefore have a major impact on how incidents are managed. In many cases the police can restrict access to premises for extended periods to fulfil their duties. It is also the police who will try to create and facilitate a situation in which the expertise of the other emergency responders can be fully focused and proceed unhindered through their co-ordination role. The most vital period to get that right is in the initial stages of the response.

Planning Foundation

A good planning foundation will reduce the response time considerably. The effectiveness of an emergency or critical incident response is determined by the speed at which key responders are alerted and begin to carry out actions to mitigate the adverse event. This also includes the speed that the appropriate control structures and co-ordination are put in place to support those key responders, be it operational responders, commanders or managers. Minimising the response delay will have a direct impact on minimising loss of life, injury, damage to property or indeed reducing the impact on any organisation. The three issues that affect that response from a planning perspective are the alert, notifications and mobilisations that determine that response time. Most of us are familiar with 'response times' and targets set to reduce those delays in recognition of the importance of an early response. The strategic pre-positioning of emergency services vehicles; both ambulance and fire service have reduced response times based upon incident risk analysis. But it is not all about being in the right place or the right time.

Alert—how do we find out?

In Chapter 3 we have discussed alert levels or trigger levels being reached in situations of increasing crisis or 'smouldering'. In these cases a degree of time and consideration can be applied and notifications and mobilisations activated as appropriate. In a sudden onset event the usual alert we are all familiar with is the emergency call 999—either via the public or affected organisation. This is embedded in our culture. With the increased use of mobile telephones there is an assumption that within a few minutes the emergency services will be alerted and begin to respond, in many cases these calls come from the victims as well as members of the general public. This is spontaneous and there is little scope to 'manage' that alert apart from general public information and using the 999 system appropriately.

Other emergency situations are more structured, for example in industrial or transport emergencies where pro-active action is required by the operator to alert the emergency services as soon as possible set against agreed criteria to determine what is an 'emergency' or a 'major incident' for them, which we have discussed earlier. How can that alert be managed to ensure it is prompt or immediate? First, by ensuring that there is confidence that the alert will occur immediately, and not be inhibited by factors such as trying to prevent reputation damage to the organisation or trying to avoid litigation or regulatory sanctions—keeping it hidden in the hope things will get better or nobody will notice and 'we can keep it in-house!' Other inhibitors could be process supervisors not being trained properly, trying to avoid blame, panicking or simply not having the confidence to make that decision and push the button. There is little that can be done externally to guarantee a prompt response as this situation is dealt with 'in-house' through monitoring by regulators and partners but the EPO can press the operator and fellow partners to seek written reassurance reinforced by regulators that clear systems and proper authority is devolved to the right personnel to make those decisions on the spot without having to get clearance from the CEO or MD, who may not be available. The message is get the alert out as soon as possible not as soon as convenient!

Notifications—who do we tell?

This is an area where more control can be exercised and managed, particularly by the emergency responders. All notifications will be agreed in advance during the planning phase. Have all those who need to know been identified? In turn—in a cascade notification, are we sure that they will tell who they should and so on. But are we sure we are using the right contact details. This is where *only* a no notice notification exercise (Communication Exercise—see later chapter) will tell if those details are current and correct. Notification exercises should be a regular feature of plan maintenance, at least annually, as it will be notifications that in most cases will cause a plan to fail totally. The more accurate the contact details the faster the response.

Mobilisation—getting going!

Once the information is out to the right people, how quickly can they respond? Again, this needs to be tested in real time with no notice to get a true picture—virtual mobilisation or pre-positioning is really a waste of time in terms of testing mobilisation. This type of exercise is not uncommon but requires umpires in place to 'stop' the exercise as soon as the asset moves. When the notification comes in—to whichever organisation—where are the right people? Where are the vehicles and equipment? How long before the 'control' or co-ordination centre is active? Only real time live testing will provide the true picture. Using assumed or notional assets is a false and dangerous path to tread. This is the area where most delays will occur in emergency response. It is worth at this stage thinking again about the 'Golden Hour'. It is not the Golden Half hour—because it has taken an extra 30 wasted minutes in hesitant alerts, pointless notifications because contact details are wrong and mobilisation of assets that are not there.

The 'Golden Hour' as we have seen, is typically used to describe the critical time within which most lives will be saved following an incident. It can also be viewed as the most important period within which the adverse impact of the event can be reduced. That can also be extended to mean preventing property loss or enhanced business resilience response. That initial response, or the 'Golden Hour' to any land based spontaneous (sudden impact) emergency presenting a threat to human welfare is typically led by the emergency services who respond immediately and their response activity will diminish over a relatively short time, usually starting with the ambulance service followed by the fire service and the police. Organisations like the local authority and the business community usually take more time to mobilise but remain involved for longer, in some cases years into the recovery phase.

KEY POINT

Maximise the 'Golden Hour' by having the most efficient alerts, most accurate notifications and assured assets in place at all times.

Emergency and Recovery Phases

Incident response is divided into two distinct phases. The 'Emergency' phase and the 'Recovery' phase are almost self-explanatory. The emergency phase is usually co-ordinated by the police and is the period within which there is or exists a threat to public safety, personal safety or damage to property (except cases where disease is the primary threat, in which case health professionals will lead). The recovery phase, or return to normality, is the period following which there is consolidation, investigation, remediation and recovery. It should be noted that 'Recovery Management' begins at the start of the incident and is managed by the multi-agency Recovery Co-ordinating Group (RCG) as we will discuss in detail later in the Chapter.

The phrase 'return to normality' is somewhat of a misnomer in that following a major emergency, in particular where lives have been lost or serious environmental damage has been caused, there is no return to 'normality': That will change forever. The longer term impact following an emergency could have effects lasting many years and affect not only the community and business infrastructure but individuals and family groups at a psychological level too. It is usual that the recovery phase will be led or co-ordinated by the local authority in whose area the incident took place. This handover from police to local authority is a formal process undertaken within the SCG or Strategic Co-ordinating Group that we will explore later. The RCG running from the beginning of the incident will continue into the recovery phase. There is UK national guidance relating to recovery which can be found in a document called *National Recovery Guidance—Recovery Plan Guidance template*, on the HM Government website 'UK Resilience'. This document is used to 'localise' a tailored recovery plan to a particular emergency. This will be discussed in more detail in Chapter 5. Figure 4.1 represents the response and recovery phase in a graphical form. Note how responder organisations respond and their roles diminish. Blue lights are typically fast responders but their response is relatively short compared to those with longer term recovery issues to address.

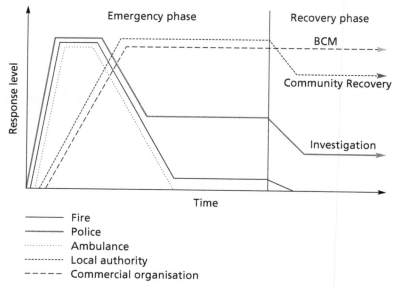

Figure 4.1 **Emergency Response and Recovery Phase**

Emergency Response Terminology

Attempting to categorise the scale and nature of any incident will be difficult and is often at best a subjective judgement based on partial and incomplete information. But there are certain definitions that attempt to clarify the nature of an incident for management purposes. Before describing the emergency response in detail and categorising what type of incident is being dealt with it would be useful at this stage to introduce the terms used to identify incidents and show how using a common emergency response language can assist communication. It is fair to say that emergency management terminology prior to the CCA was largely parochial leading to confusion and misunderstanding. An important feature of the CCA guidance is the introduction of a 'lexicon' or dictionary of words and phrases specifically prepared for emergency management. This is vital as it enables everyone to literally speak the same language and so enhance communication. But it is important to understand some key words which form the basis of the emergency response. They are described briefly in the following paragraphs.

Emergency—the defined term was introduced by the CCA 2004. In fact the Act defines emergency in a number of contexts within Part 1 and Part 2 of the Act. Part 1 focuses upon preparations by local responders for localised emergencies as outlined in the lists later. Part 2 is designed for use in very serious emergencies where a threat is posed to an English regional area or areas, Scotland, Wales or Northern Ireland where emergency powers may be

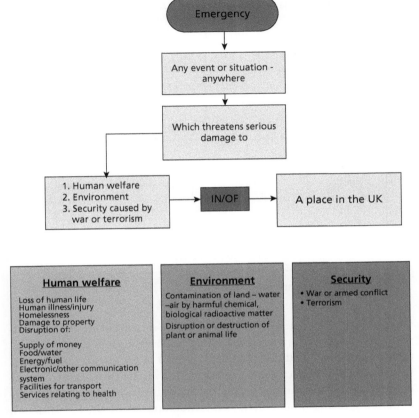

Figure 4.2 What is an 'Emergency'?

considered to manage the emergency. But for practical purposes the Part 1 definition applies for our purposes. Figure 4.2 illustrates the definition.

The range of incidents specified in the CCA is very wide ranging which Category 1 responders must prepare for when fulfilling their civil protection obligations or duties. What other terms are common in defining an 'emergency'?

Major Incident—is a term that the emergency services have used for many years, which is well understood in terms of the nature of the response required to manage an incident.

It should be noted (see Figure 4.3) that under the umbrella of the CCA definition of 'Emergency', the term 'Major Incident' still exists, although unwritten. 'Emergency' redefined the general or generic term 'Major Incident' as outlined in the document *Dealing with Disaster* but a major incident definition remains important as it defines what is a major incident for an organisation and should be unique to each organisation. A major incident definition

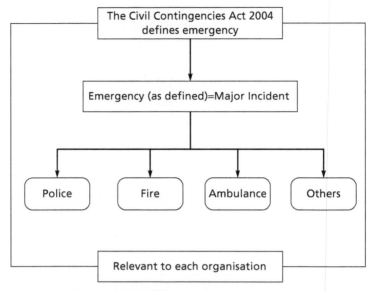

Figure 4.3 What is a 'Major Incident'?

is essential to all emergency responders but this should extend to all organisations that have plans, including businesses. There must be a means of recognising when, for that organisation, there is a major incident and indeed who will make that decision to declare it. This will be the trigger to invoke or implement special arrangements to manage the incident. Remember the importance of that initial alert, notification and mobilisation—without a definition of what constitutes an emergency or major incident the alert is likely to fail. In other words each organisation whether it be an emergency responder or a business must create a definition of a set of circumstances or conditions that will initiate a planned response for them. It will trigger a set of actions and responses that begin to manage the incident.

These terms are closely related and their relationship must be understood to apply them correctly. More complete explanations and their application follow in this Chapter.

The final term that may be encountered is 'Critical Incident.'

Critical Incident—for completeness this term is included here. This term is used by the police to describe any incident where police action may have an impact on the confidence of a victim, their relatives or the wider community. This term is often used in situations of racial tension. However, this is a term that requires caution in its use. It can arise from time to time in other contexts. It is used by some organisations to describe a level of incident or circumstances that may fall short of a major incident or a condition that precedes a major incident. It is a term that causes confusion and must be used and applied in the context intended by the organisation using it.

Sometimes allied to critical incident is the term *'Serious Incident'*—again this is used to describe a situation that may not justify a major incident designation. It is now quite easy to see how confusion can creep in and compromise communication.

There is also one more set of terms that are important. They are the Government definitions requiring Government direction or assistance. Again, this defines a set of triggers for the Government to respond—remember, as we have said, each organisation needs a set of criteria or conditions that will alert or activate their emergency response arrangements. The Government is no different, see Figure 4.4. This topic is covered in some detail in the government UK CONOPS.

Whatever terms are used it is important that the significance of the terms is understood by those who are using them. In an ideal world there would be a fixed terminology or lexicon but in many areas these terms are embedded in tradition and local practice which are well understood. Staying with the common terms may be the lesser of the two evils!

But the CCA has endeavoured to achieve a common language in civil protection and for the EPO it should be followed where possible. Constant use of the correct terms will eventually become embedded. It is vital that the lexicon is used. But it is also important to be aware that where local or organisational terms have been in use for many years changes are made gradually and with widespread notice and consultation with emergency responders otherwise confusion will occur. It is not uncommon for senior members of an organisation to 'import' terms and procedures they are familiar with from other organisations they have worked for and effectively impose them. In some cases the proposed changes make sense or add clarity but that advantage can easily be lost if everyone is confused. Making such changes will have serious logistical impact on plans, training and consulting with partners. This must be avoided in the short term. If changes have to be introduced they should be gradual and fully sanctioned, usually through the LRF. The CCA lexicon can be found as an appendix to the CCA guidance document *Emergency Response and Recovery*. Too much change carried out too fast is a recipe for disaster—literally!

Many of these terms will be mentioned later when we examine the emergency response and how those terms are applied. One of the first building blocks of successful emergency management is scene management. We will now look a general scene management layout. The terminology around scene management is agreed between all the emergency services to ensure that there is a clear methodology and approach to every incident. A schematic scene management layout can be seen in Figure 4.6 later in this chapter.

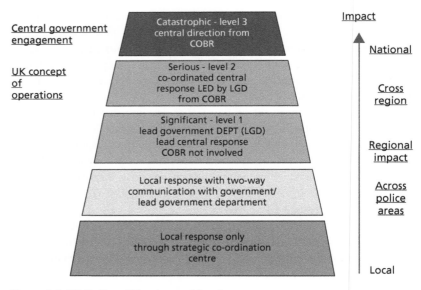

Figure 4.4 UK National 'Emergency' levels

> **TOP TIP**
>
> As an EPO take every opportunity to ensure the correct national lexicon of terms from agreed national guidance and policy is used. Local variations should be phased out slowly.

Using common terminology assists the police to manage effective co-ordination at and around the scene if all those responding subscribe to the same emergency management principles the response will run smoothly. The terms used and an explanation of the key facilities will be introduced as we build the picture of the emergency response. In terms of a national approach to scene management the police set out their emergency procedures (EP) policy in a document produced by the Association of Chief Police Officers (ACPO). This document sets out guidance across the whole emergency management process and provides a consistent approach for all police forces in England, Wales and Northern Ireland.

The configuration of the scene management structure and the terms used have changed in recent years to deal with new threats such as chemical, biological, radiological and nuclear-type incidents (see Figure 4.6 later in this Chapter). To that extent the ACPO EP guidance was revised in 2009 in the light of the new threats and to accommodate the CCA.

Having established the basis for these terms we will now consider their practical application in both planning and the emergency response itself.

The Emergency Response

The first few minutes of an incident, as we enter the 'Golden Hour' will inevitably be chaotic as the situation unfolds but the emergency services will quickly begin to meet to discuss immediate priorities and implement the appropriate co-ordination or command structure as required to manage the incident. One of the first considerations will be whether it is a 'Major Incident' (MI).

What is a major incident?

As already mentioned this term still dominates the emergency planning world and each organisation should have a set of criteria which describes their own major incident triggers.

The reason is because it describes for an organisation what is for them a situation that requires a special response. Why is this important? Declaring a major incident will:

- initiate plans;
- mobilise and alert support organisations and other emergency services;
- release resources;
- focus attention;
- drive the operational response;
- combine multi-agency response; and
- define a command or management structure—internally.

But a major incident for one service may not be for another. For example, a major plane crash with no survivors will not create a major incident for the ambulance service but will for others involved in the response. The health service may experience excessive demands for hospital beds which could be a major incident for them but no one else. This is where the principle of **'Combined Response'** is adopted. The combined response principle ensures that the overall response is co-ordinated. The 'unaffected' services will liaise closely to determine their response—full response, standby or stand-down in support of that agency. This will avoid 'catch-up' for a service that would not be routinely informed. It is for an individual service to determine if they are needed at a scene and it is *not* for another service to stand them down or decide they are not needed. For example, the police should not make operational assessments on behalf of the fire and rescue service and visa versa or any other combination of organisations. Each individual organisation must decide if they can assist.

TASK 4.1

Can you think of five emergencies that would not require all three of the three emergency services?

Recognising a major incident may not be so easy to determine in the early stages of an incident. It is important for all organisations to understand the circumstances that will trigger a 'major incident' for their organisation otherwise they may not be able to respond effectively or they could become confused as to what is or is not a major incident for them. That hesitation can create delays and confusion across all emergency responders.

How would an organisation define its major incident? The first consideration in defining a major incident is to understand that major incidents are about consequences and not cause. It is the impact and effects of an incident and how it affects an organisation that will determine at what point to move to declare a major incident. Issues to consider for determining a major incident may be:

- The response required to manage the incident falls outside your daily capability.
- Whether or not it requires additional resources or special arrangements to deal with it.
- Whether or not it is large scale and having serious and widespread impact.
- Whether or not it puts your ordinary service delivery at risk.

TASK 4.2

Thinking about the organisation you work for or have worked for—what do you think would constitute a major incident for them? Define it.

Some organisations refer to a major incident as requiring additional resources outside what they term as 'business as usual' or 'normality'. Some police forces use the term 'steady state' to describe their day to day activity. Remember that building a major incident response must be integrated into that 'steady state' and emerge from that as a seamless incremental increase in activity and management (see Chapter 3).

Once an organisation has determined what for them constitutes a major incident they should then define what criteria will trigger that response. This may be a staged response moving up in levels eventually reaching 'major incident'. Each level will determine a course of action that will appear in the plan, which we will consider later.

A key point here is not to confuse 'major' with 'unusual'—in many cases the unusual can be dealt with quite easily. For example, a helicopter crash in open rural countryside is an unusual event but in terms of management it is quite straightforward in terms of resources.

KEY POINT

Do not confuse 'major' with 'unusual'! The response is determined by the consequences not the cause of the incident.

Who will declare a major incident?

The CCA is quite clear about how this process occurs for 'emergency' and requires a plan to include the following information:

1. Which post holder will declare the emergency.

2. How they will be advised of the incident.

3. Who is consulted.

4. Who they will inform.

It is suggested that this is a good basis also for allocating responsibility and clarity as to who has the duty or responsibility to declare a major incident within any organisation. The early recognition and declaration of major incident is crucial to the effective management of the incident. Although the CCA directs an individual to be identified it is often quite ambiguous who that person is in reality. Traditionally emergency service organisations have left that decision to the first responders. It could be argued that for the more obvious incidents such as a major plane crash or train crash it is quite easy but some major incidents are 'slow burn', 'rising tide' or 'smouldering' incidents and it is not quite so simple or obvious. First responders are often too involved in scene management and rescue to be in a position to assess the overall impact of the incident, the availability of their resources or indeed if all the conditions and criteria apply to call a major incident. There is no doubt that the first responder would inform the decision to call a major incident but a more reliable and robust method would concentrate that decision on a management level. For example, a duty or on-call manager within the organisation or duty officer perhaps in a control room environment. Often these decisions can be assessed or quality assured more thoroughly through control rooms—people who have the detailed overview of the circumstances and probably the experience to make those subjective decisions at the earliest opportunity.

In the author's experience it is often the delay in declaring a major incident that inhibits that early response and the 'Golden Hour' effectiveness. It is suggested that by default the decision to declare a major incident should be integrated into a managerial function.

Having determined that a potential major incident response involving threat to life, property or public safety is taking place we will now consider the key roles of the primary emergency responders, beginning with the police. Note that the word 'operational' is used as the emergency response always builds from the operational or routine response first and escalates rapidly or in slow time depending on the circumstances.

The Police—Category 1 Responder

At this point it should be made clear what is meant by the 'police'. This book concentrates on emergency procedures in England and Wales and therefore the focus is on police co-ordination as outlined in the ACPO Emergency Procedure and Command and Control Guidance as already described. There is no significance to the term 'Police' or 'Constabulary'. Historically city and borough police forces used the term police and county police used the term constabulary. Some county forces have now adopted the term police perhaps as it is perceived as more modern. The other main police forces in England and Wales are outlined in the following paragraphs.

The Civil Nuclear Constabulary (CNC)

Until 2005 the CNC was called the UK Atomic Energy Authority Constabulary which focused on guarding civil nuclear sites and nuclear material in transit. It receives its strategic direction from the Department of Trade and Industry (DTI). There are approximately 750 police officers and staff working from 17 sites in the UK. They are routinely armed. Post the terrorist attacks in New York in 2001 and coupled with the subsequent increased terrorist threat posed against civil nuclear sites the CNC was expanded considerably and have enhanced security levels at all nuclear sites that previously were not staffed full time by CNC. They typically have jurisdictions up to several miles around nuclear sites and have close links with their colleagues in the local police area with agreements or memoranda of understanding (MOU) relating to combined incident and emergency response.

The CNC also have responsibilities in relation to the transport of dangerous nuclear materials. The CNC co-ordinate the National Arrangements for Incidents Involving Radioactivity (NAIR) in case of a release in transit and can alert the nearest 'expert' nuclear site to attend and manage the incident. The NAIR scheme is there primarily to assist the police and it can be used for any radiological related incident for which there are no other set arrangements in place. Another scheme co-ordinated by the CNC is the RADSAFE scheme and it again provides 24/7 advice and response to accidents involving civil nuclear material in transit but excludes military nuclear material which is managed by the Ministry of Defence (MOD) (see next in this section).

Ministry of Defence Police (MDP)

The prime role of the MOD police is armed security at approximately 100 MOD sites throughout the UK. Every officer is trained in the use of firearms. The MOD has special arrangements and responsibilities for managing MOD nuclear incidents or accidents and has the Nuclear Accident Response Organisation (NARO) in place to respond if needed. NARO works closely with all civil agencies. They are involved in the transport and security of MOD nuclear assets.

British Transport Police (BTP)

The BTP, a Category 1 responder, is made up of approximately 2,700 officers supported by Specials Constables (250, approx.), Police Community Support Officers (210, approx.) and Police Staff (1,200, approx.) (circa. 2011) They cover the whole rail network including the London Underground, Docklands Light Railway, Glasgow Sub-Way, Midlands Metro, Croydon TramLink and Eurostar. They work very closely with train operators and Network Rail and with each local police force.

In terms of co-ordination, protocols and MOUs exist between these forces and the main 'Home Office' forces to ensure that roles and responsibilities are clear when dealing with major incidents.

In general the role of the police as co-ordinators does not mean they are 'in-charge' of other services or agencies. They act more like a conductor of an orchestra ensuring that the score (or plan) is followed and the right instruments (resources) are used. They co-ordinate in a truly multi-agency environment or setting, involving the other blue light services and other response agencies including the voluntary agencies and private industry as necessary. Increasingly the private sector is becoming an important contributor to major incident response in particular where their specialist knowledge can assist critical decision making. This may take the form of technical or organisational information. And of course for any agency or business being at the centre of decision making can have a profound effect on the ability of any company to survive the incident commercially.

What all police forces have in common is the use of the Strategic (Gold), Tactical (Silver) and Operational (Bronze) (STO) or (GSB) command structure which we were introduced to in Chapter 3 but we will look at in some detail in Chapter 5. Understanding STO or GSB and its application is essential to all those engaged in emergency planning, no matter what organisation they come from.

The police ranks are included here for general information to assist in recognition. Although as we will see 'rank' is not a critical factor in using STO or GSB, rather it is about role. However, rank does tend to assign a level of experience and knowledge which will inevitably mean the more complex the management role the higher the rank. It is useful for non-police responders to have an awareness of rank for identification purposes (see Figure 4.5).

KEY POINT

The police are not in charge of any agency apart from their own—they co-ordinate the multi-agency response.

The primary role of the police as we have seen in emergency management is to co-ordinate the response. Without effective co-ordination the response, will be inadequate and probably fail entirely. The primary functions of the police service can be summed up generally as:

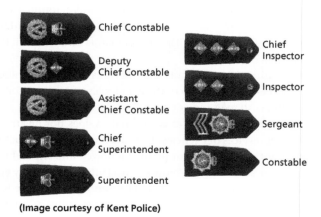

(Image courtesy of Kent Police)

Figure 4.5 Police Ranks—the terms in brackets refer to the Metropolitan Police Service

- To protect life and property.
- Co-ordination of the emergency services and other support organisations.
- To investigate, gather and present evidence of criminal activity and enforce the criminal law.
- To identify those involved in major incidents or disasters.
- To collate and disseminate casualty information and inform relatives.
- To investigate death on behalf of the coroner.
- To co-ordinate evacuation.
- To identify, along with the Ambulance Service, a suitable location to accommodate those involved or surviving an incident to receive support and enable documentation to take place, known as a Survivor Reception Centre (SRC)*.

The police priorities will be:

1. To ensure the emergency services and other emergency responders can perform their tasks effectively by:
   - facilitating inter-agency communications and consultation at the scene—initially at the Forward Command Post (FCP)*;
   - facilitating access and egress in and around the scene;
   - setting up traffic management and diversions;
   - setting up appropriate cordons—both inner and outer;
   - managing RVPs* and Marshalling Areas*;
   - dealing with the media.

These terms will be fully explained as the emergency management co-ordination structure develops.

2. Protecting and assisting the public by:
   - providing support and assistance with care for the welfare of survivors;
   - establishing the identity of persons involved in incidents;
   - co-ordinating any evacuation;
   - assisting with warnings, advice and information;
   - protecting property.

3. Establishing or assisting in the establishment of the facts of the incident by:
   - protecting and preserving the scene and any deceased persons;
   - identifying witnesses/suspects;
   - investigating or assisting in the investigation.

It should be noted and appreciated that the police will secure a scene to obtain evidence or assist others to get evidence such as the fire and rescue service, forensic services and the Health and Safety Executive (HSE). It is their duty.

Being prepared for this type of disruption is an essential part of business continuity planning and one the emergency services must consider when assessing the impact cordons may have on communities and businesses. It could mean that getting access to the scene may be restricted or excluded for hours or even days. This is an important factor for businesses. How will their business survive? This is a good reason to ensure that where possible businesses should engage with the police and other emergency responders at an early stage of planning for emergency and crisis. This can be achieved by having key managerial staff in non-blue light organisations or large businesses trained as 'liaison officers' by understanding the emergency management process. This will allow them to slot into the process more easily.

The priority of all the emergency services at a scene is to save life and prevent injury as far as possible. The first response will be an operational response by the emergency services. The operational response is activity on the ground, what would be actually seen and is described as the routine response. That will entail vehicles and personnel attending the scene. Upon arrival at the scene of an emergency the police will use the following list to assess the scene; this is known as SAD—CHALET:

- Survey, Assess and Disseminate. Think....
- Casualties—number, severity contaminated?
- Hazards—fire, chemical, explosion risk, gas?
- Access—identify safe routes.
- Location—be precise.
- Emergency services—in attendance or required? Or Evacuation required?
- Type of Incident—RTC, explosion, CBRN?
- Safety—do not put yourself at risk!

Incident Scene Management—General Initial Response

To illustrate the co-ordination function of the police we will look at the process as it begins from a 'typical' spontaneous (sudden impact) incident. In this case it will have potential to be a major incident, although that decision will follow from a process of observation, assessment and professional judgement by the most senior police officer attending the incident in consultation with multi-agency colleagues. Initially however normal on-site police management will occur with no obvious need to involve others. When it becomes apparent that further co-ordination is required because of the scale or potential scale of the incident the police will begin to invoke structure around the scene.

Having carried out the initial assessment and reported to their control room the police at a scene will initially arrange a **Rendezvous Point** (RVP) in liaison with the Fire Service (if they are present) in a safe area. Near to that a **Forward Command Post** (FCP) will be identified. The FCP is the initial control where Commanders (Incident Officers), with appropriate identifiable tabards, from other blue light services meet and decide on operational priorities to manage the incident. It should be noted that the term 'Forward Control Point' is sometimes confused with Forward Command Post. The Forward Control Point is a location at which individual services set their initial assets and 'service brief'. This means where each respective service will brief their own staff. They will then meet at the Forward Command Post to initiate that co-ordination role. The Forward Command Post as FCP is endorsed by ACPO. For our purposes when you read FCP assume Forward Command Post.

An FCP is intended to be the first management building block to accommodate the police and other agencies to achieve multi-agency co-ordination at or near the scene, a place where they can meet and discuss options and priorities. In reality this initial inter-agency discussion can take place at any convenient location and is often within one of the emergency services rapid response command unit vehicles or even on the ground. Most emergency services have their own 'command' vehicles which could be used in the initial stages of the incident to fulfil that FCP function.

The FCP is set in a location as close as safety permits and the RVP is where responders will meet before being directed to the FCP. The RVP and FCP will be supported by a **Marshalling Area** (MA) which will hold resources until as and when needed at the incident site. These locations are managed by the police as part of their co-ordination role. See Figure 4.6 Access Control.

KEY POINT

The FCP, RVP and Marshalling area are the building blocks co-ordination of a sudden impact emergency threatening to life or serious damage to property.

Cordons and access control

Although an important feature of scene management cordons can take a relatively long time to implement fully, simply because of the logistics involved. Cordons are put in place for very good reasons. They are usually maintained by the police and the fire and rescue service and are very resource intensive to maintain their integrity. Usually there are two cordons, an inner and outer cordon. In addition, the terms hot zone, warm zone and cold zone may be used to manage a scene involving contamination, but essentially these zones

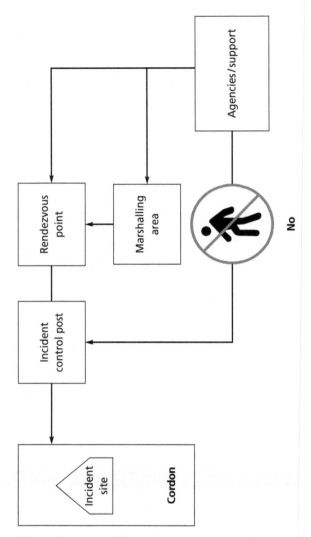

Figure 4.6 Approaching a scene/access control

are cordoned areas. Each cordon has 'access control' to ensure only author-ised people can gain access. Security is maintained by the police and the inner cordon safety management is usually left to the fire and rescue service. Cordons are there for safety reasons primarily, in which the fire and rescue service have overall primacy within the inner cordon unless it is a terrorist related incident in which case the police will take primacy.

Another term used at a scene and a term often used by the fire and res-cue service is 'sectors'. Breaking a large scene down into manageable sectors each managed by a 'sector commander'. 'Sectorisation', as it is known, is a geographic means of incident management whereas the police use a functional approach by means of Operational or Tactical Commanders looking to activity based roles, for example, traffic management, cordons, RVP, Marshalling Area, and so on.

In terms of cordons, which are still understood and used by the fire and rescue services, as a general rule cordon distances are initially set as follows:

- 100 m for minor explosive risk (letter bomb) or the edge of detected contamination
- 200 m for a moderate explosive risk (briefcase or parcel)
- 400 m for a serious explosive risk (vehicle bomb) or Chemical Biological Radiological Nuclear (CBRN) device not yet activated. {Note—a nuclear device would not require cordons! –Author's note]

(*NPIA ACPO Guidance*, p. 49—Emergency Procedures 2009)

However, it is critical that 'expert' advice is sought as soon as possible to verify or confirm the appropriate cordon distance for that particular risk as there are so many variables. For example, the fire service for toxic plumes or the military if explosive devices are evident.

Unless the incident is a result of a terrorist action, the police cannot force people to leave cordon areas or force evacuation but clearly it is sensible to follow police advice as it will be backed up by other agency advice such as the fire and rescue service or health professionals. The police obtain their powers to impose and enforce cordons following terrorist incidents from sections 33–36 of the Terrorism Act 2000. The police do not impose cordons lightly.

In non-terrorist cases the establishment of cordons rests in common law. In this case the police can cordon an area to protect public safety, keep the peace and protect a crime scene, or at the request of, and with the consent of, the landowner (*NPIA ACPO Guidance*, p. 48—Emergency Procedures 2009). There are also some powers given to the fire and rescue service to enter premises to extinguish fire. However, in reality it is difficult to envisage a situation in which force would be required in the context of a civil protection situation.

At the FCP, located between the outer and inner cordon, the police, fire or ambulance services may require the assistance of other agencies, for example, the local authority, utility companies, Environment Agency or even a company representative, to name but a few. They will be asked to attend the Rendezvous Point and will be brought forward to the FCP by the police (see Figure 4.6).

Beyond the cordoned areas there will be traffic management in place. This will restrict access to a general geographic area. Clearly the objective is to keep people away for safety reasons but there will be occasions in which staff need to attend a site, a scene or a police co-ordination centre to offer assistance. Many non-blue light organisations have a legitimate need to attend incident scenes. A frequent issue arises from those who cannot gain access. How to get through police cordons? Getting through police lines can be an interesting experience! This is why it is important to brief those who may be 'on-call' or called out to an incident as to the correct approach to adopt when trying to access cordons or navigate police traffic management. If there is a genuine reason to request access through a police line the person requesting access should make it clear to the officer the reason why they need to get through. Production of photo identification is essential. The person requesting access may also ask that a message be forwarded to the police co-ordination centre or FCP advising them of the request to get access in order to get authorisation. This approach may seem excessive but non-blue light emergency responders may have real difficulty persuading an officer that their role is essential and only by verification via control can this be confirmed. Requesting a police escort to get through traffic is generally unrealistic unless it is arranged in advance at the time of call out or the attendance is vital to save life.

TOP TIP

Without photo ID access to *any* emergency facility or site will be refused.

During the initial scene management process police officers will be appointed with specific jobs to do, such as implementing cordons, managing RVPs, marshalling areas and cordon access control in order to protect the area. They will be engaged on traffic management to assist in controlling traffic in and out of the area too. This is a very resource intensive time, the level of resource needed can easily be underestimated. As we will see later, during exercises it is often an important issue to ensure those taking part in the exercise are given 'realistic' levels of staff and equipment to reinforce the level of resources needed to manage even a relatively small scene.

In and around the incident site the activity will be frenetic and it is important that key managers and commanders are readily identifiable with high visibility jackets. It is vital that they are easily identifiable to other response agencies and take an active, decisive and robust role at a scene to co-ordinate the activity. The police will wear 'Incident Officer' jackets to indicate their role. More detail about the role of the police Incident Officer will be dealt with in Chapter 5.

An example of a comprehensive scene management structure is shown in Figure 4.7 No two scenes will be the same and the exact positioning of various facilities will vary but the diagram gives an overall impression of the general layout.

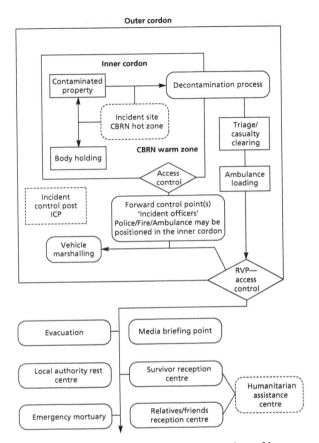

Figure 4.7 Scene Management—An overview of key facilities

TASK 4.3

Research the legal powers that give the police authority to enforce cordons.

Scene management structures have remained fairly constant for a number of years. That changed when planning began to cater for CBRN threats. The scene management structure shown in Figure 4.7 includes additional features designed to enable a CBRN incident to be managed. Essentially a CBRN incident has many similarities to a hazardous material incident or HAZMAT incident.

Chemical, Biological, Radiological and Nuclear (CBRN)

These terms are now common place in emergency planning and have very different impacts if used. It is not intended here to give a definitive clinical explanation of their effects on humans or the environment but they have some characteristics that the EPO should be aware of from a planning perspective.

More detailed information can be obtained at: http://www.gov.uk/government/publications and http://www.hpa.org.uk/ or various readily available publications.

HAZMAT v CBRN

Many emergency planning officers will be very familiar with dealing with HAZMAT or hazardous materials incidents and all emergency services organisations have dedicated specialists working in HAZMAT environments. HAZMAT incidents are sometimes mistakenly associated with CBRN incidents in terms of management. HAZMAT incidents are caused by accident, negligence, disregard for instructions or incompetence in handling hazardous materials and are random in location, whereas CBRN is defined and motivated as a deliberate murderous act designed to kill and deliberately targeted. Therefore scene management is different in that CBRN will be a crime scene and managed as such by the police whereas HAZMAT are usually led in the investigation by the fire and rescue service and the HSE where evidence recovery is less rigorous.

In CBRN incidents the substance will probably be unknown whereas in HAZMAT situations that can be quickly established. CBRN can involve simultaneous multiple sites as a co-ordinated attack—HAZMAT does not. CBRN may involve unexplained casualties just falling down—usually HAZMAT does not. In CBRN incidents emergency responders may be targets too and secondary devices must be assumed and perpetrators may in fact be casualties—this can be discounted for HAZMAT.

Having said all that, all HAZMAT officers will have a good general knowledge of HAZMAT and indeed CBRN scene management. Depending on their organisation their HAZMAT knowledge is a specialist role of their overall function within that organisation which will have a different emphasis or focus to other HAZMAT specialists. It is mentioned here to avoid complication and confusion across the blue light services in terms of HAZMAT scene management.

The police HAZMAT officers tend to concentrate their HAZMAT knowledge in terms of enforcement of regulation usually transport. The ambulance HAZMAT officer tends to concentrate on the clinical effects and casualty management. The fire service HAZMAT officer concentrates on substance identification, protecting the public, mitigating the harmful effects through the application of special techniques, recovery (in certain circumstances) or assisting in recovery. To that extent they are better placed to manage the scene and advice both the police and the ambulance service. In short CBRN is different to HAZMAT but we will now look more closely at CBRN management taking into account those differences.

KEY POINT

HAZMAT and CBRN are different although they both involve the dispersal of hazardous substances. CBRN is malicious and deliberate.

CBRN incident management

Turning to a CBRN incident, as it is managed as a crime/terrorist scene the police will have primacy in scene management but they do work very closely with all emergency services and specialist contractors. The police service is now fully trained and equipped for CBRN response and can quickly mobilise across the UK in response to an incident as can the fire and rescue service and ambulance services.

Essentially, the objective in a CBRN response is to deal with contamination effects resulting from chemical, suspected biological or radiological substances. It is worth considering the effects these substances have in the initial stages of exposure. The C of CBRN, chemical substances, will have an immediate effect as people inhale the toxic substance or it is deposited on the skin. Effects will vary depending on substance type, concentration and quantity. Effects will be influenced by location, topography, wind strength and direction, and building lines—all affecting distance travelled and concentrations of the substance. Those affected by toxic chemicals will present with symptoms quite quickly if not within minutes.

The B of CBRN, biological, and R, radiological exposure, will be far less dramatic with the harmful effects emerging within a matter of hours, or indeed probably days. The N, nuclear aspect, of CBRN is a nuclear explosive device that will create catastrophic devastation instantly followed by some limited radioactive contamination or 'fallout'. Fortunately these devices are very complex to manufacture and would probably require state-sponsored support to effect an explosion. This is opposed to a radiological device, which is intended to spread radioactive material around by means of conventional explosive—a dirty bomb. In these cases physical explosive injury may also present issues for emergency responders and awareness of secondary devices is essential. It should also be noted that low level radioactive deposition may be carried out covertly and only emerge following a warning, in which case many people may be contaminated without knowing it. The term CBRN E may also be seen. The E stands for explosive.

The emergency services have access to radiation detection devices to alert their own staff if exposed to radiation and so can pass warnings to the public very quickly. The emergency services also use a system of CBRN incident approach called Steps 1–2–3. This ensures that as few emergency services personnel are affected as possible. In effect it is used in chemical type attacks—as we have seen the biological and radiological substances may not be that obvious.

STEPS 1–2–3

This system was developed to assist emergency responders approach a scene safely by making them alert to potential chemical attack situations.
Step 1—if one casualty down—normal procedure
Step 2—if two casualties down—approach with caution
Step 3—if three or more casualties down, without obvious cause—do not approach. Possible chemical attack.

Steps 1–2–3 are an ideal solution if it can be applied in a measured and calm set of circumstances but the reality is likely to be a situation of confusion and uncertainty. The expectation is that some emergency response personnel will become casualties and it is indeed their initial reporting that will prevent further emergency service casualties.

A point to note is that the CBRN decontamination procedures now extend also to the accidental or negligent spillage or discharge of these substances (HAZMAT) and not just terrorism. The focus of the response concentrates on the effective and speedy de-contamination of those exposed; in particular the new role of the ambulance service as the primary decontamination agency supported by the fire and rescue service to deal with mass decontamination. The key concern in these situations is keeping the public calm and reassuring them to remain where they are at the location to undergo decontamination and so prevent the spread of the toxic substance. If the emergency services apply steps 1–2–3 the likelihood is that in the initial stages there will be few if any emergency service personnel there to offer advice and reassurance anyway. If they are there it will present another problem, as most of the emergency services giving out those messages will be protected in CBR suits which are not very reassuring to the public and are likely to frighten them. There is a growing recognition that many people will leave a suspected CBR scene and not wait for full decontamination. Decontamination can be described in four main categories:

1. Clinical—individually by trained health professionals using design built equipment.

2. Mass—fire and rescue service using design built equipment.

3. Interim—using standard equipment prior to using design built equipment.

4. Improvised—anything to hand! 80% contaminant will be removed by taking clothing off. Washing and/or spraying will remove more.

Interim decontamination will be the quickest form of managed decontamination at the scene but improvised decontamination is likely to be a significant option for personal decontamination for those affected. DIY personal decontamination information is likely to follow through the media in that case. For the EPO the challenge is putting in place effective public communication in a situation which is dynamic and charged with anxiety and potentially panic.

On a planning level, every LRF will have in place a multi-agency CBRN plan based upon specialist guidance issued centrally. This has matured over the last decade with numerous exercises and training sessions which address many of the unique challenges presented by CBRN.

Whilst the use of CBR remains a credible threat it should be noted that the prospect of the delivery of suspect packages and letters containing CBR and explosive substances remains an issue for many organisations. The delivery of suspect letters or packages is something that can originate from non-terrorist sources. These 'white powder' incidents could result from personal issues from previous employees or aggrieved customers or anyone with an axe to grind. Some organisations with 'sensitive' affiliations or connections such as political, law enforcement, environmental or animal rights issues for example may be subject to such attacks and indeed they have a duty of care if their risk assessment highlights such a threat, either from past experience or ongoing intelligence, to prepare for such attacks. They of course should be aware of that and have arrangements in place to identify and intercept such packages. They should also be able to respond to such events quickly using trained staff and tested procedures to assist the blue light response. Special arrangements exist co-ordinated by the police to risk assess and manage such incidents. The response arrangements to 'white powder' incidents are capable of escalation to a full CBRN incident if the need arises.

Having looked at the main emergency response features and structures we will now look towards the support that can assist that response and expand on those definitions.

Facilities and People that Support the Response

Forward Media Briefing Point—FMBP

The media, as we have seen, are a primary support organisation when it comes to passing information and warning the public. They do however, have responsibilities to report and gather news; one of the crucial facilities for them is the 'The Forward Media Briefing Point (FMBP)'. The FMBP represents the focal point of media activity around the incident site. The demands of 24-hour news media require a robust and facilitated approach to meet those demands. Although remote Media Briefing Centres (MBCs) still form an important facility in managing large numbers of media personnel the emphasis has certainly shifted. Some LRFs are pre-identifying potential Forward Media Briefing (FMBP) locations strategically placed across their areas to enable a rapid media set-up that can offer all the facilities and logistic support that is needed. Places to consider are hotels, conference venues, clubs, police stations, local authority facilities, sports and leisure centres. Each one is then surveyed and a basic set-up plan is prepared in terms of layout, reception, security, IT facilities, accommodation, parking, access, etc.

Allowing access to safe locations to enable filming and live broadcasts from the incident site is now an expectation that needs to be met. This can be achieved by pooling and managing the media through briefing at the Forward Media Briefing Point and taking them forward to a safe location. Issues of 'good taste', in terms of what is filmed, are a matter for negotiation and agreement between the media and primarily the police. There is no doubt that there is mutual benefit to be gained by both the media and the police having a joint consensus in media reporting arrangements from an incident site. Media footage can also be a useful tool to assist an investigation. The police will have media arrangements in place to manage the media demand which will involve consultation with other agencies resulting in a co-ordinated approach to managing the media. The LRF will also have joint media response arrangements in place.

Media co-ordination for a large scale incident will be managed through a Strategic Media Advisory Cell or SMAC. This group will meet at the Media Co-ordination Centre (MCC). The SMAC is usually chaired by the police who will then report and sit within the SCG (discussed later). The SMAC is made up of media liaison officers from all participating organisations, who can, through the SMAC, contribute and where necessary resolve any issues of conflict in terms of media output. It is important that any one agency does not unilaterally address the media without reference to the SMAC and SCG. If that occurs there is a real danger that confused and mixed messages will be released that may compromise the overall response.

Social networking

Dealing with the media has matured and developed around well established agreements and protocols over the past decade based upon mutual respect and benefit, however, the proliferation of social networking in the form of Facebook, Twitter, Blackberry and others has introduced a new dimension to emergency management which fall outside an ability of the authorities to manage or monitor effectively. In terms of mobilising the public for good or bad this is now a real concern for emergency planners. Access to social networking sites can warn, inform, communicate, reassure and offer advice but they can also spread rumour, misinformation, alert people to ongoing incidents and mobilise those intent on disruption which may create public order difficulties for the police in managing cordons and traffic.

It is a difficult issue which is being assessed and considered by the emergency services and civil protection bodies at the time of writing, but it is a significant emerging management issue for the EPO. The benefits of rapid and widespread information sharing with the public are obvious but the potential to create panic and anxiety is also there.

Rest Centres (RC)

The provision of Rest Centres is a matter for the local authority supported by the police and voluntary services. The centre will provide food, drinks, non-emergency medical support and children's facilities. In many cases provision for pets will have to be considered as being separated from pets will cause some people to be very anxious and many people will not like being accommodated near to animals. Another issue related to Rest Centres and animals is the management of contaminated animals. Animals that have been exposed to contaminates, for example chemical or radiological may have to be destroyed—an emotive issue often overlooked.

Siting Rest Centres, like Forward Media Briefing points, many LRFs have pre-identified suitable locations and facilities to act as Rest Centres. They tend to be local authority facilities such as leisure centres or community buildings. The concept of a Rest Centre is to accommodate those who are temporarily displaced from their homes. Although an essential facility in those circumstances many people faced with evacuation will try to find accommodation with family and friends or indeed go to a hotel. In many pre-planned contingency or emergency plans hotels are often approached to offer emergency accommodation in the event of evacuation or emergencies. Large hotel chains are often willing to do this as a PR exercise and offer genuine support and assistance to their local communities. The prospect of sleeping in a Rest Centre environment can be distressing for many people who will feel insecure and vulnerable. It is therefore important if a Rest Centre is operating that the police provide that level of reassurance and security where possible by being present and visible.

Those attending a Rest Centre will be documented by the local authority and voluntary services to ensure that they are accounted for and details can be passed to enquiring relatives and friends. Many local authority documentation forms are also compatible for police casualty bureau purposes in the event that the situation requires a Casualty Bureau to be opened and the data can be transferred to the Casualty Bureau without having to re-interview those already documented.

Medical Rest Centres (MRC)

The MRC or mass casualty treatment centre is a relatively new concept under development but describes a facility which in effect is a field hospital to accommodate large numbers of 'walking wounded' patients. This could be as a result of insufficient beds in hospitals or a need to isolate patients due to disease—designated as a mass casualty incident. The facility would be equipped by the ambulance service and staffed by the local health providers.

Survivor Reception Centre (SRC)

Survivor Reception Centres are temporary facilities which are set up near an incident site to accommodate those who have been involved in the incident and could be classified as 'casualties'. They are distinct from Rest Centres and serve a different purpose. Following an incident involving many people the Ambulance Service will sort or triage those involved and those requiring hospital treatment will be taken to designated hospitals. There may be significant numbers of people who are not physically injured or with very minor issues but who need general comfort, support, assistance and advice. The location of the SRC is made spontaneously by the Ambulance Service and the Police. Any suitable local building will be used. Casualties will need to be documented there by the police for 'Casualty Bureau' purposes (see later) and investigative reasons. A point to note here is that those at the SRC are there voluntarily. There is no power to require a person to stay or attend at a SRC unless other circumstances apply in which the police will take the necessary action.

TASK 4.4

Can you think of a situation where you could have a 'Rest Centre' operating and a 'Survivor Reception Centre' operating at the same time?

Friends and Relatives Reception Centre

The Friends and Relatives Reception Centre (FRRC) is complementary to the SRC. It is a location chosen to enable those concerned about their family and friends who have been involved in an incident to go to and seek information. It is a natural reaction for people to do this which the authorities must be able to manage. In many cases it will involve large numbers of people. As with the Rest Centres and Forward Media Briefing Points pre-identification can be a valuable exercise in speeding up the set-up process. The best locations tend to be hotels as they have accommodation, catering and large rooms for briefings and interviewing families. Also bear in mind that following a major incident the local hotels will be block booked by the media very quickly.

The FRRC is a location where police Family Liaison Officers (FLO) will attend and begin the support process for the families involved (see further discussion of FLOs later in this section). The key point for a FRRC is 'information'. The provision of 24-hour TV broadcasts and regular briefings by the police or local authority are essential to keep everyone informed. Even if a briefing states that there is nothing to add this will reassure and ensure that everyone feels involved. Police teams, often supported by Social Services Crisis Teams will take details from the relatives and friends to inform and assist in the identification process for those involved (see Casualty Bureau).

A point to note is that holding reunions of families and those involved within the FRRC can be distressing for those who have not been reunited. Also, for emergency personnel engaged in mortuary duties, they should not share the same accommodation as the families and friends. This can be distressing for them.

Humanitarian Assistance Centre (HAC)

This facility although having some similarity with the FRC is intended to provide longer term support offering practical advice and guidance to those involved in the incident, whether it be individuals, families or communities. Indeed, support should extend to rescuers and response workers too. It is a truly multi-agency activity tapping into the health services, local authority, faith communities and the private sector, such as insurance companies. Detailed guidance can be found in the UK Government website at <http://www.gov.uk/government/publications>.

Emergency/temporary mortuary

An incident involving many fatalities (or many body parts) may require the setting up of an 'Emergency Mortuary' as hospitals may become overwhelmed by the number of deceased persons. This is a responsibility of the Local Authority. The decision will be a joint one as to the need for an emergency mortuary made between the Coroner and the police. The need is also determined by the number of probable body parts as opposed to persons missing. This is because each body part for administration and processing purposes is treated as a person for identification purposes. Extensive emergency mortuary planning has already been undertaken in advance of a potential influenza pandemic and following concern over mass fatalities resulting from a CBRN-type attack. The options for an emergency mortuary can vary from pre-designated sites to temporary structures erected on secure sites. Each LRF will hold plans outlining their approach and policy.

Having looked at the key facilities we will now look at those key roles in support of a major incident.

Senior Investigating Officer

The **Senior Investigating Officer** (SIO) is a police officer and is responsible for the overall investigation of an incident where there is potentially any criminal liability associated with the circumstances. Where fatalities occur the police will act on behalf of the Coroner to inquire into the circumstances of the death. As a result of that investigation prosecutions may follow. As we have seen the police will also support and investigate with other agencies such as the HSE and Department of Transport. The SIO commands a large team of officers covering many investigative disciplines such as gathering forensic evidence and it is for that reason that the SIO must be involved in major incident management from the very start. The guidance and advice offered by the SIO is invaluable to secure and preserve evidence wherever possible once every possible effort has been made to save life. The SIO will arrange for the scene to be forensically searched, examined, witnesses to be seen, suspects to be detained or arrested and interviewed. All these activities have implications for the multi-agency team managing the incident. It is therefore important that the SIO or deputy is part of the Strategic Co-ordinating Group to assist in decision making (see Chapter 5).

If the incident is a terrorist incident the SIO will act as a member of a much larger counter-terrorist response involving regional counter terrorist units, the Metropolitan Police and security services. Terrorist response arrangements are led by the Home Office based upon guidance in the Home Office Counter Terrorist Manual.

Senior Identification Manager

The **Senior Identification Manager** (SIM) is a police officer and this is a relatively recent role which emerged following the *Marchioness* river boat disaster on the Thames in London and the subsequent Lord Justice Clark report into issues relating to identification of the deceased. The SIM is a very senior police position alongside that of SIO. The SIM will work with the SIO and the police Gold Commander in developing strategies and tactics to complete the identification of all those involved in an incident, both fatalities and those injured.

The SIM in collaboration with the Coroner and supervising pathologist will ensure that the deceased are correctly and properly dealt with, in terms of efficient identification which is appropriate and respectful, ensuring the families are involved throughout the process. The SIM will oversee all activity at the mortuary, the Casualty Bureau (if deaths are involved) and the role of the Family Liaison Officers (FLOs). Again the SIM or deputy should have access to and be part of the SCG.

Family Liaison Officers—FLOs

FLOs are police officers, often supported by Social Services crisis support teams, who are allocated to a family who have suffered bereavement in circumstances in which the police are investigating or where a family member is missing. They are essentially evidence gathering which will include identification enquiries for example DNA and physical descriptions. They are also there to support and offer advice and guidance to families throughout the identification and investigative processes. It can be a very emotional and difficult job taking many months.

Casualty Bureau

The Casualty Bureau is a police facility set up to manage the identification of those involved in an incident. This can include those who have died, have been injured or are missing and unaccounted for. Casualty Bureau facilities are often shared between police forces and linked in terms of call handing to ensure sufficient call takers are available to manage the demand for those seeking information about relatives and friends involved in incidents. Technology has enabled direct electronic input from remote sites such as hospitals and emergency mortuaries and from FRRC with information provided by relatives and friends.

The Casualty Bureau concept is straightforward. It is there to match up information from someone who is missing or dead compared against information from those reporting them missing hopefully leading to a positive identification. See Figure 4.8.

TASK 4.5

Police Family Liaison officers supported by Social Services Crisis Support Teams care for the needs of those affected by major incidents involving injury and death. Using the CCA guidance and information available from your LRF website and other material research their role and responsibilities.

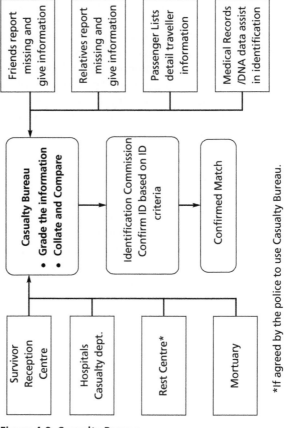

Figure 4.8 Casualty Bureau

When an incident takes place resulting in loss of life or injury it is understandable that close friends and family will be anxious for information concerning their friend or relative. Depending on the circumstances and numbers involved the police will decide if a Casualty Bureau is required. If an incident is a 'closed' incident, for example a small aircraft where all the passengers are known with certainty a Casualty Bureau may be dispensed with. If they decide to open a Casualty Bureau, usually a free phone number is released through the media. The police will activate the pre-planned arrangements and call takers will be positioned to handle the incoming calls. These could in fact be in different locations across the country within police forces subscribing to a national or regional scheme. In this way the number of call takers can be scaled up or down to meet the demand. All incoming information will then be channelled to the designated or 'home' Casualty Bureau. Although the police will issue a number for the Casualty Bureau or information centre, in many cases with large transport undertakings such as airlines' and rail operators' protocols exist to share and collaborate with information sharing.

TASK 4.6

Establish what Emergency/Temporary mortuary arrangements apply in your LRF area.

How does the system work?

When a relative reports someone missing and they assume that they have been involved in the incident the police will grade that information. The grading will be decided by the SIM and colleagues such as the casualty bureau manager. The grading can be, for example 1–5, 1 being that the person reported missing is very likely to have been involved and 5 unlikely. For example, if it is a train crash, the relative may have actually put the person on the train in question so they are certain that they were on it—which is graded at 1. On the other hand a relative may report that they are aware that their relative is touring in that area and always uses trains. That may be graded as a 5 and depending on the level of certainty any grade between 1 and 5 will be used. Casualty Bureaux will also have a pro-active team who actively re-contact relatives and friends to establish if the person they reported missing has turned up. This is often overlooked by the reporting person as they are so relieved they forget to tell the police!

This information is then compared and collated with information coming in from various locations such as hospitals, SRCs and later in the process, mortuaries. To make formal positive identifications an 'Identification Commission' is established to assess the identification information and make

Primary	Secondary	Assistance
DNA	Personal jewellery/effects	Visual ID
Fingerprints	Medical Records/X-ray	Photographs
Odontology	Blood Group	Personal Description
Distinctive Deformity	Distinctive Clothing, tattoos	Body location
Distinctive Medical	Marks and scars	Clothing
	Physical disease	

a decision. They will use a combination of Primary, Secondary and Assistance means of identification.

TOP TIP

Proactively checking missing person reports will reduce the number of missing persons

---

For example:

A positive identification criteria combination may be any 2 primary or a minimum of 3 secondary. Assistance only means support to primary and secondary and cannot be taken as reliable. It should be noted that visual identification in itself cannot be a positive identification. 'Viewing' the body or indeed part of the body is a matter for the relatives to decide as it may greatly assist them coming to terms with their loss. Although viewing a body may be very traumatic often relatives are counselled prior to the view to prepare them for the task.

TASK 4.7

Can you think of reasons why visual ID is not a primary form of ID?

Once identification is confirmed by the Identification Commission that will be communicated to the relatives. This is done by a personal visit which will involve the police or by the Family Liaison Officer (FLO).

Having looked in depth at the police response we will now examine the role of the other emergency services and key support agencies.

Fire and Rescue Service—Category 1 Responder

For general information, the fire and rescue ranks are included in Figure 4.9 to aid in recognition. The fire and rescue service has undergone major change in recent years, in particular in relation to their role in responding to large scale catastrophic events in the wake of the terrorist attacks in New York in 2001, under the New Dimensions programme. They now have substantial equipment strategically placed across the UK to respond to major incidents including decontamination units and high capacity pumps.

The fire and rescue services have scene management arrangements that are configured on creating sectors with a sector commander in charge of each one (see Figure 4.10).

Figure 4.9 Fire and Rescue Service Ranks

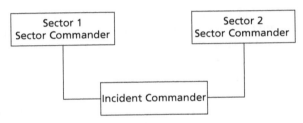

Figure 4.10 The Sector Commander

As mentioned earlier in relation to cordons, the fire and rescue service will approach a scene and 'sectorise' it into manageable areas but the system is still compatible with overall co-ordination, as the Incident Commander will liaise with the other emergency services on site. Other developments have included changes in working practices and the way equipment is managed and deployed.

The primary areas of fire and rescue service responsibility at a major incident are:

(a) Life-saving through search and rescue (including water rescue).

(b) Fire-fighting and fire prevention.

(c) Rendering humanitarian services.

(d) Providing and/or obtaining specialist advice and assistance where hazardous materials are involved.

(e) Salvage and damage control.

(f) The provision of specialist equipment, e.g. pumps, rescue equipment and lighting.

(g) Safety management within the inner cordon (hot and warm zone).

(h) Provide equipment and manpower to support the mass decontamination of the public in support of the NHS.

(i) Provide manpower and equipment to perform urban search and rescue.

(j) Initiate environmental protection measures.

TASK 4.8

The Fire Service Operate a system of Sector management. Will this conflict with police co-ordination?

Fire and rescue detection, identification and monitoring (DIM) capability

A recent innovation by the FRS has been the introduction of DIM Teams and vehicles. As of 2011, 17 specialist vehicles and support officers can respond rapidly to any HAZMAT or CBRN-type incident. They can enter the inner cordons or 'Hot Zones' to render assistance, identify substances and monitor levels of contamination.

The fire and rescue service provide a wealth of data relating to hazardous and toxic environments and as such should be the primary initial source of information relating to risk management.

Ambulance Service—Category 1 Responder

The ambulance service like many other public sector organisations has undergone rapid change in recent years, again being touched by the effects of the terrorist attacks in New York in 2001. The ambulance service is now the primary body responsible for casualty decontamination, working closely with the fire and rescue service to decontaminate large numbers of people.

The primary areas of responsibility for the ambulance service at a major incident, may be summarised as follows:

(a) To save life in conjunction with the other emergency services.

(b) Provide treatment, stabilisation and care of those injured at the scene including decontamination of casualties.

(c) Initiate casualty decontamination procedures at the scene including mass decontamination arrangements in conjunction with the Fire and Rescue Service.

(d) Provide sufficient medical and other staff, equipment and resources.

(e) Establish effective triage systems to determine the priority evacuation needs of those injured.

(f) Act as a gateway to all NHS services and co-ordinate NHS activity at the scene.

(g) Provide communication facilities for NHS resources at the scene, including communication links with hospitals and other control centres.

(h) Nominate and alert appropriate hospitals to receive casualties from the incident.

(i) Arrange for the provision of a Medical Incident Officer and Mobile Medical/ Surgical teams and provide transport to the scene where necessary.

(j) Provide appropriate means of transporting those injured to hospital or other treatment centre.

(k) Maintain an emergency service throughout the county and return to a state of normality as soon as possible.

(l) To assist setting up of Medical Rest Centres (if operating)

TASK 4.9

Who has primacy for decontamination? What is the distinction if any?

We have already seen the use by the police of SAD CHALET for assessing an incident site. The ambulance service and the NHS use METHANE.

M Major incident. Standby or Declare

E Exact location

T Type of incident

H Hazards

A Access

N Number of casualties

E Emergency Services

Essentially the information is similar but in a method preferred by the ambulance service.

KEY POINT

The ambulance service act as the gateway into the wider NHS in the UK.

Ambulance service—Hazardous Area Response Team (HART)

This new capability offered by the ambulance service provides specially trained paramedics who can enter the inner cordon or 'Hot Zone' to render first aid and assist casualties. They are also trained to manage complex transport incidents and urban search and rescue, particularly in confined spaces.

They combine to form a front line response service working closely with the police and fire and rescue services at the heart of the incident.

Maritime and Coastguard Agency (MCA)— Category 1 Responder

The primary role of the Maritime and Coastguard Agency is to co-ordinate the emergency response off-shore. This can cause some confusion as to where the police and MCA co-ordination starts and finishes. In practice the MCA will always control areas covered by water and dry areas by the police. In the area from high water to low water it will be a combined effort. Their role can be summarised as follows:

(a) To control and co-ordinate the response to major maritime emergencies until such time as the emergency is closed or has become a mainly land based operation.

(b) To mobilise, task and co-ordinate declared and additional SAR facilities, which include:

- RNLI and other lifeboats;
- Military Search and Rescue and other rotary and fixed wing aircraft through the military Aeronautical Rescue Co-ordination Centre (ARCC);
- Maritime and Coastguard Agency resources including boats, vehicles, beach, mud and cliff rescue teams;
- vessels and support units in the vicinity;
- Port Authority and associated resources, e.g. tugs, pilot vessels, etc.

(c) To alert other relevant emergency services local authorities and organisations.

(d) To arrange the embarkation of survivors and casualties to nominated landing points. To agree with the police the location for landing any deceased.

(e) To provide an early warning system for oil, chemical and other forms of sea and coastal pollution, including the alerting of the Regional Operation Manager—Counter Pollution and Salvage (ROM-CPS) of the MCA, and local authorities. To assist with counter-pollution and clean up by providing co-ordinating facilities and communications.

The RNLI have become more prominent in recent years, in particular in relation to flood emergency response. In 2000, three Emergency Flood Response Teams were formed made up of 20 volunteers to respond on a 24/7 basis. Although many fire and rescue services do have a water rescue capability too (<http://www.rnli.org.uk>).

Local Authority—Category 1 Responder

The Local Authority provides a vast amount of resources and support in major incident management. It must be remembered however that they are not a blue light emergency service and must be given a very early call out to allow them to mobilise themselves and the voluntary agencies that support them.

The primary areas of responsibility for local authorities are:

(a) To support the emergency services and those engaged in the response to the incident.

(b) The provision of a wide range of support services and social care.

(c) To activate the voluntary agencies bearing in mind the time taken to respond, and co-ordinate their response.

(d) To provide suitable accommodation at Rest Centres for those evacuated or otherwise displaced from their homes including the documentation of those displaced.

(e) To provide support at a location used to care for and provide support to those involved in or surviving an incident, known as a Survivor Reception Centre.

(f) To provide facilities and location(s) for relatives and friends of those involved in an incident to enable information, support and reuniting, known as a Friends and Relatives Centre. Including Humanitarian Assistance Centres.

(g) Will provide, in consultation with the police, emergency mortuary arrangements (Emergency/Resilience Mortuary).

(h) Will facilitate the remediation and reoccupation of sites or affected areas.

(i) To lead the recovery and return to normality, whilst at the same time maintaining services at the appropriate level.

(j) To activate faith groups bearing in mind the time taken to respond, and co-ordinate their response.

The local authorities have certain responsibilities relating to flood management in particular relating to flash flooding and water runoff and drainage inundation. This work is sometimes contracted out to United Utilities. In addition, local authorities will be taking a more active role on public health provision.

From April 2013 the role of the local authority as it extends to health protection will increase with the role of the Director of Public Health moving from the NHS. See later for more information.

TASK 4.10

Establish the emergency planning structure for your local authority—is it County, Metropolitan, Unitary or District based?

Support Agencies

Having looked at the primary emergency response agencies we will now look at other key support agencies. Government restructuring in 2010/11 has led to many changes across government departments and some changes remain to be embedded and ratified but core responsibilities remain in the following key response organisations.

The Food Standards Agency—FSA

The FSA is an independent government department offering a range of services relating to food safety generally including advice and guidance relating to food affected by contaminants. They also monitor radiological safety as it relates to discharges into the environment and its effect on the food chain.

The Department for Environment, Food and Rural Affairs (Defra)

Defra is the government department responsible for policy and regulation on the environment, food and rural affairs. Defra covers such topic areas as the environment, food and farming, rural and countryside, wildlife and pets. They have a particular responsibility for flooding incidents.

The Department for Energy and Climate Change (DECC)

This department was brought together in 2008 to bring together 'energy policy' and climate change mitigation policy, previously dealt with by Defra. It oversees policy in relation to nuclear power generation and as such incorporates the Nuclear Emergency Planning Liaison Group (NEPLG) formerly part of the Department of Business and RegulatoryReform (BERR).

DECC main objectives, though, are to ensure energy is secure, affordable and efficient. To bring about a low carbon country and agree international agreement of climate change.

The Food and Environment Research Agency (FERA)

This is an executive agency of Defra established in April 2009. It provides analysis, research and advice to assist Defra and other government departments to sustain and secure the food chain, a healthy environment and protection against the deliberate release of Chemical, Biological, Radiological or Nuclear material (CBRN). It now incorporates the **Government Decontamination Service** (GDS). The GDS offers non-compulsory advice and information with regard to 'clean-up' from incidents resulting from CBRN or hazardous materials releases following HAZMAT incidents. They hold a database of approved specialist contractors able to carry out decontamination work.

Animal Health and Welfare

Formerly the State Veterinary Service, part of the Department for Environment, Food and Rural Affairs (Defra).

Many major incidents, in particular where contaminants are involved, will have a serious impact on animals, from domestic, to farm animals to wild animals. Animal Welfare has a number of offices across the country that will provide advice and guidance relating to animal welfare issues.

National Health Service—Overview

The NHS of the UK is one of the largest and complex organisations in the world. It seems to be under constant political scrutiny, review, reformation and restructuring. However, it forms the core of emergency response in terms of providing life saving support immediately and during any incident and offering long term support for survivors and those affected.

In recognition of the changing nature of the NHS further up to date information about NHS structures can be found on the relevant websites but to provide an understanding and context for the NHS an overview is provided here. The most recent changes have been included here together with the previous structures to illustrate the significant changes and interactions that have occurred. This will allow the reader to move from the old to the new as smoothly as possible.

For emergency planning purposes it is important to understand that, whatever the shape or procedures the NHS adopts in terms of emergency support, emergency access for emergency responders to the wider NHS is through the Ambulance Service.

Department of Health (DoH)—Category 1 responder

In the event of a national or international incident which is deemed to be complex and of a serious nature the DoH will take control of NHS resources. This will be managed from their Emergency Preparedness Division Co-ordinating Centre. This will provide the necessary co-ordination for the NHS as a whole and offer support to Ministers.

Clinical Commissioning Group (CCG) (Previously Primary Care Trusts (PCTs))—Category 2 responder

PCTs provided or co-ordinated a range of health services such as doctors (GPs), dentists, opticians, mental health professionals and pharmacy services. The PCT worked with Local Authorities and other agencies that provide health and social care locally to ensure that the needs of the community are met. PCTs within the LRF area often nominated a lead PCT to co-ordinate other PCTs and they sat on the LRF to ensure an effective PCT response following an emergency. New arrangements from April 2013 saw PCTs abolished and replaced by Clinical Commissioning Groups (CCG). CCGs became Category 2 responders as opposed to the PCTs who were Category 1 responders. CCGs retain some responsibility for co-ordinating emergency response for their locality health provider services (those who deliver front line health care) and acute trusts (hospitals). The term Emergency Preparedness Resilience and Response (EPRR) is used in the NHS as a term to describe their resilience duties.

To oversee the CCGs and new commissioning responsibilities is NHS England who are a Category 1 responder acting through NHS England Area Teams (ATs) across England. The ATs broadly fit LRF areas and discharge their EPRR duties at strategic level through Local Health Resilience Partnerships (LHRP). This group is made up of representatives from all health commissioning CCGs (who contract the provider organisations to deliver health care), health providers, public health and local authority social care stakeholders in a AT area. This group will link directly into the LRF. On a local level some CCGs within health economies have health economy resilience groups (HERGS) in place to act as their operational and tactical arm of the LHRP to implement policy.

The NHS England AT will be responsible for ensuring that all CCGs and provider organisations of the NHS are prepared for emergencies and will facilitate monitoring to ensure they are fully prepared.

Acute Trusts—Category 1 responder

Hospitals are managed by acute trusts. They have:

- arrangements in place via A&E in dealing with emergencies as receiving hospitals for casualties;

- tried and tested Major Incident procedures in place and can link into police casualty bureau systems and technology to assist in identifying casualties;
- clinical response capability to an emergency;
- mobile response capability to incident scenes.

Some acute trusts are foundation trusts which essentially mean they have more financial autonomy.

NHS England Area Teams—Category 1 responder

In 2013 Strategic Health Authorities (SHA) were abolished and the NHS England Area Teams adopted their role including their previous EPRR role. NHS England Area Teams EPRR role includes (overview):

- Ensuring the local role out of the LHRPs, coordinating with Public Health England (PHE) and local government partners.
- Ensuring the NHS has integrated plans across their areas and with local health economies.
- Where appropriate develop joint plans with PHE and local authorities.
- Seek assurance that effective information governance agreements are in place to share information.
- Ensure that NHS funded organisations can respond to and be resilient against emergencies that cause increased demand or disruption to patient services.
- Discharge local NHS England EPRR functions locally (a role for some CCGs).
- Ensure the NHS are represented at LRFs locally.
- Have the capability to lead the NHS response to an emergency.

Note that the PCT was a Category 1 responder and the SHA a Category 2. In effect the CCG that replaces the PCT is now a Category 2 responder and the SHA as replaced by NHS England is a Category 1 responder.

Local Health Boards (Wales)—LHBS—Category 1 responder

The LHB is responsible for local co-ordination of NHS emergency planning and response. They are the lead health co-ordinator over a wider area covered by each LRF and report and liaise with the Welsh Government's Health and Social care department to support a pan-Wales response.

Public Health

Directors of Public Health (DsPH) from within the NHS transferred over to local authorities in April 2013. The new arrangement aims to integrate and streamline health protection for the population by combining existing local authority public health duties and those previously positioned in the local NHS PCTs. DsPH responsibilities will include, amongst other things, ensuring that emergency plans set out clearly defined roles and responsibilities for all key partners within the local authority, Public Health England, NHS Area Teams, CCGs and health providers for responding to disease outbreaks and emergency response. This will include arrangements for 24/7 on call rotas, exercising and escalation protocols. However, there will be occasions within which the lead for a given health emergency may be jointly managed.

It can be seen therefore that at a response level there are many stakeholders with specific emergency and social care responsibilities. It is the LHRP that will ensure full and effective integration takes place between stakeholders to deliver a robust health sector response.

In Wales, public health advice is provided by the National Public Health Service for Wales.

Public Health England—PHE (formerly The Health Protection Agency—HPA)—Category 1 responder

At the time of the NHS restructuring in 2013 the functions of the HPA transferred to Public Health England, a category 1 responder and an executive agency of the Department of Health. Overall the role of Public Health England (PHE) has been established to protect and improve the nation's health and wellbeing and to reduce inequalities. They work closely with both DsPH in local authorities and the NHS.

The role of the PHE in EPRR are (overview):

- Set a risk based national EPRR implementation strategy for PHE.
- Ensure they support partners in responding to a public health emergencies at all levels.
- Work with health partners in developing plans and provide specialist advice in doing so.

Port Health Authorities (PHA)—Category 1 Responder

The focus in collaboration with other agencies is the control of infectious diseases, protecting the environment, import controls on foods and general hygiene on vessels.

The Environment Agency (EA)—Category 1 Responder

The Environment Agency's role is to protect and improve the environment in England and Wales by:

- Prevention or minimisation of the effects of an incident upon the environment.
- Investigating such incidents and prosecuting where appropriate.
- Pursuing remediation, clean-up or restoration of the environment.

Their primary role relates to flooding where they are responsible for issuing warnings, operating flood defences and educating the 'at risk' communities to manage flood events. They will also seek to prevent and control pollution events and monitor pollutants into the environment.

They will provide advice and monitor and regulate the disposal of wastes such as diseased animals.

The Environment Agency co-ordinate air quality monitoring following the release of a toxic plume. This is a new role following the Buncefield fire in England in 2005. This information they supply to the STAC (see later) to assist in protecting and offering advice to the public.

Health and Safety Executive (HSE)—Category 2 Responder

In 2003 the police (ACPO), the Health and Safety Executive and the Crown Prosecution Service agreed a joint protocol for liaison when investigating work related deaths. The role played by the HSE cannot be over-emphasised as they have extensive powers when conducting investigations, in particular now with the Corporate Manslaughter and Corporate Homicide Act 2007 in force. The HSE inspectors should be seen as an integral part of the investigation team. HSE also regulate nuclear installations, mines, factories, farms, hospitals, schools, offshore gas and oil installations and other workplaces to ensure a safe working environment for both the workforce and public.

Department of Transport (DoT)

The DoT carries out accident investigations relating to transport incidents. The main branches are:

- **Air Accident Investigation Branch (AAIB)** is part of the DoT and investigates all civil aircraft accidents and incidents. Its primary aim is to establish the cause and circumstances of accidents to preserve life and make improvements for the future. It is not to apportion blame or liability.
- **Marine Accident Investigation Branch (MAIB)** is a separate branch within the DoT. It is not part of the Maritime and Coastguard Agency (MCA). There is a Memorandum of Understanding however between the HSE, MCA and the MAIB to ensure full co-operation and collaboration during investigations.

- **Rail Accident Investigation Branch (RAIB)** is an independent body within the DoT. It reports directly to the Secretary of State. It was established by the Railways and Transport Safety Act 2003 following the Ladbroke Grove rail accident in 1999 and recommendations contained within the Lord Cullen report into that incident. Again the RAIB has extensive powers of investigation and will work closely with the police (British Transport Police) relating to incidents on railways involving the death of a person, serious injury to five or more people or extensive damage to rolling stock, the infrastructure or environment.

Ministry of Defence/Military

The military have taken a much higher profile in becoming engaged with assisting and planning for civil emergency matters, in particular following the flooding events of 2007 and 2014 in the UK. Every LRF will have a military representative within their group called the Joint Regional Liaison Officer (JRLO). MOD support to the civilian authorities has been available for many years. However military operational commitments both home and abroad have a significant effect on how the military can respond to civil requests.

Arrangements have existed under the terms of what is known as Military Aid to the Civil Authorities (MACA) which is divided into:

MACP—Military Aid to the Civil Power, which is concerned with national security and counter terrorism. For example using special forces to support the police. MACP also includes the role of the military in bomb disposal duties or EOD Explosive Ordinance Disposal. EOD have specialist training in CBRN-type incidents.

MACC—Military Aid to the Civil Community which involves supporting the civil community, for example building bridges and sand bagging. This support is further divided into categories. Category A which is defined as emergency assistance, Category B which is routine military assistance and Category C which involves attachment of volunteers.

MAGD—Military Aid to Government Departments which involves military assistant on issues of national importance. Recent examples have included the fire service strike and assisting in managing the foot and mouth outbreak.

It must be stressed that there are strict criteria for accessing military aid that can have very significant financial implications. If the situation is not directly life threatening, emergency assistance advice must be sought from the local Military Liaison Officer (JRLO) to clarify the cost implications. Military aid is usually sought through the Strategic Co-ordinating Group (see later).

Private Sector

The CCA 2004 identified and recognised the contribution certain organisations and companies bring to emergency management and designated them as Category 2 responders. These include:

- Electricity Distributors and Transmitters
- Gas Distributors
- Water and Sewerage
- Telephone Providers
- Railways Operators
- Airport Operators greater than 50k passengers.
- Ports
- Highways Agency.

Such companies provide critical support to the community and support what is known as 'Critical National Infrastructure', or CNI. CNI is broken down into nine sectors:

1. Communications
2. Emergency Services
3. Energy
4. Finance
5. Food
6. Government
7. Health
8. Transport
9. Water

The ability of these sectors to continue to provide services in the face of a malicious attack is obviously key for the national interest and as such is the subject of continued enhancement and development through the Centre for the Protection of National Infrastructure (CPNI) (<http://www.cpni.gov.uk/about/cni/>). The CPNI work across many government departments including the police to ensure facilities are protected.

On a similar theme work is also ongoing through the Cabinet Office to increase resilience of the national infrastructure from natural hazards.

For the EPO this is an emerging area of work in which it is recognised that the private sector have a key role to play in national resilience and can be viewed as a partner in that goal. This is one factor as we have seen in Chapter 1.

TOP TIP

Organisational change occurs quite frequently within the emergency planning community. For the professional EPO visiting organisational websites regularly to keep up to date on current developments and changes is essential.

Voluntary Sector

The voluntary sector, such as the Red Cross, can provide a great deal of support through the Local Authority in terms of offering support to the community generally, those involved in major incidents, casualties and friends and relatives. Voluntary does not mean amateur. The voluntary services provide dedicated professional level services at all times.

Although not specifically covered in this book detailed information relating to their role within a major incident can be found on their respective websites and by referring to the LRF. As a matter of good practice every EPO should regularly update themselves on current developments within all emergency response organisations.

Faith Communities

Connected to voluntary work is the support offered by many faith groups from diverse denominations and religions. This support is normally co-ordinated through the Local Authority. Their advice and guidance can be invaluable in terms of understanding cultural or language issues. In particular, many faith leaders and community leaders can assist in communication with sections of the community that would otherwise be less effective.

Managing Change in Emergency Response Organisations

It must be recognised that change within any developing and evolving organisation is inevitable for many reasons, perhaps financial, political, restructuring, amalgamations or mergers. However, in every case real thought needs to be applied to the impact such changes will have on resilience and the potential 'ripple' effect such changes can realise not only in the changing organisation but those partners and stakeholders who rely on or interact with them. There is a real danger that corporate 'memory' may be lost in both personnel and changes in process and procedure. These processes and procedures often need reviewing or indeed a complete re-write to 'fit' the new organisation. This will of course require the re-training of key personnel, exercising and evaluating new systems. It will also mean informing and consulting at all levels with partners and stakeholders. This can often involve changes to those organisations too, caught in the ripples. Embedding new knowledge, processes and procedures will take time to settle down. Moving too fast or too far in a change process will result in the obvious loss of knowledge and skill but it can also result in lack of confidence of staff to act, disengagement, frustration and ambiguity as systems, roles and responsibilities change. An EPO caught up in significant change processes must be mindful of the possible impact and be prepared to voice those concerns and be a central figure within that process to minimise the adverse impact.

There will always be a period of uncertainty during and following change. This change requires careful management and recognition that the work of the EPO will 'spike' and grow exponentially during that change and embedding period to ensure essential retraining and exercising takes place.

TASK 4.11

Can you think of the kind of support the voluntary sector can provide following a civil emergency? List at least 10 activities.

Summary

You should now understand:

- How the emergency response is structured and the activities of the emergency services and support agencies.
- The police response and how they combine their management arrangements into overall co-ordination.
- How scene management operates giving you an insight into the arrangements you may have to support or plan for.
- The key roles of response organisations.

Conclusion

Understanding the role of the emergency services and all the agencies that make up the multi-agency approach is vital to the EPO. Working together in a co-ordinated way will greatly enhance the effectiveness of the response and therefore reduce the impact upon the community. The number of response agencies as we have seen is large and without co-ordination the overall effort will fail. Effective co-ordination may however be compromised by 'change'. It should also be recognised in the changing world we live in that change is inevitable. Managing change is challenging and is crucial for the resilience of the community and the EPO.

Chapter 5 examines in detail how effective co-ordination is achieved. The focus will be on the police and how they create the environment and facilitate co-ordination from the start of an incident.

Co-ordinating the Emergency Response

Overview
In this Chapter we will cover:

- Police co-ordination
- Invoking and using STO/GSB effectively
- Police Incident Officer—PIO
- Technical Co-ordination Centre (TCC) and the Tactical Co-ordination Centre Co-ordinator
- Activating management levels
- Strategic Co-ordination Centre—SCC
- Multiple tactical commanders/managers?
- Two essential SCG sub-groups
- The return to normality
- Area/Regional and National Co-ordination
- Lead Government Departments
- Managing within the TCC and SCC/SCG—Recording and sharing information
- Recording information/the 'Loggist'
- Crisis meetings
- Running meetings
- Resourcing police co-ordination centres (external agencies)
- Criminal liability
- Co-ordination—Putting it all together (a practical example)
- Creating your own 'Incident Room'/'Emergency Control Centre'

In this Chapter we will expand further on the co-ordination of an emergency.
The term Command and Control is a well known emergency planning phrase

whose meaning will emerge in greater detail as we explain co-ordination. Co-ordination is perhaps less well understood but is vital for the successful management of any emergency. In fact the term 3 Cs is gaining currency in the emergency planning community in recognition of the importance of co-ordination—Command, Control and Co-ordination. The term can be seen as expressed as 'C3'.

As we now operate in a multi-agency environment the key to being an effective EPO is to fully understand the relationship, interaction and responsibilities of each organisation and perhaps most importantly where they and their organisation fit into the whole picture. The range of response agencies is quite extensive as we have seen. Each Category 1 and Category 2 organisation including many private sector organisations will have detailed 'tried and tested' internal procedures based upon their own plans for dealing with crisis, major incidents and civil emergencies developed over many years and it is not intended to go into detail here about individual organisational approaches to procedures, primarily as they are so diverse, ever changing and evolving as new information becomes available or lessons are learned.

However, this Chapter is about describing how effective multi-agency co-ordination is achieved from the initial response right up to government level in bringing together what is, or can be, a wide range of different plans. This Chapter will also describe how support organisations including the private sector can effectively engage with the overall co-ordination process to add value and indeed support their own organisation in surviving the incident.

We have already seen how important it is for all organisations to support the police and align themselves with the nationally agreed methods of co-ordination outlined in the CCA guidance, UK CONOPs and ACPO guidance. However, this process of alignment should be one that does not replicate or confuse existing guidance but should be compliant, complementary and fully integrate with that guidance. This will ensure a clear understanding of the primary response focus.

KEY POINT

Incident or emergency arrangements put in place by non-category 1 or 2 responders must not compromise and confuse the UK national guidance of emergency response.

For most organisations the process of supporting the police through the STO method of incident management is quite straightforward in that they react to requests from the police to attend and participate within one of the management levels be it at Strategic level, Tactical level or Operational level.

Having recognised and designated their own staff to one of the three levels in advance, as mentioned earlier in the book, eases that collaboration process considerably.

We will now review some important issues regarding police co-ordination.

Police Co-ordination

For the purposes of familiarisation only we have considered a simple summary of the role of the main emergency response organisations together with the initial scene management and key considerations from Chapter 3 and 4; however the role of the police is examined even further now as this will shape the whole emergency response. As already alluded to, this focus is on the police primarily because it is the police who are charged with the responsibility for the overall co-ordination of the emergency response. On a few occasions this lead will not rest with the police, as in certain disease issues, but being able to understand that co-ordination role as generally managed by the police is vital for any EPO in terms of preparing plans, exercising and training, as the principles remain the same whoever is leading.

To enable co-ordination to occur the police have adopted and developed the Strategic, Tactical and Operational (STO) or Gold, Silver and Bronze (GSB) Command and Control system, which is now fully incorporated into national guidance. This system is fully integrated into day to day police practice and is capable of incremental development to manage major incidents. This is accepted nationally. As we now know STO and GSB describe a flexible management structure which separates management activity. It creates Operational activity known as Bronze, Tactical activity known as Silver and Strategic activity known as Gold. This can be further described as 'What to do'—Strategic, 'How to do it'—Tactical and 'Doing it'—Operational.

For the purposes of this book the terms Strategic, Tactical and Operational will be used in conjunction with Gold, Silver and Bronze but recognising that STO is a more appropriate model to describe the management functionality and is preferable to GSB.

Most people associated with emergency response will at least have heard of the STO/GSB system and indeed many will profess to understand it fully. The difficulty is that over time it has been interpreted and shaped into many forms and formats. It was always envisaged as a flexible and simplified system of incident management that recognised the need to separate out the Strategic, Tactical and Operational or Gold, Silver and Bronze elements in order to make the decision making process clear and unambiguous. It is dependent on function and role, not rank or position. The reality is however, that the distinction is now becoming blurred with a mixing of the elements and inevitably, rank seems to impact upon the effective operation of the system. Indeed, the configuration of GSB within the police service is further manipulated depending on the nature of the incident being managed. For example, incidents relating to firearms, public disorder and major incident management all have variations in the application of GSB. To avoid confusion, STO/GSB only as it is applied to the management of major incidents or civil emergencies will be dealt with in this book.

KEY POINT

The police not only have to manage their own resources but co-ordinate the emergency response where there is an immediate threat to public safety.

An important point to remember is that the police must operate a command and control system that not only delivers effective co-ordination for all responding agencies but it can also manage their own resources too. The command and control training for police managers is therefore quite comprehensive and the whole police command and control process has been reviewed to make it less ambiguous and more consistent across the UK which is reflected in the most recent edition of the ACPO Emergency Procedures Guidance 2009.

Invoking and Using STO/GSB Effectively

There is no mystery to STO or GSB. To begin, consider how a problem is managed in everyday life and how decisions are made. When presented with a situation that requires a solution we initially think: 'What is it I need to do to resolve this?' We weigh up our options, consider alternatives, we look at the implications of taking that course of action. Having decided what needs to be done by assessing all the options we then consider how we will achieve what we have decided to do. What methods are available to us, which are the best economically and practically? Having decided our preferred method we then implement that by actually doing what needs to be done to resolve the situation. In effect—we have been thinking strategically…'what needs to be done'. We have been thinking tactically…'how I am going to achieve this'….and finally we have been thinking operationally…'doing it'. Our decision making has comprised three components but we hardly think of it in those terms because it is so natural and intuitive. We have simply described the process of STO/GSB.

So it can be seen that in normal everyday situations the three components can easily be accommodated because the tasks faced are generally simple and not complex. Consider:

• Problem/Issue: I am thirsty.

- What to do? (strategic thinking) I need a drink.
- How to do it? (tactical thinking) Get a glass and go to the tap and pour water into it.
- Doing it? (operational thinking) Drink the water.
- Problem/Issue: Solved.

In fact, in the majority of situations the strategic and tactical thinking or elements will be a small part of the overall activity as we know what needs to be done and how we are going to do it. The bulk of the resolution, being operational...doing it is hardly given a second thought.

But consider a situation in which the issues are more complicated, involve many people, impact upon many resources; the environment; the media; or have major financial implications....not quite so simple now! In this situation it may be necessary to separate out the components to be able to manage the situation effectively. It is simply too much to deal with by one person. Their 'span of control' is compromised. Their ability to manage these complex multi-dimensional tasks and processes is too difficult—information overload begins, communication breaks down and inevitably mistakes are made. It is critically important, as we shall see, to understand that the three management levels are truly not rank orientated—indeed you could have three members of staff each of equal rank allocated one management level to deal with. This is one reason that the GSB is falling out of favour as it implies a status or rank aligned with precious metals. The association with high rank or position is usually related to their ability to direct secure support and resources, and they will probably have more experience and training. The latter two attributes can also apply to someone of relatively low rank or position because of the specialist nature of their knowledge, in which case they usually act as advisors to designated decision makers (Tactical Advisors).

Moreover, the key to successful integration and usage of STO/GSB is recognising the need and the point at which to separate and invoke the levels of management as the situation directs. The implementation of STO/GSB should be seamless and a logical progression based upon the needs of the situation. Management levels are dependent on complexity not the nature of the incident. Recalling the explanation of what is a 'major incident' it can be seen that a helicopter crash is a very unusual event but in many respects could be managed as a 'routine' incident by the emergency services, but how many times would a full STO/GSB management structure be imposed for such an unusual event?

In the event of a spontaneous large scale emergency (or major incident) the application and use of STO/GSB is quite straightforward and easily understood. It is obvious from the outset that all management levels will be required because of the nature and magnitude of the event. Take for example a major aircraft crash. It would be obvious that this catastrophic event needed a full STO/GSB management structure in place immediately. Therefore, all the management levels kick in at once. But what about something less obvious and at what point would STO/GSB kick in and up to what level? This is where the difficulty lies which we need to clarify. This is where the critical role of police in co-ordination begins—facilitating and invoking the most appropriate level of multi-agency emergency management. The EPO needs to know this and be able to explain it.

It is worth at this point making clear that we are considering the spontaneous (sudden impact) events, the unexpected and unplanned; the events which threaten immediate danger to the public. Planning for and managing forthcoming events in many respects is easier as the consequences and events are largely predictable notwithstanding that an unexpected event may occur. Therefore, the management structure can be designated and facilities put in place in advance. Management layers can be agreed in terms of strategic decision making and tactical application of the strategy is clear and delivery at the operational or bronze level is planned. The challenge therefore is being confronted with an incident with no notice and implementing arrangements and obtaining resources to manage it as the incident develops.

The spontaneous event is characterised by starting with the operational response and building as the issues unfold. The incident may jump to a full STO/GSB response immediately as in the case of a large scale incident but in other cases can begin as a routine or normal incident (we will consider such an example at the end of this Chapter) and only gradually increase in seriousness. It is this latter incident where the skill in co-ordination should become evident. Therefore the difficulty arises in operating the STO/GSB system spontaneously when it develops from a 'normal' incident as it escalates and the need for and recognition that appropriate management levels are required. These could be described as 'slow burn' or 'rising tide' incidents, a gradual escalation of an incident that falls between a full STO/GSB response and a 'normal' response or within the 'steady state'. You will notice that the gradual application of STO/GSB has similarity with developing plans that can move seamlessly from day-to-day activity to a full emergency response see Figure 5.1. Getting this part of the response wrong is where effective co-ordination can fail. This is primarily an issue for the police but understanding the process and the triggers that initiate the necessary management levels is important for any EPO from any background as it is this process that has

Figure 5.1 Gradual escalation of an incident

such an impact and influence on the response overall. It is this period of uncertainty that can stall an effective and timely response. In most cases the decision of the police to move to another management level will in fact be prompted by a non-police agency.

To explain this process it would be useful to look at this from the police perspective and how incident management should build and develop from a simple incident into a major incident and the thought processes that will inform the decision of the police to invoke the various levels on management to achieve optimum co-ordination. The implementation of these management levels can affect everyone with an emergency response responsibility. The key here is not to view STO/GSB as a stand-alone, off the shelf procedure that will solve all the complexity of major incident management—the magic bullet that will be fired when things start to get tricky. It must be fully integrated into daily activity and fully understood by all those with an emergency response role, in particular those in managerial or command roles, for example those who designate or will call a major incident.

TASK 5.1

Think of everyday tasks and apply the STO to each component of the decision. For example,

Issue/problem—I have to get rid of the household rubbish

Strategic—I will have to put it outside for collection—*what has to be done*

Tactical—I intend to go to the yard, get the bin and wheel it out to the kerb—*how to do it*

Operational—I walk to the yard and take it to the road—*doing it*

Try to think of three more everyday tasks using this process....

It is the consequences of the incident that matter, not necessarily the cause. Incidents should be managed and decisions made at the lowest appropriate level, known as *subsidiarity*, in fact the CCA endorses this view in the guidance document *Emergency Response and Recovery* by saying 'co-ordination at the highest necessary level only'. In other words, the response and management levels must be proportionate to the incident and only taken to the level at which effective co-ordination works. It must be remembered too that STO/GSB does not predetermine rank or status but acts as a descriptor of function. Where the Bronze or Operational level is not seen as inferior, low status or low rank—it simply says: 'I am operating and managing this incident at Operational level—dealing with any Strategic or Tactical issues as they arise'. 'The operational response will usually deal with most incidents or events'.[1]

---

[1] *Emergency Response and Recovery*, CCA 2004, p. 22.

In some situations that do not justify a full STO/GSB response there seems to be a desire for some police officers to notionally appoint themselves as Tactical or Strategic Commanders—just in case, as if there is a need to tick all the management boxes, although they are detached or isolated from the incident and in many cases it is not required. Phrases like, 'I am the Gold Commander, if you want me I am at home' have no place in management. There can be no notional commanders. Commanders, if required need to be in their appropriate command positions at all times. It must also be remembered that unnecessary command or management structures will complicate, confuse and blur accountability.

Commanders are mentioned a great deal and in particular within command and control, but what does command mean in the context of co-ordination? Command is a term more often seen in organisations such as the police and military services but it simply means 'management'. A commander is a form of manager but it is important not to use the term 'Commander' in inappropriate situations. Those officially and generally understood to be commanders are those who have undergone specialist leadership training in dynamic crisis situations and will probably have considerable frequent exposure and experience in that area—hence the blue light and military services. The commander element infers an element of authority under fear of punishment if an 'order' is disobeyed. That rigid style of management in the civil context is diminishing in favour of more consultative and collaborative approaches. The Fire and Rescue Service for example have removed all 'ranks' and replaced them with roles and managers, e.g. Crew Manager, Station Manager, but retaining 'Commander' for emergency management. To designate a role as 'Commander' to anyone means that that person must possess those skills or attributes—to have earned their 'spurs', otherwise there is a danger of being accused of 'bigging-up' the person or the organisation which could cause a little resentment and is not conducive to good multi-agency relations. Command function is about people, and refers to people, those who manage, command, facilitate or make decisions on behalf of their organisation.

As we have seen, control on the other hand is about places or facilities to enable effective command or management to be administered. The police co-ordination centres, in a multi-agency response at tactical and strategic levels are used to support commanders or managers and are usually police stations or other permanent locations usually operated by the police. They are there to facilitate and manage co-ordination of both their own police resources and that of response organisations, in other words a multi-agency response.

Specially constructed and adapted vehicles are termed 'command vehicles' but can be confused as 'Co-ordination Centres'or 'Controls'. Command vehicles are just that—they are used by individual organisations to control and support their own resources—they are not multi-agency co-ordination centres.

Multi-agency co-ordination centres need to have administrative support, space, seating, heating and communication for several organisations to use for multi-agency purposes. It is difficult to envisage a vehicle with that capacity. Therefore, many police forces now designate fixed site Tactical Co-ordination Centres (TCC) and Strategic Co-ordination Centres (SCC) at specific locations within their areas. In this way they are ready to open at short notice. The exception to this is the Forward Command Post (FCP) (or Bronze Control) which is the initial point of first multi-agency communication and consultation which may involve the use of a suitable vehicle or convenient building until a more permanent location is agreed (see Figure 4.7, Scene management).

Co-ordination centres support and service the needs of commanders. Commanders should not become involved in the administration of co-ordination facilities They must be free agents to position themselves at the most appropriate location to manage the incident. The decision to open a police co-ordination centre will be made by the relevant police commander in liaison with other agencies; this decision normally begins at the incident site where an FCP has been designated. Remember this may only be a vehicle with basic accommodation initially.

The Police Incident Officer

In the previous Chapter mention was made of the Incident Officer. The term Police Incident Officer (PIO) is common throughout the police service and requires explanation within the context of STO/GSB

The PIO represents the means by which co-ordination is achieved; in particular where it is not immediately obvious what management structure will be needed. The PIO becomes the focus and point of reference for all agencies responding at and around a scene of an incident. This applies to small scale incidents right up to major incidents. The PIO must be conspicuous, pro-active and dynamic at the scene to provide that point of contact for responding agencies and ensure that co-ordination is begun at the earliest stage. It is the PIO who will make those first assessments and decisions in building an effective co-ordination structure.

KEY POINT

Although the police lead on co-ordination—the decision to invoke and move to management levels is a multi-agency activity.

Any incident at its beginning will be attended by a police officer. They will be the incident officer, as they are dealing with the incident. They could be of any rank and if the incident remains low level and non-complex that PIO will remain in place and conclude that incident without the need to escalate or invoke additional management levels, such as STO/GSB, or seek more senior support.

It could be a road traffic collision, assault, minor public order incident, a theft, or indeed many types of incident. That officer may require some assistance and will agree some tasks with colleagues or indeed speak to other emergency services at the scene (see Figure 5.2), but their span of control can cope with the incident.

On arrival at an incident the first police officer will make an assessment as we have already seen. From that point in time that officer is the PIO and will be assessing and if required will be reporting information using the SAD–CHALET system and will begin liaison with any other agencies that are in attendance.

Co-ordination begins at that point. It is the responsibility of the police. The PIO will continue assessing, making judgements and liaising with other Incident Officers from the other services. At this point their span of control is effective and manageable, in that they can effectively communicate instructions, assimilate information and process that information and they have sufficient resources. It is from this process that a management structure will begin to emerge.

To effectively become the focal point of co-ordination that officer should make themselves readily identifiable by wearing a PIO jacket or tabard. This may sound a little pedantic but without this identification other services will not know who they should be speaking to and co-ordination breaks down. More often than not incident scenes can look like a sea of yellow jackets. The PIO can change from person to person as more senior or experienced police officers arrive on scene and this must be logged. It is the PIO who will begin to invoke the necessary level of management. Initially, the PIO will be dealing with all aspects of the incident at STO/GSB combined. However, there may come a point, which could be immediate or after several minutes or hours that the PIO declares that there is a need for a tactical level of command and co-ordination. Why should that be?

The issues that would affect that decision could include:

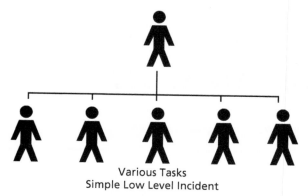

Various Tasks
Simple Low Level Incident

Figure 5.2 The Police Incident Officer

1. If a Major Incident is declared.
2. If multi-agency co-ordination is required.
3. There is a need for significant additional resources.
4. Their span of control is becoming too large.

Having made that decision to invoke the next management level, the PIO will assume the role of police tactical commander (or Silver) and begin to designate and delegate tasks to others who now occupy the Bronze management level through one or more Bronze commanders. In terms of a fixed incident scene the police Tactical Commander should remain with the scene and in liaison with other services.

The police Tactical Commander will summon resources to the scene, which may include the support of a command vehicle to assist them in scene management and communication. This vehicle could well become the FCP or indeed another emergency service vehicle may be used. The police Tactical Commander may also call for the establishment of a multi-agency Tactical Co-ordination Centre (TCC) to support them and facilitate multi-agency co-ordination. So where will the police Tactical Commander go if they open a Tactical Co-ordination Centre?

Tactical Co-ordination Centre (TCC) and the Tactical Co-ordination Centre Co-ordinator

The Tactical Commander should remain where the incident scene is fixed. If the scene is widespread, for example flooding or a moving toxic cloud it may be more appropriate for them to move to another location or into the police TCC. To manage the TCC, a Tactical Co-ordination Centre Co-ordinator will be appointed by the Tactical Commander or another senior officer to administer and manage the facility. The Commander should be free to command. When the TCC is operating it will require support and attendance from other services and possibly other organisations, such as a business, to assist with information as to who is involved in the incident or other specialist advice. These people will be liaison officers from those organisations and not designated commanders who will be too involved in managing the incident scene.

KEY POINT

Those attending TCCs are usually liaison officers from agencies as tactical commanders or managers need to be able to attend the scene if required. SCCs are usually attended by strategic or senior managers or commanders and remain in that location. Rarely will a strategic commander or manager need to attend a scene.

To recap, at this stage there is a Tactical Commander and Operational Commanders in place. Co-ordination is active through on-scene liaison meetings with operational and tactical commanders at the FCP, supported by a multi-agency TCC managed by a police Tactical Co-ordination Centre Co-ordinator. As the event develops and circumstances change the police Tactical Commander may accept direction from senior officers or make a judgement and a recommendation that a Strategic or Gold level of management is required.

Again, this decision is informed by liaison with other agencies and senior officers recognising a need to separate out the strategic elements. Issues that would be considered in informing that decision may include:

1. Is a multi-agency TCC being opened?
2. It is a large scale major incident?
3. Is the incident highly complex—for example nuclear release?
4. Are there multiple sites?
5. Are there multiple Tactical Commanders (see later)?
6. Is co-ordination of a tactical response required? That is the introduction of additional Tactical Commanders to deal with specialist issues such as the identification of the dead or the investigation.
7. Regional or national impact?
8. Significant policy decisions to be made?
9. Potential major expenditure?
10. Necessary to agree a policy framework with other agencies?
11. High profile media reaction?

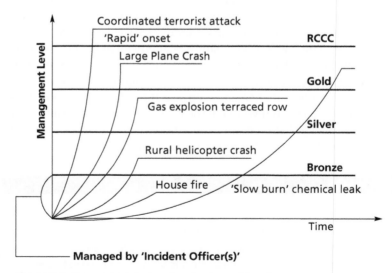

Figure 5.3 Response curve and management levels

12. Multiple casualties?

A full command structure is illustrated in Figure 5.3.

Activating Management Levels

The activation and implementation of the correct management structure is determined by need. It is managed at the lowest appropriate level (subsidiarity) with 'co-ordination at the highest necessary level only'. In a spontaneous (sudden impact) unplanned incident the management structure will grow, sometimes almost instantaneously. At other times very slowly as the facts emerge. The incident management structure will plateau at some point within the incident response. The diagram in Figure 5.3 illustrates this by comparing different types of incident and the management level development. Some incidents are rapid on-set and some are slow, breaching the management thresholds if necessary.

TASK 5.2

In terms of sudden impact or rising tide incidents—make a list of five scenarios for each. What is it about each incident that would define it as such?

When a decision is made to invoke the next management level under STO/GSB the police will agree this with all responding agencies and designate a time and location of the relevant Co-ordination Centres be it Tactical (Silver) or Strategic (Gold). TCC arrangements will vary between police forces but the EPO should make themselves aware of local practice.

It will be noticed that some incidents remain in the Operational region and are co-ordinated by the Police Incident Officer without recourse to implementation of a formal STO/GSB management structure. On the other hand some incidents will rapidly reach beyond Gold requiring sub-national or even national co-ordination through the Cabinet Office Briefing Rooms (COBR) at Level 3 in the UK CONOPS designation of events (see Figure 4.4). In the example it is a terrorist related incident but could be a licensed nuclear site emergency event.

Strategic Co-ordination Centre—SCC

Having implemented the correct management levels—through Operational, building through to Tactical, the next level is Strategic. If the Strategic Co-ordination Centre (SCC) is operating it can be assumed that the incident is one that is very serious requiring significant strategic input and deliberation. It becomes the focal point or the centre for decision making at policy level and therefore will have very senior representatives from all organisations managing the incident.

Before looking in detail at how a multi-agency SCC operates it is useful to look more closely at the nature and context of the SCC. The SCC facility is usually located at police premises, generally at headquarters on the basis that the police lead the co-ordination function during an emergency response. It makes sense in respect of its functionality in that often the police will activate their SCC at three levels.

Firstly, in relation to a police only managed incident—which may not be multi-agency, for example a firearm incident or even an internal BCM issue. Secondly, in relation to a blue light managed incident involving key Category 1 responders only—such as major road terrific collision. Thirdly, as a full multi-agency managed response such as major flooding, a COMAH or REPPIR incident. In this respect there is a seamless transition up the co-ordination levels.

In terms of the facilities provided to agencies within any SCC across all police forces it can vary enormously. Some are excellent, others lack facilities to sustain a full multi-agency response requiring perhaps 10–12 agencies including their entourage. The police forces that have nuclear facilities within their areas have developed more robust multi-agency facilities, primarily due to the legal requirements to test nuclear emergency response plans at set periods (3 years) and in many cases these facilities have been assisted by financial support from the nuclear or chemical operators. For COMAH requirements again this had led many SCCs to expand and develop in terms of functionality under similar requirements to REPPIR. The positive spin off has been that these police forces have in effect created excellent facilities as a result.

However, this is not the case across all police forces. The REPPIR and COMAH requirements were put in place to respond to wide area toxic releases and engage the local community in preparing for the event. Those police forces that did not have such sites in general did not have the incentive or possibly the resources to achieve the same capability—which can be considerable. Nevertheless, the prospect of a CBRN-type incident happening in any location demands that such multi-agency SCCs be established across all police forces, taking into account the potential widespread impact such an event will have. In effect, developing SCCs to offer a common minimum standard (CMS) to all agencies wherever the incident takes place.

There is an emerging view, and indeed a case to support the view, that such facilities are now falling under the response remit of LRFs. As such, perhaps support, development and investment should be a multi-agency responsibility jointly financed across all responding agencies.

It should be noted that TCCs run on very similar lines to SCCs but on a smaller scale and many of the arrangements to be described here apply to

TCCs also. In any event, the SCC remains the key facility for overall complex co-ordination and command.

Opening the SCC is a significant event for all agencies. Hopefully, through LRF support and training most attendees will be familiar with operating practices within the SCC. When the SCC, as it is correctly known, is opened the Police Strategic (Gold) Commander will chair multi-agency Strategic Co-ordinating Group (SCG) meetings. The SCG will agree policy and strategy and will delegate that for implementation by Tactical Commanders through the TCC. All management staff in police co-ordination centres should be identifiable by tabards displaying their role within the centre. This simple requirement is important for those attending the SCC and a TCC who may be unfamiliar with the key staff running the centre.

The SCC is a strategic co-ordination centre. Note the word co-ordination is emphasised. Each participating agency will have its own *strategy* which may have been agreed within their own organisation but the role of the SCG is to co-ordinate those strategies by agreeing to accept, modify or re-configure them, if necessary, in the light of the collective aims and objectives to achieve the most effective response. The SCG will address the 'what we have to do' questions. That decision making process can legitimately contain elements of tactical functioning in offering advice on 'how we achieve what we have to do'. But there must be a clear separation. Typically, an SCC will appear serene and slow moving, with deliberation and due consideration. Whereas, a TCC will appear to be dynamic, fast moving but controlled.

KEY POINT

An emerging potential model for a combined Major Incident Co-ordination Centre is in fact a TCC within which is contained a Gold Cell made up of a small number of strategic managers/commanders. This option would reduce the resources needed to run both a multi-agency tactical and multi-agency strategic centre which are extensive and difficult to sustain over long periods. In addition, many agencies require additional specialist support staff to assist them which in many cases is making existing SCCs untenable due to sheer weight of numbers. In many situations agency personnel fulfil both strategic and tactical roles in any case out of necessity. But for now the existing model remains the national approach.

The SCC co-ordinator

An important issue to remember is that control and specifically co-ordination centres facilitate two crucial activities within the management process. Firstly, it is a decision making forum and secondly it is an information processing facility. The two must not become confused. Commanders and senior managers must not become embroiled in administration and in practical information processing. To do so would distract the commander or senior manager from decision making. To that end a Gold Commander will normally nominate a SCC Co-ordinator to take ultimate responsibility for information processing, analysis, briefing and communication. This will ensure that commanders and senior managers are free agents able to concentrate on key decisions.

The SCC Co-ordinator must also ensure that the SCC runs effectively. In effect ensuring that the conduct of the facility runs smoothly, monitoring numbers of people, ensuring messaging is being used and security is in place. The co-ordinator function at both TCCs and SCCs is vital to the effective management of the incident.

Figure 5.4 illustrates a typical large scale SCG arrangement. The membership will of course vary but the illustration gives an insight into the scale and nature of what to expect.

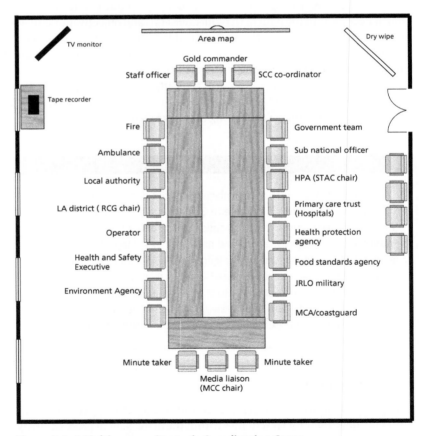

Figure 5.4 A Multi-agency Strategic Coordinating Group

TASK 5.3

Look at the membership of the SCC in the diagram and familiarise yourself with the organisations represented there. Who are they, what do they do? Research outside the book content if necessary.

Multiple Tactical Commanders/Managers?

In many complex large scale major incidents, specialist Tactical Commanders/Managers are designated—where the requirement for tactical application extends beyond the scope and expertise of one individual. In as much as there can be several police Operational or Bronze Commanders or operational functions operating together to achieve a common objective there may be multiple police Tactical Commanders—sometimes referred to as multiple Silvers. This is not a concept universally accepted. Some management structures prefer instead to have one Tactical Commander supported by Operational Commanders managing all other functions.

However, some of the functions now required in major incident management extend beyond operational capability in terms of resourcing, that a Tactical Commander level is justified. For example for the police:

1. Police Senior Investigating Officer (SIO)

2. Police Senior Identification Manager (SIM)

3. Police Tactical Commander (multiple scenes)

The SIO, as we have seen is designated to oversee the investigation of the incident to ascertain if any criminal acts have been perpetrated. They are usually very senior detectives. The SIM, again usually a senior detective is responsible for the whole process of identification. This will be from body recovery and identification to assisting relatives and friends.

In addition, in a widespread event with multiple sites, a separate Tactical Commander for each site may be essential. For example, separate townships, separate terrorist incident sites or flooding sites. This is where a Gold Commander is essential to co-ordinate their efforts and make decisions relating to the allocation of resources.

The illustration in Figure 5.5 shows a diagram of a full police command structure configured to support a multi-agency response. Note the key roles at all three levels of management and their relationship. This illustration relates to a single site incident. If more than one scene is involved several FCPs may be evident and more than one TCC operating depending on the scale and geographic spread of the incident. Only one SCC will be operating within any given LRF area. Note that in this example the terms—Gold, Silver and Bronze are used.

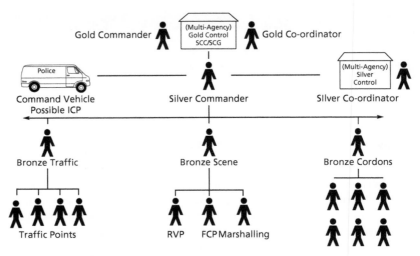

Figure 5.5 Police Full Command Structure

Two essential SCC sub-groups

A recently introduced feature of the SCC, brought about by the Buncefield Oil depot fire in Hertfordshire in 2005, was the introduction of the Scientific and Technical Advice Cell (STAC) to ensure timely co-ordinated scientific and technical advice during the response to an emergency. The STAC should be formed as a standing sub-group to offer advice to the SCG when required. The SCG will also need to identify a designated STAC lead who would co-ordinate the work of the STAC when activated. The STAC should bring together technical experts from those agencies involved in the response who may provide scientific and technical advice to the SCG on issues such as the impact on the health of the population, public safety, environmental protection, and sampling and monitoring of any contaminants.

The purpose of the cell would be to ensure that, as far as possible, scientific or technical debate was contained within the cell so that the SCG (and others involved in the response) receive the best possible advice based on the available information in a timely, co-ordinated and understandable way.

To that end there is no ideal STAC for every occasion. Each STAC will be configured to address the hazards presented. Given that a number of agencies will be involved in the response, the STAC lead and the SCG should identify the core membership of the STAC, as well as any other membership that may be required on an ad-hoc basis. To ensure the effective working of the cell, membership and attendance should be strictly controlled by the cell lead. STAC meetings must be controlled effectively and not become a quasi-SCG. It is for that reason that the designated chair should be the person sitting on the SCG and not a delegate sent from the STAC.

TASK 5.4

Can you list ten situations where a STAC would be useful?

The illustration (Figure 5.6) shows a typical STAC arrangement. Note that the configuration can change and often does as the situation changes and more or better informed participants are required to contribute. The illustration is intended to provide an insight into the composition of a STAC.

TASK 5.5

Looking at the STAC table, research each organisation there and find out their key roles—if not listed within the book, research them.

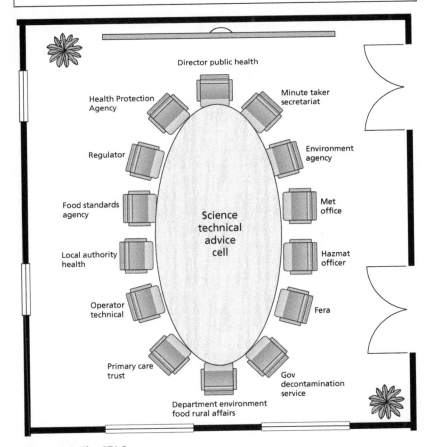

Figure 5.6 The STAC

A useful addition to the scope and effectiveness of the STAC is the Air Quality Cell, or AQC. In the event of a release of toxic substances which are potentially hazardous to the public the Environment Agency will be notified and convene an AQC, which will initially be 'virtual' in that all contributors will be collaborating by telephone. Agencies involved in the monitoring process could include for example, the Health Protection Agency, Food Standards Agency and the Met Office. The AQC will facilitate the deployment of detectors to vulnerable areas to assess the levels of contaminants and report to the STAC. This facility is reserved for the emergency phase, at the recovery phase such monitoring will be handed over to the Local Authority Recovery Co-ordinating Group.

It should be noted that in the event of a widespread incident covering more than one STAC area that is spreading across more than one LRF area, a sub-national STAC will be set up. This will ensure a consistent and non-contradictory approach to advice. This group will be monitored by the cross-SCG level by the Response Co-ordinating Group (ResCG) at sub-national level.

The Return to Normality

The term 'return to normality' is sometimes used to describe recovery, which is never the case. The impact and consequences of any significant incident will result in change at some level, as we have seen. During the emergency response phase to any incident it is important to consider the longer term recovery issues. These issues could involve impact on a business, the environment and health or welfare of a community. Decisions made during the emergency response could create longer term problems during the recovery phase if not thoroughly thought through. It is therefore crucial for all stakeholders to be at the heart of that decision making process to have influence on how both the emergency phase and recovery phase are managed.

To that end the SCG under the lead of the police will usually call for and create a Recovery Co-ordinating Group, or RCG. As we have seen in a previous Chapter this group is normally chaired by the Local Authority in whose area the incident takes place. It operates at the same time as the SCG and STAC and will consider the implications of dynamic decisions on future issues and advise the SCG accordingly.

The RCG will also provide that continuity link when the emergency phase has passed and the lead is formally handed over to the Local Authority. The RCG will become the focal point to activate all the resources and support that can be obtained locally, nationally and internationally to mitigate the effects of the incident. Appropriate grants, funding and aid will be sought using central government support. A typical post-emergency recovery committee structure is shown in Figure 5.7. Further information can be seen in the National Recovery Guidance Template issued by the Cabinet Office (see <http://www.gov.uk/government/organisations/cabinet-office>).

Each group will have a specific remit to address key recovery issues and will be co-ordinated by the Strategic RCG (SRCG). It should be noted that the Community Recovery Committee is a vital group to assist the overall recovery. The community group have a role in communicating messages and concerns which can often be overlooked by agencies not connected to that affected group.

The make-up and format of the SRCG can of course change depending on individual needs and the hazards present but an illustration in Figure 5.8 gives some indication and insight to a typical format during an emergency phase. This group would be expanded post-emergency to include all the chairs of the groups illustrated in Figure 5.8.

TASK 5.6

Looking at the RCG table given in Figure 5.8, research each organisation there and find out their key roles.

Note that the STAC chair is seated at the table.

Recovery management is as much of a challenge as responding to the emergency itself. The emergency phase is classically termed as the tip of the iceberg. For example in flooding situations the recovery phase represents a larger scale operation than the response phase and will probably take years to recover from. The impact on communities is devastating. The decontamination alone will disrupt communities, the environment and business. Strategies will need to be carefully integrated and co-ordinated to ensure the most effective and rapid means of bringing relief to those affected by the incident.

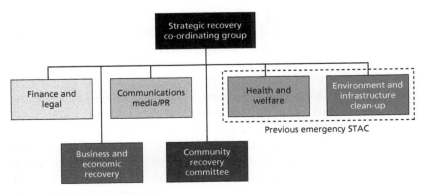

Figure 5.7 Aspects of Recovery

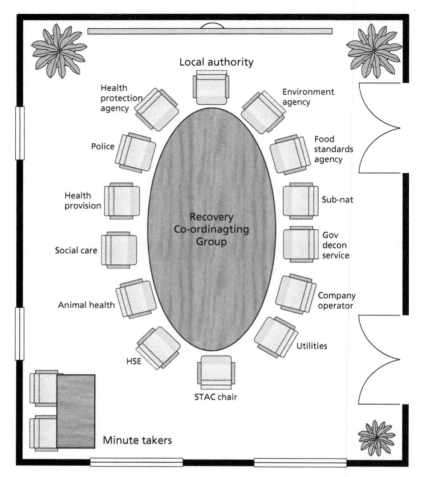

Figure 5.8 An example of a Strategic Recovery Co-ordinating Group

Recovery as an emergency management discipline is growing in terms of planning and exercising. The emergency phase always seemed to catch people's attention. For that matter the emergency services had a rather diminished enthusiasm after the event. Recovery management is probably as important a function of incident management as response, in particular for the local authorities who need to build robust and detailed plans to cater for a range of disruptive incidents within their communities as the complexity and implications of recovery emerge following real events. In particular, and as an example, following the nuclear incident in Fukusima in 2011 major reviews have taken place of UK capability to manage an incident that is prolonged and extends far beyond previous estimates in risk assessments in terms of boundaries, national and international impacts—areas that may have been underestimated in the past. Such incidents raise questions relating to risk management for the EPO. Planning for recovery is likely to become a major part of their work.

The diagram at Figure 5.9 illustrates the phasing from emergency phase to recovery. Note how during the emergency phase both the STAC and RCG offer advice and support to the SCG. Throughout the emergency phase the RCG is formulating a recovery strategy. On handover to the Local Authority the STAC and RCG form into the Strategic Recovery Co-ordinating Group.

This handover process is now very formalised with a certificate signed off by all parties to ensure there is a clear demarcation between two phases. This handover process follows when a set of previously agreed criteria have been met which signifies the end of the emergency phase.

TASK 5.7

Consider what type of issue would affect the decision to move from emergency response to recovery.

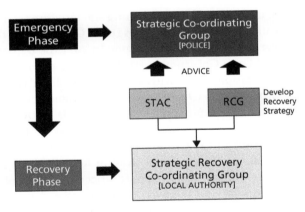

Figure 5.9 Moving to recovery

Area/Regional and National Co-ordination

Without doubt, previous experiences in the UK of wide area emergencies at either regional or national level, such as flooding or foot and mouth disease have demonstrated the need for effective co-ordination of both regional and national assets. But that is just what is required—not interference. It is well understood and heavily supported and endorsed in the CCA 2004 that the local response is the most effective with additional co-ordination as and when required. There have been occasions when the term 'Platinum' command has been used to refer to regional or national support. This must be avoided at all costs. The responsibility for the emergency response co-ordination usually rests with the chief police officer within whose areas the incident occurs when the police are leading. The regional and national input and support is essential in supporting that role but it should not be viewed as a command role.

As we have seen in Chapter 2, planning at the regional level has been restructured extensively. That not only extends to planning as described but the way in which regional support and central government become involved in a co-ordinated response.

TASK 5.8

Consider the role and function of the sub-national level of co-ordination through DCLG. Can you think of five situations in which their co-ordination would be needed?

Let us look at the new arrangements for national resilience co-ordination. LRFs remain the focal point of local planning and response arrangements across England and Wales. In Scotland it is the SCGs. Following the abolition of the Government offices of the region in 2011 the Department of Communities and Local Government (DCLG) established the Resilience and Emergency Division (RED) with an Implementation Group and a Management Group and set in place resilience teams across England. The resilience teams are sub-national groups to RED in DCLG and are divided into the North, based in Leeds; Central, based in Birmingham; South based in Bristol and a central London based resilience and emergency management team. Each has a Head of Resilience supported by Resilience Advisors and Resilience Support officers. The core of the new DCLG arrangements drives the government's localist and de-cenralist policy with a view to enhancing local resilience. Their new roles are described as:

1. Enable resilient localities—DCLG Resilience Advisors will agree with each LRF an engagement plan, based both on local priorities and the risk capability assurance DCLG undertake on behalf of the Government. They are supported by capability leads in RED for each of the national capability workstreams who work with the relevant lead government department.

2. Ensure preparedness for emergencies—to support LRFs to plan for the response to high impact and/or wide area emergencies. Where the impact is likely to extend beyond the capacity of a single LRF to cope, including facilitating the liaison between the lead department and the LRF(s).

The RED one team structure means a good practice can be better shared between LRFs anywhere in England.

3. Provide government support when emergencies occur—DCLG will provide 24/7 Government Liaison Officers to SCCs.

4. Discharge DCLG responsibility as the lead government department for specific emergencies

DCLG will also co-ordinate national recovery programmes across relevant lead government departments.

The DCLG Resilience and Emergencies Management Division embraces five areas within their role:

In effect their overall role will be to:

- act as the 'eyes and ears' of central Government in incidents;
- be available to attend Strategic Co-ordinating groups, knowledge of locality and key players;
- have a specified role in some lead government department plans;
- enable partnership working with responder organisations;
- have a capability to provide larger scale co-ordination—as required.

The new arrangements describe a government support framework specifically configured to deliver the implementation of capability at the local level through engagement with partners, providing the national context as well as feedback and challenge. The new teams will also represent the DCLG and local partner interests in the development of national policy for the capability; develop expertise in that capability; and share best practice and advice with the wider Resilience Division. (Courtesy of *DCLG RED*, September 2011)

The underpinning principle in major incident management in the UK remains that it is dealt with locally under the auspices of a chief officer of police who has overall responsibility. Government Liaison Officers (GLOS) will only become involved if they can contribute and support the response. Gathering information to brief the central government may be a key role for them. However, the greater the significance of the incident, and the press and ministerial interest, the more the GLOs will be able to provide support and assistance.

They should be made aware of significant incidents in a liaison capacity and all plans should include a notification option to alert RED of DCLG which may involve the attendance of a member of their sub-national team members to the SCG.

In terms of response and co-ordination the new arrangements bring together the relevant local LRF/SCG members to carry out an area co-ordination function, known as a multi-LRF Response Co-ordinating Group (ResCG) (note—not to be confused with Recovery Co-ordinating Group).

This is based upon a variable geography which remains flexible and not set around regional boundaries as before. It is obvious that civil emergencies do transcend or exceed fixed regional boundaries. It is also envisaged that the new ResCG will meet 'virtually' using teleconferencing and/or collaborating using a secure web-based National Resilience Extranet sponsored by the Cabinet Office.

Although the Regional Civil Contingencies Committee (RCCC) is no longer active the roles and responsibilities in the following list were assigned to them. For the EPO the list remains a relevant summary of what regional and central government should be able to deliver and provide to the LRF and SCG.

- Collating and maintaining a strategic picture of the evolving situation within the region, with particular, but not exclusive, focus on consequence management and recovery issues.

- Assessing whether there are any issues that cannot be resolved at local level.

- Facilitating mutual aid arrangements within the region and, where necessary, between regions to resolve such issues.

- Ensuring an effective flow of communication between local, regional and national levels, including the co-ordination of reports to the national level on the response and recovery effort.

- Raising, to a national level, any issues that cannot be resolved at local and regional level.

- Ensuring the national input to response and recovery is co-ordinated with the local and regional efforts.

- Guiding the deployment of scarce resources across the region by identifying regional priorities.

- Providing, where appropriate, a regional spokesperson.

One important issue must be made clear and that is the relationship between the chief officers of police and sub-national co-ordination function. As we have seen the emergency response is driven locally under the general co-ordination of the police with the delegated authority of the Chief Constable who holds responsibility for policing in each police force area. This raises the question of who is in charge of an area or regional emergency. The answer is that the individual chief police officers retain responsibility and authority in their jurisdiction but liaise closely with each other using the sub-national arrangements to act as a co-ordinating instrument. The ResCG will hold no additional authority or direction over chief police officers.

The ResCG will not interfere with local command and control arrangements, unless specifically empowered to do so by Emergency Regulations giving emergency powers under Part 2 of the CCA. The role of the ResCG is to add value to the response, usually where there is more than one SCG operating and there is a need to co-ordinate.

Therefore the CCA created a structure which has been revised but is intended and designed to mobilise the combined resources of the nation in support of the local response to any scale of event.

KEY POINT

Emergency Powers

The CCA 2004 updated the Emergency Powers Act 1920. Only in extreme circumstances will emergency powers be invoked by the Government. It involves the making of temporary legislation to apply across the UK or to any of the English regions or devolved administrations under the control of a Regional Nominated Co-ordinator or, in the case of devolved administrations, an Emergency Co-ordinator.

Lead Government Departments

In terms of co-ordination beyond the sub-national level there may be cases where the nature and size of event requires central government support. We have seen that the UK CONOPS Cabinet Office publication outlines the situations in which the government respond to emergencies based around definitions of Significant—Level 1 Incidents, Serious—Level 2 Incidents and Catastrophic—Level 3 Incidents. It must be emphasised that this function is not intended to take away the main focus of the response which will always remain local, but it is rather to add support and assistance in delivering the most effective means of managing the incident.

The Government has created a list of Lead Government Departments (LGDs) to oversee this co-ordination function depending on the nature of the emergency. By default the Civil Contingencies Secretariat (CCS) will facilitate the activation of the appropriate LGD or indeed take the lead themselves in certain cases. The current list containing the main LGDs is shown on the Cabinet Office website.

TASK 5.9

For the following incidents which would be the LGD for response and recovery and the local co-ordination lead?

1. Outbreak of smallpox

2. Civil nuclear accident

> 3. Falling satellite
>
> 4. Reservoir (dam) breach
>
> 5. US Military aircraft crash
>
> Research the relevant information.

The process of invoking central government support and/or co-ordination will normally route through the DCLG emergency out of hours arrangements. All LRF/SCG activation arrangements should have the relevant contact details in their plans.

In some cases of national emergency, or indeed where a number of LGDs are operating, the government may convene their crisis management facility known as COBR or Cabinet Office Briefing Room. You may see the term COBRA—the A stands for room A. That committee will be chaired by the Prime Minister, Home Secretary or a senior government minister. Within COBR will sit the National Security Council (NSC) for issues related to threats, hazards, resilience and contingencies. If the situation is terrorist related this group will be the Security Group (Counter Terrorism) and the response will be co-ordinated by the Home Office. An Intelligence Cell will support the Security Group if it is operating. In all cases, if COBR is operating a Situation Cell will be constantly monitoring the incident and co-ordination and preparing periodically a Common Recognised Information Picture or CRIP. CRIP is essentially a military import and a term gaining more use but simply means a situation report or 'sit rep'. The CRIP is prepared to an agreed format and circulated to key co-ordinating agencies.

The format can be different but essentially should include:

1. An introduction—including title of operation, security classification, date and time.
2. The location—description of area affected.
3. Current situation—an analysis of key events and implications.
4. Strategic aim and objectives.
5. Key decisions.
6. Co-ordination arrangements in place or planned.
7. Resource issues.
8. Communication issues—media state and 'lines to take'.

This is then updated periodically as determined appropriate. As the CRIP is added to the font ink may change colour or some other indication may be given to show there is new added material. This saves having to read the whole paper each time one is published.

Within that national group will sit key stakeholders and LGD representatives. ACPO will usually be present representing the police service and have at their disposal the Police National Information Co-ordination Centre (PNICC) to assist in co-ordinating information and resources of the police nationally. This co-ordination function will cover such areas as major public disorder or national disasters where large scale police resources need to be moved around the country.

If the Government become involved in co-ordinating centrally they will also become responsible for the national communications strategy. This communications strategy will be co-ordinated with the local responders via the SCG and MBC. The National Co-ordination Centre (NCC) will be activated to drive national media communication. The Home Office may also take the lead in managing a government media centre to deal with terrorist type incidents or a LGD for non-terrorist incidents. The NCC will co-ordinate media appearances of ministers.

Another function of the Cabinet Office is to take the lead with regard to warning and informing the public where local arrangements would prove insufficient or ineffective. The diagram shown at Figure 5.10 illustrates the framework of national emergency management and the role of the CCS.

The process of notification and activation follows from the illustration in Figure 5.10. Following activation of the SCG following a single incident the sub-national level of support and co-ordination may be invoked depending upon consultation with the SCG members and the government representative or officer (GLO) in attendance at the SCG. If the incident involves multiple SCGs in operation, for example following a flood, it is very likely that sub-national co-ordination will take place.

At that stage the CCS will be aware and there will be discussions as to the need to provide further support at national level. At this point it may only involve a

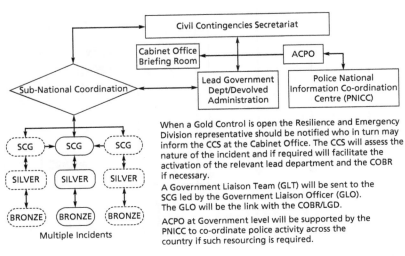

When a Gold Control is open the Resilience and Emergency Division representative should be notified who in turn may inform the CCS at the Cabinet Office. The CCS will assess the nature of the incident and if required will facilitate the activation of the relevant lead department and the COBR if necessary.

A Government Liaison Team (GLT) will be sent to the SCG led by the Government Liaison Officer (GLO). The GLO will be the link with the COBR/LGD.

ACPO at Government level will be supported by the PNICC to co-ordinate police activity across the country if such resourcing is required.

Figure 5.10 National Co-ordination

LGD leading the national support and co-ordination, however that may progress to full activation of COBR if that is seen as the most appropriate option. Each case is determined on a case-by-case basis and with so many variables it is almost impossible to give hard and fast rules as to how those decisions are made.

The speed at which each tier of management becomes operational too can vary a great deal but assuming that the incident is obviously a major event with national impact, the illustration in Figure 5.11 gives some indication as to the sequence and timescales to be expected.

Figure 5.11 consolidates the co-ordination process from incident to national level. It should be noted that the shaded area in the corner is representative of the management level at which most incidents are managed. As with most

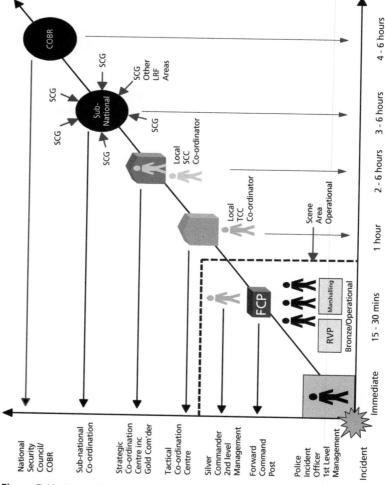

Figure 5.11 A seamless integration of management levels

aspects of emergency management only an expectation or an aspiration can be given as no two incidents are alike or will have the same demands.

KEY POINT

Be realistic in terms of structural set-up times and plan for them.

Managing Within the TCC and SCC/SCG—Recording and Sharing Information

All Control Centre(s), including the police co-ordination centres at all levels and across all response organisations will be pivotal in managing the multi-agency emergency response. Allied to that will be the control facilities operating outside Category 1 and 2 organisations in support of that function or operating to manage their own crisis. To that end capturing and recording information and processing that information is the fuel that drives the response engine. Wherever a control centre is operating there will have to be a system in place to record, assess and disseminate that information. All control centres will need a system to record and log messages, information and decisions. That can be a simple paper message form or a sophisticated computer based system. But remember that no matter how good the IT system is a paper backup is essential.

This area cannot be over-stated. All decision making must be recorded. This will require keeping a policy/decision log for each participant at a police co-ordination centre and indeed within separate controls. Recording is essential for all incoming and outgoing messages and indeed any verbal exchanges within those centres that are relevant. Documentation will be scrutinised at any follow-up inquiry and everything is subject to disclosure, which means all documents and computer records may be seized and used in evidence in some circumstances—assume it will be. Remember—'Preserve and Protect' all documentation. A clearly defined audit trail must exist. Paper flow and logging systems adopted within control centres must be tested and understood by all staff designated to perform roles within the room, which may also include advising other multi-agency co-ordination staff or those invited to attend—such as industry or business representatives. Any system used must be:

- Reliable–electronic systems can fail and crash.
- Secure from external hacking—consider wi-fi security issues or poor security.
- Capable of identifying the inputter—accountable.
- Easy to use—little or no training required.

- Capable of reproduction into hard copy—no virtual data storage.

- Tamper proof—preventing malicious or mischievous acts.

The system can be electronic but must have a back-up in cases of IT failure. There are several systems on the market but whatever system is chosen it will only be as good as those who operate the system and are trained in its use.

A simple example of a paper message form is shown in Figure 5.12 together with instructions how to use it shown at Figure 5.13 and a paper flow chart shown at Figure 5.14 which again can be adapted to suit individual needs. Ideally it should be produced in pads and on self-carbonised paper. The suggested colours are white, blue and yellow which is the scheme used in the example.

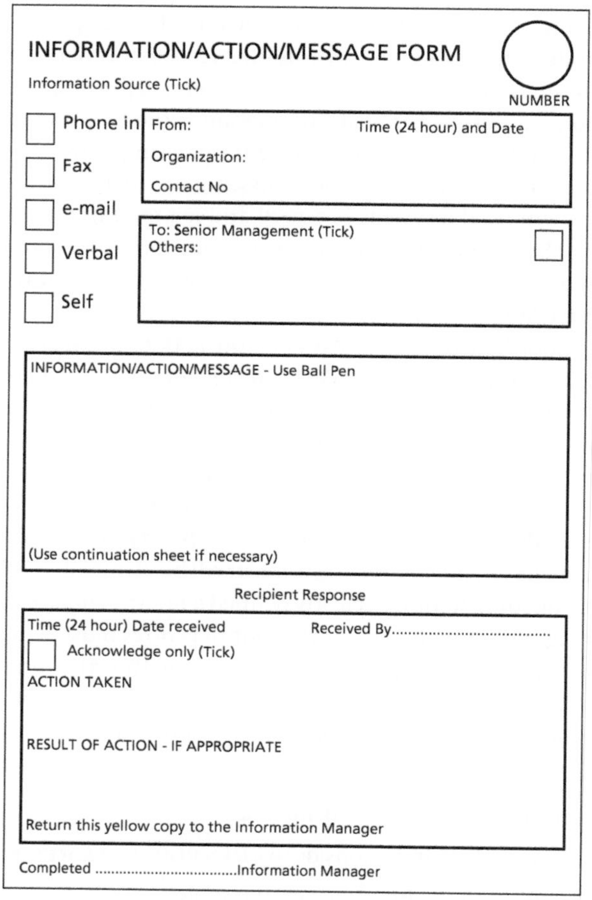

INFORMATION/ACTION/MESSAGE FORM

Information Source (Tick)

NUMBER

□ Phone in | From: | Time (24 hour) and Date

□ Fax | Organization:
Contact No

□ e-mail

□ Verbal | To: Senior Management (Tick)
Others: | □

□ Self

INFORMATION/ACTION/MESSAGE - Use Ball Pen

(Use continuation sheet if necessary)

Recipient Response

Time (24 hour) Date received   Received By.......................................
□ Acknowledge only (Tick)
ACTION TAKEN

RESULT OF ACTION - IF APPROPRIATE

Return this yellow copy to the Information Manager

Completed ....Information Manager

Figure 5.12 A generic message form

- INCOMING telephone or fax messages to the Emergency Control Centre for an action and/or passing information must be recorded on an INFORMATION FORM for central logging.

- OUTGOING messages for central logging must be recorded on an INFORMATION FORM.

- INTERNAL communication need only be recorded on the INFORMATION FORM if the information is required OR necessary for central logging.

- The message must be completed accurately and contain sufficient detail to inform the recipient exactly what is required, or what information is being passed on. One action or piece of information - one form, please.

- Complete the three copies; BLUE, YELLOW and WHITE, they are self-carbonated.

- All three copies will be taken to the INFORMATION MANAGER. The Information Manager will check that the form is fully and correctly completed. A unique number will then be issued by the Information Manager from a simple matrix of numbers.

- The BLUE form will be immediately returned initialled and endorsed by the Information Manager, to the originating organization or person. The BLUE form will be retained by the organization themselves which will act as a receipt.

- The YELLOW form, duly endorsed, by both the originating organization or person and Information Manager, will be passed to the relevant recipient where there is a need to know the information contained in the information or to take appropriate action. This will be carried out by a clerk/runner.

- The Information Manager will pass the white copy to the senior management loggist for recording on the master log, who will then hold it in a General Pending tray.

  NOTE: If one message requires attention by more than one recipient, sufficient YELLOW photocopies will be made by the clerk/runner (YELLOW paper should be available).

- The recipient willl endorse and acknowledge the YELLOW copy and indicate what action has been taken. This will be entered as an 'ACTION' and initialled. The YELLOW copy must be returned to the Information Manager without unnecessary delay.

- The Information Manager will examine the YELLOW copy to ensure it has been actioned and pass it to the senior management loggist who will record any new information from it onto the master log.

- The senior management loggist will then attach the YELLOW copy to the white copy from the general pending tray and place both forms in a file dedicated to the originating organization.

Figure 5.13 Information management system instructions

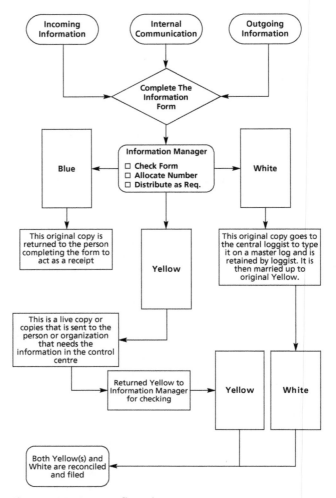

Figure 5.14 Message flow chart

It is often a good idea within a control facility to have eye-catching posters around the building emphasising the need to record information—with stark warnings of the consequences for failing to do so! Using phrases such as, 'Can you afford not to?' or 'Are you willing to risk it?'

These can be quite light-hearted but usually get the point across and are a simple nudge to keep the issue prominent.

What should be recorded?

What is committed to a messaging system for sharing is a matter of professional judgement for the individual and will be aided by appropriate training and familiarisation sessions. But it is better to encourage participants to input information than not to. It must always be remembered that in the context of an inquiry: 'if it is not written down it never happened'. It must also be remembered that many inquiries are years after the event.

TOP TIP

When running exercises or following a real event calculate the number of messages generated by each participant in a control or co-ordination centre. It is interesting how few are submitted. This information can be useful for future training and encouraging more data input.

External agencies using electronic information sharing systems must ensure that they are secure as far as reasonably possible and data protection issues are addressed. For example, personal information relating to the deceased and injured must be managed in compliance with the relevant regulations and guidance. In addition these systems must not undermine the role of the police in terms of the investigation, acting on behalf of the coroner or where circumstances direct the use of police family liaison officers (FLOs) and social service crisis support teams, who will be working closely with families affected by the incident.

If attending a police co-ordination centre message management systems will (or should) be in place for everyone to use. Although the police cannot force anyone to support or commit to such a system of recording messages or information it must be remembered that it will not be the police who are stood up in court or public inquiry if someone failed to record vital information...it will be the person who failed!

For those invited to attend such a centre there is no reason not to use their own logging system but critical information can be lost or not brought to the attention of the SCG if the in-house system is not used.

TASK 5.10

List five reasons why recording information within a control centre is good practice.

TASK 5.11

Using the format and information just discusded in this section—can you think of a paper format and prepare a system that would be better suited to your organisation?

Incident management—recording information

Recording information is a vital part of incident management for many reasons—typically this activity is referred to as the 'log'. Everyone with a decision making role must log information, either individually or by making use of a trained loggist—or a combination of both.

What is a log?

A definition of a log is given as an 'official record of events' (*Oxford English Dictionary*), which was historically associated with ships and aeroplanes but can be now extended to describe any permanent (written) record of information that may be later required to examine or review a set of circumstances or events for official purposes which may include a judicial inquiry or for de-brief purposes.

Note that the word 'written' is in brackets—we now have to accept that many records are generated by computer and as long as those records and data can be authenticated and stored securely and permanently they are becoming an accepted means of recording information. However, caution must be exercised when using computers, firstly to ensure that the inputter of the information or 'loggist' can be easily identified and secondly, remember computers break down!

A log can be further distinguished from other records too in that the nature of a log is that information is recorded at the time (or very soon after)—as the currency of the log will diminish rapidly as the time between the event and record increases. The reason being that human recollection falls away quickly and is subject to influences and biases that we may be unintentionally unaware of. The sooner a log entry is made the more accurate the detail is accepted to be.

A loggist can therefore be described as the person charged with keeping such a record. In practice this role can be wide ranging from taking instruction from a Principal (a person who needs recording support) to recording communications from a variety of sources. The loggist is not merely a person with a notepad and pen. They should understand the nature of a log as part of a much bigger process of information recording and gathering.

Who needs to log?

In effect within an organisation where logging is required everyone who has a decision making role within the incident response should keep a log. That can range from the person on-call, 'in the field' or up to the highest level of strategic management at organisational level to national support and co-ordination.

In reality, it is often impractical for such a decision maker to be able to keep accurate records without the help of a loggist.

Why do we need to log during an incident?

The Civil Contingency Act 2004 reinforces the need to keep logs for both learning and inquiry purposes in the *Emergency Response and Recovery Guidance.*

4.2 Levels of Command, Control and Co-ordination

...

4.2.9 These discussions, [in the SCG], including both decisions taken and not taken or deferred must be logged for future scrutiny.

...

4.6 Identifying and learning lessons

4.6.1 In order to facilitate operational debriefing and to provide evidence for inquiries (whether judicial, public, technical, inquest or of some other form), it is essential to keep records. Single-agency and inter-agency debriefing processes should aim to capture information while memories are fresh.

4.6.2 A comprehensive record should be kept of all events, decisions, reasoning behind key decisions and actions taken. Each organisation should maintain its own records. It is important that a nominated information manager be responsible for overseeing the keeping and storage of the records and files created during the response, and also for assuring the retention of those that existed before the emergency occurred. All document destruction under routine housekeeping arrangements should be suspended. All electronic records should be copied directly to non-volatile media.

(CCA 2004 Guidance, *Emergency Response and Recovery,* Version 3, 2010)

All organisations involved in emergency response or a business continuity response should keep records as a matter of routine. All Category 1 responders have a responsibility to record how they respond to an incident. Many organisations will do this by recording at operational, tactical and strategic response levels. Records must be robust and capable of standing up to scrutiny at any post-event inquiry. By recording information, decisions and actions organisations also protect themselves in terms of their legal obligations, duties and requirements and in so doing manage their reputation.

Why is it important to log?

The incident log can be used in a variety of ways to support the management of the incident and any post event inquiry or debrief. The information recorded in the log can be used for:

- Securing evidence for any inquiry or investigation.
- Enhancing management effectiveness.
- To justify decisions.
- To rationalise decisions.
- To justify actions.
- To populate internal and multi-agency reports such as Sit-Reps (Situation Reports) or Common Recognised Information Picture (CRIP).
- To assist handovers when changing shift.
- To brief colleagues and partners.
- To identify lessons learnt.
- To defend organisational and personal reputation.
- Protection against corporate and personal litigation.
- Protection against internal disciplinary action.
- Promoting openness and accountability.
- Demonstrating professionalism.
- Meeting the expectations of other partners as a Category 1 responder.

By recording what was done the loggist is contributing towards the overall record, and indeed the overall success of an organisation's response. If there is no record, there is no proof and the often used phase—'if it is not written down it never happened'—usually applies.

Is a log evidence?

Yes, in law evidence is information drawn in a judicial forum from personal testimony (what was perceived first hand by an individual through their senses or expert opinion), an authenticated document (including a log) or material object (an exhibit).

The accepted rules of logging are designed to reflect the standards required of a document produced in evidence. Essentially what has to be produced is a document that will stand up to scrutiny. Accuracy and integrity are vital tests to be applied and satisfied for any log.

Many organisations produce evidence regularly in the context of enforcement and the prosecution of offenders. The loggist however, is not required to understand the rigorous procedures and requirements that an enforcement officer does when operating under the strict guidance under the Police and Criminal Evidence Act 1984 (PACE). However, the loggist must appreciate the importance of the log in terms of its potential to affect outcomes in legal proceedings and the role cannot be taken lightly.

Sit-reps and CRIP

Sit-reps or situation reports are simply summaries of events so far in incident management. They enable a quick situational awareness to be achieved without going through all the fine detail. The timing and content will be for local or organisational agreement based upon the key information needed.

A CRIP or Common Recognised Information Picture is a military import. It serves the same purpose as a sit-rep but tends to contain more information and builds as a single document whereas sit-reps are numbered in chronological order. A CRIP will contain additions which will be distinguished from previous updates often by different coloured inks, different font, underlining or bold text. The format of the CRIP is again agreed locally.

Working with partners

All Category 1 and 2 responders as described in the CCA have obligations to share information, collaborate, consult with other responders and disclose information for building resilience. Being able to integrate fully into a shared incident management process is key for all emergency responders from any background to ensure the most efficient response procedures possible. This extends to any organisation that wishes to harmonise their management approach with established emergency responders.

When multi-agency emergency response co-ordination is invoked it is imperative that all affected organisations can contribute and support that response. The loggist has a role to play here. The loggist, through the process of efficient information recording, will assist in making a contribution to that process by presenting information and sharing information across many agencies—in the form of Sit-Reps, action recording and communicating information.

Apart from operating within any Control Room, a loggist may find they are assisting their Principal within that multi-agency co-ordination environment if they are required or requested to attend one. This could be at a multi-agency Tactical (Silver) Co-ordination Centre (TCC) or a multi-agency Strategic (Gold) Co-ordination Centre (SCC). This duty may also extend to assisting a Principal in a telephone/video conference situation at a sub-national level of co-ordination or perhaps at national level within an LCG.

Whatever, the venue the principles of effective logging remain the same and equally important.

To that end—all partner agencies in that multi-agency response will operate to the same exacting standards of information recording and use the same terminology and methodology as those advocated here. The loggist may within a multi-agency co-ordination centre environment be required to contribute information from a log into a wider multi-agency information management process, which will be described later.

Starting the log

Initial call out—beginning the recording process—'Incident log'

An incident will often start with a telephone call or pager alert to a person on-call. This is the point at which, for that individual and organisation, the incident begins.

That person must start recording information from that point. The information should be recorded contemporaneously (at that time) or as soon as possible after the call including:

- the exact time of the call;
- caller details including their full name and job title;
- call back number;
- details of the incident;
- any instructions, decisions or advice you offer to them.

In an on-call situation the on-call person should have a blank Incident Log Book or log sheet to begin recording information. If that is not possible, a sheet of paper or notebook will suffice but it must be retained for later inspection if required. This temporary log book should be referred to as soon as possible in the formal incident log book. This ensures that its existence is acknowledged and recorded and indeed formally referenced by a number—in much the same way as an exhibit e.g. BJD [person's initials] 1. For example, a subsequent entry in the incident log book may read...'12/03/12. 0645 – 0848 initial incident logging completed in BJD1.' In addition, if strategic or policy decisions were made these may need to be transferred into a Decision Log Book later.

This incident log will be continued by that person and retained as this forms part of the overall incident log. The on-call person may then direct another person (a loggist) to take over this task at a convenient point. If an incident log has been started this can be continued seamlessly. If not an incident log must be started.

Bear in mind that many incident logs may be running in parallel by different people at different locations. It is the co-ordination of the incident that will bring together the information from those logs into a coherent sit-rep.

Using digital recordings

A digital audio recording can be made at this early stage but this will have to be transcribed and authenticated by the maker in due course. The recording itself will need to be preserved and not deleted.

Attending a scene—incident log and/or using an operational loggist

Even as a senior manager or officer it is not uncommon to be called to the scene of an incident initially. In this case an incident log can be started in a similar way to being called out. Alternatively, the person attending the scene may choose another person to act as a scribe or operational loggist. Again, using an incident log book or log sheet is the best option but a notebook will suffice. In this case the Principal, the decision maker, will indicate and advise the loggist what they should record for them. Recording information at a scene is vital as it informs the possible escalation of the incident and contains key early decision making. It is usually these early stage decisions that attract most scrutiny. It is also important to record health and safety advice provided to operational staff. Issues to record may include:

- those already present or required to attend at the scene;
- initial appraisal of the scene;
- the exact time of attending and leaving;
- any instructions, decisions or advice you offered and to whom;
- weather conditions.

The control room environment incident log

The information in this section applies to any Control Room environment.

Within a control room environment the individual incident log can be continued or begun for those responding from on-call or from a scene.

This environment is one where the loggist will be most active. The incident log at operational or tactical level (including temporary logs) can contain narrative relating to decision making and actions. If strategic or policy decisions are being made these should be recorded in a separate book used only for that purpose—the Decision/Policy Log Book. There can only be one strategic or policy log for an organisation managing an incident. There cannot be multiple policies or strategic decision-making originating from different locations or persons, as they will create confusion and ambiguity.

An incident log at operational and tactical level will record:

1. Incoming information to the Principal.
2. Outgoing information from the Principal.
3. Actions—direction/instructions to do something and follow up—tracking.
4. Decision making, including rationale if operational or tactical. Only strategic decision making will be later transferred to a decision log.

Remember—an incident log at strategic level will not include decision making within it. This will be contained in a separate policy or strategic decision log. This will be retained by the designated strategic decision maker who may in fact be called into a multi-agency SCC. In which case the policy/decision making log goes with them and their loggist with their incident log.

As already mentioned, it is possible that several incident logs may be operating at once, even in one location if several managers are managing an incident at various management levels or locations, such as operational, tactical or strategic. This can be confusing overall in terms of creating a situation report (Sit-Rep) or a Common Recognised Information Picture (CRIP). In this situation a Summary Log should be produced. This is a management aid only—the incident logs are of evidential value.

How is this summary log done? Every Control Room will have either one or a combination of:

1. 'time-outs';

2. structured meetings; or

3. an message/information management system.

1. Dynamic 'time-outs' present an opportunity to take stock and update the situation from inputs from the incident logs. This simply means someone standing up and calling for a very short round the room update. This is very useful in very fast moving situations. This can be transcribed onto a board, paper summary or e-mail to be circulated—this is a sit-rep. This can be combined from other locations managing the incident to create an overall incident sit-rep.

The diagram at Figure 5.15 shows multiple logs feeding into one control room which can produce local sit-reps and in turn is feeding into a central control to prepare an overall sit-rep or CRIP. The hierarchy of control rooms may fit within the multi-agency co-ordination centres, e.g. tactical and strategic or individual organisational management structures or a combination of both where they integrate.

2. Structured meetings can be minuted but minutes are not logs. Minutes are very brief summaries of discussion and any proposed actions. They in turn create a local sit-rep too. Actions and decisions coming from both time-outs and meetings must be reflected later in individual incident logs and decision making logs—minutes must not be relied upon to be accurate.

3. Message/information management systems are the most sophisticated management aid and sit-rep tool. They are usually found in multi-agency TCCs or SCCs where the number of agencies and support staff can be very large. Having a robust system to filter and process so much data is the only viable means of keeping track of the situation and not missing vital information. These systems are there to assist in

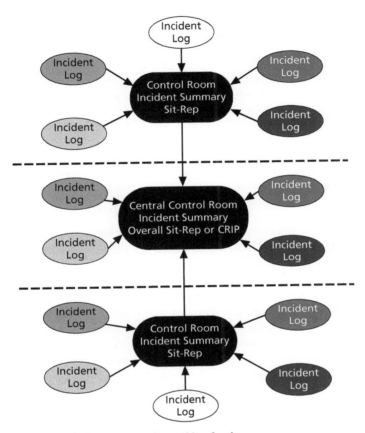

Figure 5.15 Multiple co-ordinated log feeds

information sharing across agencies/departments and organisations and ensuring as far as possible that conflict in operational priorities are minimised. Systems can vary a great deal. They can be paper based or electronic, centred on specialist software and internal (restricted) e-mail arrangements.

The loggist, who may have to operate in such an environment should familiarise themselves with the local arrangements. This is often possible and accessed through the LRF.

What else should the loggist keep?

In a Control Room setting the loggist should also consider keeping the following box files. All those files mentioned will be required to be kept in a multi-agency control room but in a single agency room another person may be allocated that work acting as a single point of reference. In a multi-agency environment however it is important to seize and control copies of these documents as they form part of and inform your own organisational log.

1. Media—any media statements that have been released.

2. Paper copies referenced in the incident log—any printed material which could include e-mail copies, temporary logs or indeed anything which is relevant to the incident.

3. All sit-reps and CRIPs.

4. Minutes of meetings.

5. Copies of messages used in a multi-agency message management system—if operating.

6. Previous logs.

All the listed documents support the content of the log.

It should be noted that if the loggist station (see Figure 5.16) is being left unattended for long periods without supervision all logging material should be secured. In addition any computer left logged on is open to tampering and as such leaving a computer like this is often a disciplinary issue for many organisations.

This role of overall administration of information as described may be assigned to a person designated as Incident Co-ordination Centre Manager, Control Room Manager, Control Room Co-ordinator or a similar title with general administrative responsibilities rather than a loggist, although the loggist term is widespread for a range of roles in control rooms.

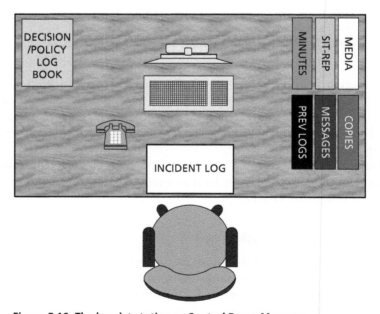

Figure 5.16 The loggist station or Control Room Manager

The sample incident log

Incident log book format is flexible and should be configured for individual organisational use—but must contain some basic information. The Incident Log Book will have a cover or front sheet (see Figure 5.17)—ideally in card and permanently bound (which avoids tampering). Each page must be numbered, for example 'Page 1 of 2' to account for each page (see Figure 5.18). The log should be A4 in size.

The inner front cover can contain instructions or rules for completing the log—a useful aide memoire.

The log sheet should be lined to fit one line of written text easily. Both sides of the paper should be used.

A minimum of three columns are required.

1. Date/time (24 hr)

2. Log Entry

3. Action taken

What makes a loggist?

A loggist requires training to carry out the role. Training should include opportunities to practise the skills and understand the 'rules' of logging. Specific courses are available to deliver those skills.

INCIDENT LOG BOOK FRONT SHEET		
INCIDENT:		
LOG STARTED:	TIME:	DATE:
ORGANISATION:	OPENED BY:	LOGGIST:
LOG NUMBER: OF:		THIS LOG CONTAINS 50 PAGES.

Figure 5.17 Example Incident Log Front Sheet

DATE/TIME 24 HR	LOG ENTRY	ACTION TAKEN
		PAGE 1 OF 50

Figure 5.18 Example Incident Log Sheet

There is no doubt that the more practice the loggist gets in training or exercising the better they will perform and, perhaps as importantly, gain confidence. As real events are so rare, regular updates and practice are essential. Becoming involved in exercises is a valuable opportunity to test and hone skills in a safe environment.

Logging skills require a person to be able to:

1. write clearly;

2. remain focused and concentrate;

3. understand and apply the logging 'rules';

4. challenge ambiguity;

5. inderstand any technology/programs being used in logging.

A loggist is *not* required to:

1. understand command skills or management issues;

2. offer opinion;

3. log for multiple Principals at once;

4. anticipate solutions;

5. contradict or influence their Principal;

6. be a decision maker;

7. analyse and summarise command discussion;

8. understand the laws of evidence.

How can a Principal assist the loggist?

The Principal is the person the loggist is dedicated to during the logging period. A Principal may not have met the loggist before and an introduction should take place so the loggist understands exactly what is required of them.

The Principal should reassure the loggist and assume a rapport to assist communication. Reassurance may consist of a reminder that the log is ultimately the Principal's responsibility, as are the contents.

Logging is an intense activity. Taking regular breaks is essential to remain alert and focused. The Principal should be mindful of this and insist on regular rest periods for the loggist where possible.

'Rules' of logging

Writing in a log should conform to some basic rules. The rules are in place to ensure a consistent looking document which is clear to read, easily referred to and is less susceptible to unauthorised amendments or changing. A log should be Clear, Intelligible and Accurate, CIA.

In all cases an incident log should be headed by the incident name, the Principal's name, the date and the name of the loggist. Black ink should be used as it aids copying later.

Each entry should be numbered in order in ascending numbers to assist later referencing, followed by the exact time in the 24-hr clock in chronological order. The person taking over the log should continue this numerical order and chronology throughout.

The mnemonic 'No ELBOW' is a useful way to remember the key rules in written log keeping.

No **E**rasures

No **L**eaves (pages) must be torn out

No **B**lanks spaces—rule them through

No **O**verwriting

No **W**riting outside the lined margins (unless it is date, time or initials)

When one loggist is finished with the log a line should be drawn across the page to indicate that change and the loggist must sign and date on the line. It is useful at this time to have the Principal endorse the log as a true record and for them to sign it. If they later disagree with the content the loggist may not be available to make the alterations which are a better option than having to do it themselves or asking another person to do it.

If however, alterations have to be made they can be made and initialled by the Principal but in doing so they must not obscure any existing text. If necessary an additional entry can be made to explain the change.

The next space allows for the narrative. Detail should be factual only. Entries should be made contemporaneously if possible recording as much direct speech as possible, in particular where questions and answers are concerned. If direct speech is recorded that should be placed in 'parenthesis'. If the log is not made contemporaneously it should be made as soon as reasonably practicable after.

Incoming and outgoing telephone/radio communication should be recorded as near verbatim as possible. Any documents containing relevant information can also be recorded in the log in summary form stating who it came from but the original document must be kept and referenced in the log, for example, 'e-mail requesting occupants details.... Ref A1, which should be written on the document and kept safely as an exhibit'. Keeping these printouts in a separate folder.

It is not expected that a loggist will record verbatim a spontaneous conversation of their Principal or be responsible for logging an entire room and several Principals. This is unrealistic. Recording verbatim is a highly skilled task for those with outstanding shorthand skills, and is a skill beyond most people. The Principal should make it clear to the loggist from the outset what they want recording and they should use suitably short concise precise terms that can be written in long hand (or shorthand, which is later written up and authenticated by the maker) so accuracy can be maintained.

It is for the Principal to decide what is relevant and what they want recording for log purposes—this is not the task of the loggist. Allowing a loggist to attempt to record an ongoing conversation in real time, to capture everything said, can lead to omissions, poor interpretation and even stress for the loggist. It could also lead to a line of questioning later in which the loggist's accuracy may be attacked.

If using an operational or tactical log—decision making can be recorded in the narrative of a general log or notebook. If it is a policy or strategy a decision log in a separate book must be used.

Figure 5.19 illustrates an Incident Log extract. The log has has five major errors. Can you spot them? (Answers at the end of the chapter.)

Audio recorded information

As already mentioned, personal voice recording is an option which presents some advantages, in particular when working from a scene or being called out when writing is not an option. However, the integrity of the recording must be maintained, in that it cannot be deleted. It will also need to be transcribed and authenticated by the person making it as a true and accurate record. Audio recording can be challenged in that it can be edited or even added to—such accusations must be borne in mind in relation to the

Date / Time Hrs	Log Entry Information [log begins for Jeff Lucas, loggist Bradley Dalton]	Action
30/2/12	Incident log commenced for Jeff Lucas EA Control @ Cricklewood relating to severe flood warning on River	
0615	Derwent and Twin Pines park. Incident site visited by Jeff Lucas EA at 0515 hrs on-call and site being	
	reinforced by local sandbagging with Local Authority operations manager Susan Keene on site.	
	Police in attendance managing traffic and warning residents. On-call log commenced by Jeff and referenced	Log JL 1 into file
	as JL 1	
0625	Information from police that police SCC is being opened at 0700 to cater for community impact and	Mr Smith Informed 0635
	possible local evacuation Simon Smith EA will be attending Police FCC SCC.	
0640	Information from site – Jeremy Tong EA that support is needed upstream at Rising Bridge – overtopping.	Inform Police
0710	Arrive SCC at police headquarters Staunton with Simon Smyth Smith 'BD'	Inform EA Control
0714	Briefing by Insp Jones (written sheet) Ref SS1. To fax to EA Control Room and police sit-rep filed	Faxed confirm 0720
0735	From Tim Elliot EA Control Cricklewood that peak levels due in 3 hours on Derwent. Will affect all flood	SCC message no.37
	risk areas.	
0810	First SCG with Chair ACC Hardwood. Evacuation called in all Twin Pines flood risk areas. Local Authority	Inform EA Control
	managing. No actions on EA. Confirmed to SCG all flood risk warnings went out at 0510	Minutes filed
0855	Handover from Jeff Lucas to Jenny Finch EA and loggist Tom Simmons EA. Returning to EA Control at	
	Cricklewood.	
0910	Handover complete to Jenny Finch EA – by Jeff Lucas ....signed by Jeff Lucas. Loggist Tom Simmons	Handover logged
0910	Assume log for Jenny Finch – Tom Simmons (Loggist) Jenny Finch agreed press release for radio / TV bulletins – copy to	
	EA Control. Filed.	
0445	Report from EA Control – EA member of staff into the water at Rising Bridge – road collapse. Fire service in attendance.	SCC message no 43
	Report of missing person.	
0955	Media seeking information on missing person – EA press statement completed by JF and released – ref JF I and filed	SCC message no 54
1010	Residents at Twin Pines complaining that EA warnings were too late and MP / Councillor Ashton asking for explanation. JF	
	issuing response via media. Ref JF 2 filed. JF press conf.	SCC message no 61
1020	EA operative recovered from water at Rising Bridge and en route to hospital. Not serious. Not wearing life belt. Media	
	aware from scene.	SCC message no 66

Figure 5.19 Incident log extract (five errors to spot)

handling of such material. For example, keeping it secured and in neutral hands until it is required.

How to record decisions

Decision making narrative can be more flexible when it comes to content. It is more flexible in that the narrative is more descriptive and explanatory. It will refer to rationale or thought processes in assessing information. It could be argued that such an approach may vary from person to person based upon their experience—this is true. But it is sufficient to demonstrate that the actions decided upon were reasonable and proportionate in the circumstances based upon the best available information at *that* time. In reality that decision may be fatally flawed because a crucial piece of information was missing, but decisions have to be made regardless, without the benefit of 20/20 hindsight.

The decision is recorded with exact time and date and should include the following considerations:

1. The issue, task or problem being addressed.
2. What information is available?
3. What is the source of the information—is it reliable?
4. Who was consulted?
5. The rationale for taking that course of action. Anticipatory assessment based upon previous experience may be used.
6. Is it a joint decision—if not, who else contributed?
7. Outline the possible options, risk assessments (often dynamic) and pros and cons.
8. The actions resulting from that decision.

The actions or conclusion (if no action) resulting from that decision will appear as outgoing information in the general log. In other words—strategic and/or policy decisions should appear in a decision log as separate from the general log. Practically, if strategic decisions are taken in the field or other situation in which a decision log cannot be completed, decisions should be recorded as soon as possible in the appropriate document. They should be timed when the entry was made but referring to the time the decision was taken and referring to any document that contains any relevant information relating to that decision making process. For example, from a notebook used prior to formally recording the decision—the notebook can be referenced by assigning it a number, e.g. BJD1 (as an exhibit).

See later for issues around decision making.

What is an 'action'?

Any action or action request is simply an instruction. It is asking someone to do something or to acknowledge some information. It must be precise in terms of who it is directed to, the time, what is required and a timescale for response (if that is required by the person initiating the action).

Can a loggist question what they are required to write?

Generally, no—the log belongs to the Principal. It is their words, verbatim or summarised, which the Principal should endorse as accurate. However, where ambiguity occurs as to meaning, acronyms or spelling, the loggist should seek clarification.

Where the loggist is recording incoming or outgoing information or actions the content will be explicit with no room for interpretation.

Some logging tasks will require recording very sensitive information. Should the loggist separate that into another document or use different ink?

No—the loggist should record information as directed or presented. Firstly, the loggist will probably not be aware what is sensitive or not and should not be put in that position to make that decision. Secondly, analysing what is and is not sensitive will come later when disclosure may become an issue at a formal inquiry, debrief or investigation. Often Freedom of Information (FOI) requests ask for logs of incidents. If disclosure becomes an issue the log content will be the subject of intense legal and policy scrutiny by experts. Any redaction (editing of text) will be their responsibility not the loggist.

Will a loggist have to give evidence at a court?

Potentially yes. The integrity of a log is sometimes questioned to ensure the information is correct, accurate, made in good time and has not been 'tampered' with. Inquiry forums where a loggist may have to attend could include not only criminal courts, but formal debriefs, public inquiries, disciplinary hearings and coroners' courts.

The information required of a loggist is usually procedural, verification or for confirmation purposes only and not the content.

Finishing the log/handing over

A point will come when the logging period for the loggist is complete but the incident is still running.

To sign-off a log the loggist will draw a line across the page and sign it. The loggist will invite the Principal to review the log and sign it—if time allows. However, this can be delayed but it is imperative that the Principal signs the log as a true record. There is a caveat here. A log can only be signed on the basis that the loggist and the Principal have produced it in good faith, to the best of their knowledge and skill and have not wilfully misled or included (or omitted) anything that they know to be untrue, false or misleading. There is no perfect log.

The loggist taking over should, where possible, be briefed by the previous loggist. This may not always be possible but the Principal should brief the new loggist every time.

At the conclusion of the incident or the shutting down of the Control Room and/or multi-agency co-ordination centre the loggist should ensure that the logs produced by them are properly signed by the Principal(s). All logs, general and decision logs should be secured and taken possession of. This will include all other documents which have been referenced in any log, this could be a written message, copy e-mail or other document mentioned in the log.

Multi-agency co-ordination centres will be subject of a rigorous document recovery process for systems operating within that facility, however, individual logs remain the property of that organisation and will stay with that organisation until or if they are required to be disclosed in any subsequent inquiry or judicial review.

Prior to that, the loggist may become part of a Document Recovery Team initiated by the organisation to locate, secure, list and archive every relevant document relating to the incident.

Documents are then secured under lock and key, with only the Incident document list being available for general reference. Only supervised examination can take place of original documents.

TASK 5.12

Using the information about logging—prepare an information sheet you would include in an incident log—perhaps as a front inner cover.

Crisis Meetings

What is a crisis? The Cabinet Office agree a definition which states: 'a crisis is an inherently abnormal, unstable and complex situation that represents a threat to the strategic objectives, reputation or existence of an organisation'. There is no doubt that an emergency/major incident qualifies under that definition in some part at least.

We use the term crisis meeting here in the context that there is an incident running and meetings are being held to resolve issues and plan ahead dynamically. Meetings are the mainstay of effective emergency management communication. They will be convened to address a very wide spectrum of issues; from carrying out simple operational tasks to high level national issues with major implications within central government at COBR. They could be single agency, organisational, business or multi-agency. What all of these meetings will have in common, in particular in the emergency phase, is that they will be dynamic fast moving and put in place to respond to issues that could be classified as critical. Understanding the new dynamic of such meetings is important for the EPO and those who will take part.

Every control centre including police co-ordination centres will conduct meetings of key responders within the organisation and/or outside the organisation to agree response options, be it strategic, tactical or operational. Effectively chairing these meetings is vital to a successful outcome. At whatever level these meetings take place the same principles apply, whether Strategic or Tactical Co-ordinating Group meetings or operational meetings at an FCP or even a meeting within a business environment undergoing a crisis event. It should be borne in mind though that crisis meetings differ from the type of meeting that most people will be familiar with in the day-to-day work environment. These 'normal' meetings tend to be more relaxed consensual management meetings as opposed to dynamic fast moving crisis management meetings. That said, it does not mean that a crisis meeting goes forward without consensus but the crisis meeting requires firm structure and discipline. After all, the issues on the table will require quick decisions, often under stressful conditions with clearly defined aims and objectives within a group who may have never met before. In many cases information will also be limited and ambiguous.

So how is such a meeting started? The chair at the first meeting will introduce themselves and explain the purpose of the meeting. In the first instance agreement is required on the composition of the group. A draft set of terms of reference (TOR) will be agreed which will set out the aim of the group and the key objectives. This will set the framework and parameters for the meetings and the TOR should be given to all those taking part. The aim of the group is important as it sets the focus for the group followed by a set of agreed objectives which will engender buy in and ownership within the group. It also prevents any 'mission shift' or distraction from the main purpose. The aim should be very short and to the point; usually a single sentence avoiding 'ands'—more detail can be added by the objectives. The chair must also be clear about the management of the meetings, timing, how they will be run—basically the rules. Discipline needs to be maintained to ensure the meetings are on time and remain focused at all times.

What needs to be appreciated by all those attending any crisis meeting that has never met before is that there is a process of bedding in of the group or team, in particular in a multi-agency setting. The dynamics of the group can and will affect the effectiveness of any decision making. Participants who are strangers will take a little time to assess each other and develop a sense of their own position and 'status' within the group. This period can in fact be quite unproductive and stressful as participants come to terms with weighing-up the others, their rank or status, their expertise and knowledge.

They may have preconceived ideas or even stereotypes embedded in their mind which create obstacles to effective communication—indeed suspicion may emerge where a vested interest or organisational agenda is being pushed at the expense of objective thinking. Some participants who are unfamiliar with this type of gathering may feel a little intimidated. However, an experienced chairperson should be aware of the issues relating to team building and ensure the meeting runs smoothly. After initial bedding in the group will begin to gel and produce as participants become familiar with colleagues and the generally running of the meeting and understand what is expected. Once the group is formed it will continue to improve but as soon as new individuals are introduced there is usually a 'wobble' where participants assimilate the new member into the group before picking up the pace again.

Apart from the expected 'getting to know you' issues an interesting feature of multi-agency meetings is the coming together of different organisational cultures. This can have a significant effect, sometimes adversely, on decision making and is often overlooked, in particular by those who are not aware of this potential obstacle. Such interaction can result in conflict and tension as competing priorities and different agendas come together for co-ordination. Some organisations will see themselves as the 'experts'. Each organisation attending a meeting will bring with them a set of values and expectations of how 'business' will be done and if the meetings are police led or in police facilities for example it can be a daunting prospect for those not used to it. Blue light organisations tend to be more accustomed to crisis management and perhaps project a style that can be perceived as mildly intimidating and can prevent some of those present from being as participative as they would like to be. The result is a decision making process that can be stifled and inhibited. Group dynamics can play an important part in effective decision making and being aware of the potential pitfalls can offset or mitigate the effects.

Some groups, in order to preserve a sense of unity and conformity within the group will sacrifice their objectivity and criticism, often unconsciously. They will defend their own organisational 'position' at all costs as being part of the team.

This syndrome can relate to any group with common values, similar ethos and status but predominantly relates to highly cohesive groups with a strong identity such as uniformed disciplined services or a very strong bonding culture. In particular where there is a disciplined and well ordered hierarchy, where the tendency is to default to conformity. To that group should be added the police but although they should not be singled out, but simply acknowledge that it is they who generally occupy the chair when it comes to co-ordination. It must also be added at this point that group cohesion will not inevitably lead to adverse decision outcomes. The key to equality and effectiveness in decision making is to promote an environment of openness and honesty, allowing for the decenting views and embrace them as valuable checks and balances.

Seeking this openness however should not lead to a situation in which the decision making process becomes bogged down in protracted generalised consensus. Rather than acknowledging the potential human factors that can restrain open discourse and ensuring that all views have equal validity and are encouraged. This becomes even more relevant in the de-briefing process reviewed in Chapter 10. Leadership in this context is not about exerting pressure, brow beating, embarrassing and degrading a view. That style and approach will create a dangerous precedent and lead to poor decision making.

TASK 5.13

Research the term 'groupthink'. This has significant impact on group decision making.

Commentators and researchers have indeed claimed that group dynamics in decision making has been underestimated. Be aware and account for it!

Another tactic to avoid adverse group dynamics would be to loosen tightly cohesive groupings by promoting regular and structured multi-agency interaction. This is best achieved by joint training and exercising where organisations can begin to understand and appreciate the views of others. In that way inward looking and narrow decision making will diminish and become defused as relationships develop between organisations and agencies. Organisations, within the emergency planning community who continue to ignore or even acknowledge the importance of multi-agency working will become susceptible and vulnerable to adverse group dynamics as they become more isolated and marginalised. All organisations must feel confident and comfortable to be able to express their views and opinions that may not always concur with the group consensus in a multi-agency context. This is probably the strongest argument for the inclusion of key business and private partners in engaging together with the wider LRF community through training and exercising to develop resilience across their organisations. Those with a BCM, crisis or emergency management role will feel isolated, vulnerable and probably overwhelmed in a real event if they fail to develop and maintain those relationships.

Running Meetings

In terms of running meetings always ensure that they are minuted and if possible tape recorded. A common error with such meetings is that they are too long in session and too far apart. Regular meetings, say every 1–2 hours, which are short focused meetings of no more that 30 minutes are ideal.

The chair will initially bring to the table the latest CRIP or sit-rep. The chair will then need to address the following:

- Ask everyone present to give a short summary of issues currently affecting them, or requiring urgent action, including any other agencies if they are present, including the police.

- Establish common objectives. Address any conflicts and co-ordinate effort. Identify any actions—be explicit and identify where the action lies. Write it down on a board.

- What are the medium and longer term issues that can reasonably be foreseen? Try to anticipate—what provisions have to be made to address those issues? Resourcing is a key issue—management resilience.

- Ensure that media considerations are addressed and agree a media strategy—remember that the police will co-ordinate the media but you have a say how the media will be managed. How press releases, interviews and conferences will be approached. Be explicit as to the parameters as to your media requirements without compromising the police objectives. Push for an early press release.

Everyone attending the meeting should be aware of the meeting objective(s). Being aware of what is required will allow those attending to prepare and it will reduce time wasting on trying to agree what the meeting is about.

Stand up or 'bird table' meetings

Meetings at which the participants stand up are intended to keep the business focused and the meetings short. They emphasise the dynamism of the meeting having originated from a military style of battlefield briefings. Stand-up meetings are sometimes called 'bird table' meetings. Stand-up meetings should be no longer than 15–20 minutes long and everyone should stand (unless of course a person is unable to). Taking longer than 15–20 minutes will result in participants being uncomfortable and affecting the business. It is also useful to provide clipboards for those attending to allow them to take notes if that style of meeting is chosen. Stand-up meetings, it could be argued, are a poor substitute for having a strong chairperson who can focus the meeting avoiding irrelevant discussion and remain focused without relying on keeping the participants uncomfortable to speed things along. It is a matter for the chair and group consensus what style the meeting takes.

Resourcing Police Co-ordination Centres (External Agencies)

When the police open co-ordination centres there is an expectation that other agencies can fully support them—and therefore the multi-agency response. That also includes an obligation upon the police who may be required to position their own liaison officer in other control centres operated by other organisations and agencies. This is part of the overall co-ordination and liaison arrangements. The initial planning considerations are: Can that commitment be resourced over a sustained period? Have personnel been identified in the planning process? Have those people been trained? If operating a single TCC and SCC agencies may have to provide two representatives 24/7 as a minimum at each site—a significant undertaking.

The police will, as a matter of priority, set up a logistical cell in an SCC to manage their own staff and resourcing. Other responding agencies must do the same from their own support controls, not only to support the multi-agency response but for their own BCM.

For agencies attending police co-ordination centres it can be a daunting prospect and that can sometimes be overlooked by the co-ordination centre staff. Police staff must try to ensure that agencies attending are afforded full support. That will include providing them with appropriate parking and efficient and courteous reception arrangements. To have agency colleagues without parking, in particular when carrying equipment, or being kept waiting is unacceptable.

Agency colleagues require efficient reception and briefing procedures upon arrival and to be afforded comfortable surrounding within which to work. This also applies to any liaison officer or manager attending any other control centre, be it police or any other organisation.

Everyone attending a multi-agency co-ordination centre should be fully briefed or given a sit-rep or CRIP if that has been produced, as they arrive. The method used is a matter for local practice. This is a police responsibility if they are operating a multi-agency co-ordination centre. Methods of briefing may include:

1. Briefing sheets, sit-rep or CRIP handed to them upon arrival and registration.

2. Briefing by a designated 'briefing officer'.

3. Self briefing from a display board—either dry wipe or electronic.

Details of briefing methods should appear in the relevant centre 'User Guide'—see later.

KEY ISSUE

Effective briefing is vital to the success of a multi-agency co-ordination centre. It is probably the single issue most complained about by agency personnel.

Criminal Liability

Another important issue in particular for non-emergency response personnel, for example company representatives attending co-ordination centres, is an ever increasing concern relating to their potential criminal liability and therefore their ability to participate. Although this may sound strange, in many circumstances where there are fatalities, a company representative connected to the incident in a police co-ordination centre may feel or perceive themselves to be treated a little like a suspect or feeling not as included within the management process as they would expect. This can result from situations where the company representative is excluded from certain meetings or conversations seem a little 'guarded' with them. Why is this? In the early stages of an incident there may be potential issues related to criminal culpability, which will focus on the companies involved, for example a transport or industrial process. It could be argued that such companies may compromise the inquiry and/or incriminate themselves in any future proceedings. This has to be expected but can be managed.

Firstly, dealing with the issue of potentially compromising any inquiry, the priority in all cases is to save life and prevent further distress and injury to those involved. If using the knowledge and experience of a company representative to alleviate or reduce that injury or distress there is little reason to exclude them at all, indeed it would be difficult to defend.

In addition, being compromised will only result from issues relating to the cause of the incident resulting in the fatality, injury or other consequence, so avoiding comments or opinions on that subject should avoid any compromise. Addressing the consequences is the key and if the company representative feels at any time that they are being excluded they should challenge this and seek a clear explanation for that behaviour and make a note of what was said and by whom. On the other hand, can a company representative incriminate themselves?

The answer is potentially yes. It is possible that a company may be criminally culpable and anything said 'can be taken down and used in evidence', to coin a phrase; but again, if that is the case the company still has a responsibility to offer assistance to reduce the impact on those involved and indeed to be seen to be assisting. This could ultimately be critical to the company's survival after the incident notwithstanding that they may face criminal charges. Again, the key here is to avoid becoming involved in answering incriminating or compromising questions. They should focus on the here and now and managing consequences and avoid references to what caused the incident or any procedure leading to the incident. There are no fail-safe rules as to what can or cannot be said but a little foresight and common sense should be applied. There are specialist advisors and trainers who can assist in training company personnel on these issues. The key phrases to consider when pressed about a cause of an incident within an SCC or other centre may include such replies as:

- 'At this stage it is difficult to be certain what happened—it will become clear when a full investigation is carried out.'
- 'I cannot answer that because I don't know all the facts as yet.'
- 'I think anything said now would be speculation. We must now resolve this situation quickly.'

Any phrases of a similar type will avoid being drawn into guessing and speculation about the cause of the incident and so avoid being 'quoted' in later proceedings, or indeed by the press.

Potential prosecution for manslaughter, including breaches of Health and Safety legislation is now a real possibility for many senior managers and company directors and must be taken seriously. An unguarded comment, an opinion or a guess, even well-intentioned could be very damaging on many levels.

The comments made by Mr Tony Haywood following the BP oil spill in April 2010—in which 11 men died—which related to him 'getting his life back' certainly created great controversy and is a lesson in thinking through any comments carefully.

TOP TIP

Anyone required to attend a tactical or strategic multi-agency co-ordination centre must undergo basic familiarisation training. This can be facilitated by the local resilience forum.

TASK 5.14

Reflect on some of the issues that may face an industry representative attending a police co-ordination and write down what they are.

The Incident Room

In this section we will look at some issues related to setting up a viable incident or control room, specifically for those who are not one of the overall Category 1 or 2 responders. For those involved with the emergency services or industries that are subject to regulatory requirements they will almost certainly have a dedicated 'Incident Room', 'Emergency Room', 'Major Incident Room' or 'Emergency Control Centre'as a focal point for their emergency response. Whatever name is used and is deemed suitable to the organisation it is acceptable as long as it can be identified easily and is compatible within the overall multi-agency emergency response structure; review Chapter 3, Figure 3.3.

For our purposes and clarity in this section we will refer to incident room as the non-police single agency or organisational/business facility. Remember, of course, that the term 'control' is a generic term for any location where response is managed. The police will facilitate the tactical and strategic co-ordination centres, the TCCs and SCCs. All Category 1 responders should have adequate and efficient facilities which will, or should have been tested through exercises on many occasions. In *most* cases they will have evolved over time into quite sophisticated facilities. Note the use of emphasis on most. In many cases however, they leave a lot to be desired and in fact many organisations simply do not have any facilities, the private sector particularly preferring to use existing office space or worse still, they fail to understand the importance of having any control arrangements at all. There is little doubt that EPOs and Business Continuity Managers will be familiar with their own organisations' emergency facilities, so why is this subject of relevance to them?

EPOs and BC Managers will regularly become involved in exercises, debriefs and real incidents involving many organisations, large or small within the private, public or voluntary sectors and will have occasion to experience their Incident Rooms, or indeed the obvious lack of an incident room. Many of these facilities will raise concern but understanding the basic principles of an efficient incident room will assist the EPO or BC manager in offering general advice and guidance in considering upgrading or creating a new facility. This is specifically directed at the local authority EPO or BC manager who may well have a duty under the CCA to offer BCM advice when requested. However, it is relevant to all those who operate in this BCM, crisis and emergency management world. Acquiring an incident room extends into organisations who simply want a BCM facility but as we have seen the resilience of an organisation is based upon sound BCM with emergency response procedures which require a different approach—depending on the nature of the organisation's activities. In this respect we are referring to organisations that have recognised the benefits of engaging with all stakeholders in managing and mitigating the impact of an event that impacts directly upon them or are involved in assisting in that role or both. Having an emergency facility integrated into BCM, crisis and emergency management ensures that an organisation is prepared and can respond quickly and effectively by using a good control facility.

How will an organisation know if they need an incident room? Quite simply, if they have a plan to cater for BCM issues and/or emergency arrangements—they need one. The number of facilities, their scale, sophistication and investment will be driven by the nature and seriousness of the issues that have emerged in their risk assessment processes and their statutory obligations. Risks may involve dangerous industries, providing public services such as transport or acknowledging potential terrorist attacks. Those statutory obligations may come from the Health and Safety at Work Act 1974, a co-ordinating role such as the police, or numerous regulatory requirements to operate safe industries or general working practices—in short having employees or dealing with the public.

The end result of a detailed analysis will indicate the type of facility required. The essential strategic questions are:

1. **What role will this facility play in the overall management of our worst case scenario?** It will be the critical focal point of decision making and information exchange.

2. **Who will need to be in there?** All those within the organisation who will be involved in decision making, administration, collating, processing information and implementing the plans. There may also be a requirement for external agencies, partners or contractors to support the response by coming in or going out, acting as liaison officers at other facilities.

3. **How will it fit into the organisational structure?** In terms of the scale of the organisation—will it fulfil an operational role or a strategic role for example? Will there be a need to create more than one facility each with a separate distinct function or management role? Remember, if it is not part of the multi-agency response allocating the facility a Gold, Silver or Bronze title may confuse multi-agency arrangements. Better to stay with a generic name with the examples listed earlier but recognising that the functionality of the facility. Is it a combined GSB? Is it Operational only or Strategic only, or a combination? Define its purpose, location and position within the management response.

We have already considered in detail police managed multi-agency co-ordination facilities and the associated management committees and groups. Control facilities of all shapes and sizes go to support the overall multi-agency response. We know that Category 1 and 2 responders will, or should, have well developed emergency control facilities to manage their own resources, using their own plans within their own premises, sending out trained liaison officers as required to multi-agency co-ordination centres, such a police SCC and TCC or indeed to a scene.

Many organisations, in particular those who do not have an emergency response role do tend to over look the importance of having a designated permanent incident room (or whatever it may be called), to be activated against a set of criteria that for them describes a major incident. It could be a large business, who need it primarily to assist managing a BCM crisis or it could be a university or college with thousands of students who may become a target for terrorism or a large fire where managing emergency procedures need to run hand in hand with their BCM issues. In many cases the realisation that they do not have a functioning incident room facility that would have enabled them to respond more effectively, engage with the emergency services more efficiently, manage their casualties and better recover will always be a profound source of distress and regret.

As we have seen, many organisations are required by regulation—such as COMAH (Control of Major Accident Hazard) Regulations and REPPIR (Radiation Emergency Preparedness and Public Information Regulation)—to have on-site emergency facilities, but many organisations do not and could find themselves struggling to cope with a major incident on their site or property.

The key business case for such a facility clearly surrounds having better control of the incident and better chances of business recovery, which also includes caring for staff who may be injured or been killed by the incident. Setting up a basic but effective facility is not difficult. Clearly the size and scale of the facility is determined by the scale and nature of the anticipated events—which will be based upon that comprehensive risk assessment, as we have already discussed.

Many of the administrative and meeting procedures already described can be applied to a smaller scale single agency incident room. The critical success factors to achieve an effective incident room could be summed up as:

1. Effective external liaison and engagement

2. Location

3. Functionality

4. Set-up

5. Liaison officers

6. Communication

7. Information sharing

8. Decision making

9. Resilience

10. 'Managing the business' BCM

1. Effective external liaison and engagement

Many businesses often fail to recognise the significance of the role external agencies have in their plans and fail to engage with them, not only in preparing plans but seeking advice and guidance in setting up an incident room and how it can be configured to assist and provide support to them whilst at the same time facilitating effective internal BCM and emergency management. It is important to ask—to what extent have external agencies contributed to your plans? For any organisation that sits outside the greater LRF family, to what extent have external agencies assisted with, been consulted by or contributed to the organisational plans? Involving the external responders is essential to ensure that plans are compatible and complementary.

In addition, what experience have your senior management team had in working with external partners? The question is: how prepared are senior managers to be able to understand and interact effectively with external agencies? What emergency management training is offered to key staff in the organisation?

2. Location

The position of the room is important. As we have mentioned, the room must not be capable of being compromised by the incident. If that is the case a fall back facility must be identified. Ensuring that the room can be secured and remain secure prevents unauthorised access without it being too restrictive to access by outside agencies. Parking is often overlooked for responding staff and can be a cause of frustration for visiting agencies.

Depending on the nature and scale of the incident or incidents identified by the risk assessment it may not be necessary to have the room permanently set up, it may be better to have it ready to go—'plug and play'. In some cases it is unrealistic to have such a dedicated facility, in which case a room can be set up and converted as and when required. But this set-up must be practised and all equipment checked on a regular basis.

A final point on rooms—try to ensure that there is adequate ventilation, with air conditioning or the ability to open windows. An incident room can become very warm and stuffy very quickly. As oxygen levels fall so will concentration!

3. Functionality

What needs to be in the room? The most important contributing factor for effective functionality is having a 'User Guide'. All control facilities must have a User Guide. A User Guide will contain every piece of information needed to run an efficient room. It can be viewed as a manual or instruction book covering everything from switching on the lights and heating to the most sophisticated information management systems and IT equipment. It will contain floor plans, seating allocation, messaging system information, briefing arrangements, conduct of meetings, administration help guide, sit-rep (CRIP) formats, etc.

A complete detailed list of actions will be included and, if not permanently set up—how to set it up with positioning of equipment, tables and seating clearly illustrated in the guide. Every incident room, whether it is within a small private business environment or a large multi-agency facility needs to have a User Guide. An incident room without a User Guide will fail, in particular where external agencies may be using the facility. In any case systems change and the User Guide needs to be up to date and be treated as an Emergency Plan.

TOP TIP

It is also good practice to circulate and exchange User Guides with partners and stakeholders.

What else needs to be in the room? The following list gives a broad outline of what to consider:

- Equipment—telephone, copier, seating, desks, stationery
- Space/capacity/layout
- Ambient noise
- Quiet rooms
- Refreshments
- Clocks—sync
- Safe environment—Health and Safety
- Large scale maps and icons
- TV coverage/monitor
- Access to CCTV—critical areas
- Role tabards
- Designated room manager/co-ordinator
- Pre-formatted status boards

We will now look at each in turn.

Equipment—telephone, mobiles, internet, copier, seating, desks, stationery

Sufficient telephones will be needed for each position in the room including any external agencies that may be written into the relevant plan and User

Guide. Internet access is now an important issue and is indispensable for emergency use. Many organisations expect online access to information and often to access their own secure data from their own organisation from secure servers. Hard wired internet access is better than wi-fi. Wi-fi can be accessed and hacked into with relative ease. In addition, mobile telephone reception can be sporadic and must be tested within the incident room—in particular on different networks. Information must be made as secure as possible.

A communications board (see later) will act as a reference for all those on a communications network. In other words, how you can get hold of everyone quickly. Having created the communications board (see later) other issues need to be considered in relation to communication.

Is there an onsite radio network? If so, ensure there is a base station/hand set in the incident room at all times and all batteries are charged. As already touched on, are there sufficient numbers of telephones for each key member in the room? Using different exchange lines also offers a fall-back in case one system fails to operate.

TOP TIP

The best communications equipment is only as good as its power source! Charge batteries and have spares.

Has access to any multi-agency radio networks been agreed and are there handsets available, for example Airwave or Satellite phones? If so, have the operators been trained in their use?

Space/capacity/layout

The first question will be: is the room large enough to accommodate everyone who needs to be in the room, including some external representatives who could include the emergency services or local authority? The BCM/emergency plans will collectively outline the likely responders who may need to be within your incident room. Space is an important factor and is always underestimated. Acquire the largest space available. Calculate the most efficient way of setting out tables, information boards or screens for viewing. Consider grouping those who will need to liaise on a regular basis, consider bottlenecks and easy access for those moving around. Label each desk clearly by organisation and put up direction signs to assist those not familiar with the layout—including the toilets and kitchen—most important!

Ambient noise

Even large open plan spaces will become very noisy as numbers increase and each person is vying to be heard. Consider headsets for telephones and physical screening if possible to contain noise. Calling regular time-outs to update participants is another way to bring down ambient noise. Probably the most obvious way of controlling noise is to ensure that only those who should be in the incident room are there and no one else. This is where your co-ordinator can intervene and politely remove those who are just taking up space and making noise.

Quiet room(s)

Related to ambient noise is the need to have separate quiet rooms in the vicinity of the incident room. It is important to have a place where people can go to discuss perhaps confidential or sensitive issues, or indeed just to 'time-out' think.

Refreshments

Often underestimated as an important factor in bonding, team building and general comfort. They are essential to keep participants hydrated and fed to keep up energy levels and can be quite a morale and mood lifter. Being considerate in terms of dietary and cultural requirements is important, as is the time of day. Producing a curry meal for breakfast may not go down too well in some cultures!

Clocks

Synchronised clocks are essential to ensure all messages within the incident room environment are the same. This could be critical in later analysis or debriefing.

Safe environment

Once the room is set up a full environmental/office risk assessment should be carried out to ensure a safe working environment for those attending—bearing in mind some people may not have been in that room or building before and will be unfamiliar with it. This will mean carrying out a risk assessment. For example, consider that document drawer behind the door; perhaps that trailing cable between desks or that coffee percolator at the edge of the desk. A serious point to remember is that you will be responsible for creating a safe working environment for those using your facilities so a documented risk assessment will be necessary.

Large scale maps and icons

This is essential to 'visualise' and clarify issues and operational proposals. How images are shown is a matter of local practice. Up-to-date hard copy maps or projected images, including large flat screens, all work well but it is a matter for local agreement and investment. The ability to see a 'picture' of unfolding events is a very useful asset to have and if resources and key facilities are overlaid on the images, so much the better. For example, where is the FCP? How is the scene sectorised? Where are the cordons? Where is the plume moving to with that wind direction and speed? From simple pins on a map with drawn lines to ultra-sophisticated virtual computer 3D simulations, they all serve the same purpose. Access to Google maps and other Ordnance Survey (OS) maps are very useful and the OS service provides such a service for emergency situations.

TV coverage/monitor

Live monitoring of television news channels is helpful to inform any media strategy and moderate any press outputs. Although all TV companies will record and keep news broadcasts it is useful to be able to capture and archive as many relevant broadcasts as possible. Reviewing previous footage may be useful in a debrief or training situation in the future. However, be aware that additional usage of TV footage in a commercial sense will probably require permission.

Access to CCTV

When choosing the incident room, if CCTV is available onsite this should be easily accessible from the room, if not actually positioned in the room. In particular, when monitoring an incident on an enclosed site, CCTV can be critical in helping to deploy resources and indeed time lapse security CCTV can be vital in investigations. The inquiry following the explosion at the Buncefield petrochemical/storage site in 2005 was greatly assisted by CCTV footage.

Role tabards

Being identified within an incident room is another means of aiding good communication. This is especially important to those visiting the room who may not be familiar with those present or their role. Tabards should also be available for those who attend in a liaison capacity—such as the blue lights or local authority. Wearing a tabard also creates a mind-set that the wearer is 'involved' and an inclusive member of the team. Consider using different coloured tabards for specific roles—do not forget to include that information in the User Guide.

Designated room manager/co-ordinator

As we have already seen, it is vital to the smooth running of the incident room to have a person designated to administer all the procedures and ensure all information is captured and made available to those who need to know. The co-ordinator should have detailed knowledge of the User Guide and be able to provide support to all those using the room.

Pre-formatted status/information boards

Finally, having pre-formatted status boards which create a visual, at a glance, situational awareness across a number of areas are important and will greatly assist in understanding the general management of the incident and continuous briefing that follows.

Essential dry wipe boards could include an Incident Briefing Board. Computer screens, if the software is available, are also useful but are not imperative. The board would contain all key information in summary form—an example is shown at Figure 5.20.

Another board should include all communication information. An example is shown in Figure 5.21.

Being able to locate a person and speak to them or identify a facility, such as an FCP, is obviously essential to effective management. A simple board is all that is required to achieve that.

TASK 5.15

Create relevant boards for your organisation. What should they contain?

Another consideration may include a Casualty Board. An example is shown in Figure 5.22

Although formal casualty identification will be the role of the police, having an update board in their own incident room can be very useful from an organisational point of view. This will ensure the provision of family support and welfare in liaison with the police and local authority is carried out.

An additional board not illustrated here is a 'Resource Board'. This will set out the actual resources available for deployment and/or the current location of those resources. This can apply to both people and equipment assets. It is

INCIDENT BRIEFING		
INCIDENT DETAIL:		
OCCURRED TIME: DATE:	LOC:	GRID:
CASUALTY NUMBER FATAL:	INJURED:	OTHER:
REST CENTRE:	LOCATION:	CONTACT INFO:
SURVIVOR RECEPTION:	LOCATION:	CONTACT INFO:
FRIENDS AND RELATIVE CENTRE:	LOCATION:	CONTACT INFO:
	RVP - LOCATIONS:	
RVP 1		CONTACT INFO:
RVP 2		CONTACT INFO:
RVP 3		CONTACT INFO:
FORWARD CONTROL POINT:	LOCATION:	CONTACT INFO:
MARSHALLING:	LOCATION:	CONTACT INFO:
MULTI-AGENCY BRONZE/OP	LOCATION:	CONTACT INFO:
MULTI-AGENCY SILVER/ TACTICAL	LOCATION:	CONTACT INFO:
MULTI-AGENCY GOLD/ STRATEGIC	LOCATION:	CONTACT INFO:
UPDATED BY:		
	TIME: DATE:	

Fig 5.20 Incident Briefing Board

COMMUNICATION

Name	Organisation	Role/ Function	Radio CH	Mobile Number	Phone Number	Location

Figure 5.21 Communications Board

CASUALTIES

	Surname	First Name	M/F	DOB	Status	Location	Information
1							
2							
3							
4							
5							
6							
7							
8							
9							
10							
11							
12							
13							
14							
15							
16							

Casualty Bureau Activated

Casualty Bureau Number			Liaison Officer Number	
SIM	Name		SIM Number	

Figure 5.22 Casualty Board

often used in exercising as we shall see later. It is an easy way to keep track of resources as they are swallowed up by the event and are a very useful aide memoire for managers.

4. Set-up

The next consideration is the ability to 'set up' the facility quickly and supported by the right people who are properly trained in all the procedures required. Issues to consider are covering in the following paragraphs.

Response times

What are they? How quickly can the room be set up? This can only be tested in real time. Testing should take place in hours and out of hours. Allied to this is speed of activation of a core emergency response team who will run the incident room. Is there a rota with 24/7 cover? Are those response personnel trained?

If the room is not permanently 'ready to go' and has to be set up from scratch this will require a real time test, including all communications, desk positioning, desk labelling and telephone tests.

5. Liaison officers

Those who act as 'Liaison Officers' to external agencies must fully understand their role. They act as the conduit of information flow with the police multi-agency co-ordination centres and their role is vital to information sharing in the incident room.

6. Communication

Communication—as opposed to the use of technical communication equipment—is the ability to pass information. Effecting good communication is heavily dependent upon robust and confident use of telephones, radios, the internet as already described earlier; but communication also involves the ability of people to articulate and present information in a way that is understandable to all those sharing the incident. This is where the more scientific and technical disciplines require careful wording and expression so as not to confuse. It also involves people not resorting to 'in-house' jargon and phrases that again will only confuse and mislead.

Good communication is critical in the next two issues.

7. Information sharing

Information sharing is achieved, as we have seen, in a number of ways including messaging systems and effective logging but which also include:

- Briefing on arrival at the incident room
- Reading status/update boards
- Using the messaging system provided
- Logging all information correctly
- Minuting meetings and recording actions
- Robust & timely liaison with outside agencies
- Media strategy—linking in to police

All of theose listed are key communications issues and assist those taking decisions at all levels by having available to them all the information upon which to make those decisions.

8. Decision making

Decision making is the core of effective emergency response. Often it is very difficult to make decisions with limited or incomplete information; which is usually the case. Trying to identify the facts from the 'noise' is a difficult task. But some basic principles should apply to add some structure to the process.

   Decision making tools are available to assist a Principal in making decisions and the factors to consider. One such model is listed as an example to assist the loggist recognise them when they occur,

Social

Technological

Economic

Environmental

Policitical

Legal

Ethical

Another useful model was developed under the UK Joint Emergency Services Interoperability Programme and is finding widespread use in the UK. It is a simple model as outlined in Figure 5.23

   This model is self-explanatory but provides a structured approach and a logic to taking key factors into consideration.

Recording the information used to make a decision

Sometimes decisions have to be made with what information is to hand. In hindsight those decisions may well be seen as ineffective or even foolhardy. The subsequent debriefs or inquiries will without doubt analyse those

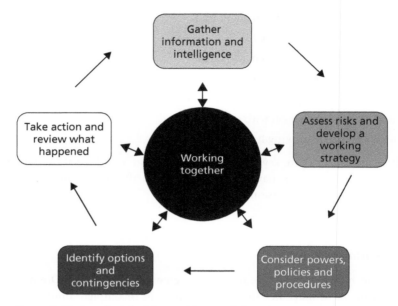

Figure 5.23 A typical decision making model used across many UK agencies

decisions in great detail and in many cases attempts will be made to point the finger of blame at those who made those decisions. In addition, many people will 'forget' that conversation they had with the decision maker if the going gets tough. It is therefore important that all the available information to hand when the decision is made is recorded. The importance of minute takers, loggists, messages recording systems, PAs or staff officers are all vital in this role.

One of the first tasks many senior commanders or senior managers do when accepting command is assign a 'scribe' to take timed contemporaneous notes for them throughout their duty. See the logging section earlier in this Chapter for more information.

Recording data—sometimes technical

Part of the process of recording information must include technical or scientific detail. Many lay people will not understand such detail and tend to disregard it. But those presenting that information—often from the STAC—must 'translate' that information into understandable terms. In addition they must, and should be reminded to, keep all technical information in raw data form for later examination by experts.

Managing meetings

We have looked in some detail about managing meetings but, unless the person is a seasoned chairperson, keeping control of a crisis meeting can be tough. Those who do not routinely engage in crisis meetings should seek out opportunities to practise, perhaps through exercises, and role play within their own organisation prior to the real event.

Tracking actions

During any meeting 'actions' will be agreed and recorded and those under-taking those actions will normally go away in slow time to progress the task. The difference with crisis meetings is the nature and dynamism of the actions. They will need to be progressed rapidly and reported back very quickly. To emphasise this, creating an 'action' board or flip chart within the meeting room to record what those actions are and who is leading is a good way of remaining focused. Although the actions will also go with the minutes, crossing off the actions from the board engenders a sense of progress and accomplishment.

Audio/video recording

Allied to the need to record information, there is an increasing use of audio and video recording of key meetings. Obviously such recording mediums offer the ideal and best record of the conversations but are also a useful means of moderating the tone and behaviour of the meeting.

9. Resilience

There is always one issue that compromises an effective incident room—resilience. Having enough trained staff available is always a problem and an important BCM issue also. This is a particular problem for an organisation that is not 'geared' to emergency response as the norm. This is a good area to test in an exercise. Bearing in mind that operating in an incident room is a stressful environment, incredible concentration is required and few participants can operate effectively for more than a few hours. People will also continue to work, apparently relishing the excitement and atmosphere, but will be running on adrenaline and will suddenly crash. Being realistic about resourcing is important. There are also important welfare issues to be considered.

10. 'Managing the business' BCM

For those engrossed in an incident focus will shift away from the mundane routine day business—'taking your eye off the ball'. Implementing your BCM plan is important. Designating someone who will undertake that role who is remote from the incident room will ensure there is that connection but also sufficient detachment to view the bigger organisational picture. Neglecting the

BCM will soon impact upon the ability to sustain an emergency response—in particular getting sufficient resources lined up to continue the response.

Having a 'control facility' is important to manage any incident from a small business environment to COBR and everything in between. The critical success factor is linking all of those 'controls' with effective management and communications that is fully integrated to the UK national co-ordination guidance on emergency management. Achieving that goal leads to reducing adverse impacts, saving lives, mitigating damage and enabling many businesses, that would otherwise have failed, to continue. In other words a community and society that is resilient and empowered.

What follows is a simple example to illustrate the application of the emergency response to an incident that starts off quite simple but becomes complex.

Co-ordination—Putting it All Together (A Practical Example)

We will look at an incident that encompasses many of the processes and procedures we have looked at so far. Understanding emergency management co-ordination across the whole range of organisations that would or could become involved underpins the effectiveness of the EPO.

To illustrate the initial co-ordination processes an example scenario has been chosen to show how a management structure will emerge from a routine incident. It is designed to describe an escalating incident, probably the most difficult area of emergency multi-agency co-ordination to understand.

It is 11 September, a police officer is out on routine patrol on a 'normal' day going about their duties dealing with incidents, making decisions and resolving situations. It is a 'steady state' situation. Remember the simple decision making examples earlier, dealing with the three components, STO or GSB and finding the solutions within the scope of our experience and knowledge in an operational context.

The officer is called to a small car fire on a garage forecourt and the fire and rescue service is already there and there are no injuries reported. The officer has spoken to the Fire Incident Officer (Crew Manager) and there appear to be no complicating factors, quite routine. The police officer decides what needs to be done, and that is to protect the public by keeping them away and manage nearby traffic congestion whilst the fire service deals with the matter. The police officer knows how to do that and is able to do it alone. They are the police 'Incident Officer and are effectively operating at the operational level, managing any strategic and tactical issues as they arise—all relevant issues are within the 'span of control' of the officer. Remember, that STO or GSB is not rank but role orientated. They can do this because the situation is simple and 'manageable'.

Suddenly the owner of the car returns to the garage clearly upset that his car is on fire and informs the police officer that there are three oxy-acetylene cylinders in the boot of the car. On hearing this information the Fire Incident Officer (Crew Manager) orders a 400-metre cordon around the car and the immediate evacuation of all those in and around the garage. The police officer immediately recognises the need for more resources to carry this out. They need to pass this information to the media because of the potential traffic congestion this will cause and the potential damage should the cylinders explode and they need to warn the public to keep away.

The officer calls for support and immediately directs arriving colleagues to a safe Rendezvous Point (see Chapter 4, Scene Management and Figure 4.6) and assigns various tasks to fellow officers to assist in evacuation and traffic management. The police officer retains regular communication with the Fire Incident Officer (Crew Manager) at an agreed FCP and they decide there is a need for an ambulance on standby in case of injuries. The ambulance service is told to send their ambulance to a Marshalling Area which has been agreed by the police officer and Fire Incident Officer. The police officer knows what to do and how to do it and is co-ordinating the incident effectively but it becomes apparent that they are unable to actually carry out all the operational tasks.

The officer decides that it is necessary to become solely 'tactical' to focus upon how the situation needs to be managed and not get involved operation-ally. The officer is also satisfied that the strategic elements are within their scope and understanding, which senior colleagues are now aware of and agree. The officer now declares a major incident for the police and informs all others services via their control. They now assume the role of Tactical Commander (or Silver), delegating operational tasks to other officers via a Bronze Commander. For example, Bronze cordons (400m), Bronze traffic management and Bronze evacuation. In this situation the tactical command function is discharged from the scene, as it is the most effective location to co-ordinate the scene. The officer uses the police patrol vehicle as the initial FCP at a safe location away from the garage.

There is no strategic level of management at this time. The current Tactical Commander is joined and replaced by a more senior officer who formally takes command. The previous Tactical Commander remains as the new Tactical Commander's staff officer and makes notes of decisions being taken by the Tactical Commander as a 'decision log'. The Tactical Commander is dealing with any strategic elements at this time. The situation is now consolidated and effective cordoning and traffic management is in place. The officer has directed that a TCC is opened at the police station to assist in tasking and man-agement. The Tactical Commander asks for a Tactical Co-ordinator to be desig-nated to manage the TCC and that all relevant agencies are made aware of the TCC being open and requesting agency liaison officers to attend there as soon as possible. The TCC user guide is used to ensure the facility is set up correctly.

As the driver of the car is spoken to by the police it becomes apparent that the driver can offer no reasonable explanation as to why the cylinders were in the boot. Further enquires reveal that the driver is suspected of association with known terrorist groups and the car may be in the process of being made ready for use in a terrorist act as it is the anniversary of the terrorist attacks in New York in 2001. At this point the implications of this development would direct the Tactical Commander to consider the need for a strategic level of management or command. To assist them in making that decision they may take the view that this case has:

- exceptional circumstances;
- large scale implications;
- regional, national and possibly international impact;
- significant policy decisions to be made;
- potential major expenditure;
- and it is necessary to agree a multi-agency policy framework.

The Tactical Commander, in liaison with senior officers, agrees to move quickly to a Gold Commander level of management in the light of this information and open a multi-agency SCC and Media Briefing Centre (MBC) to assist and deal with the strategic elements of the incident. The police also activate the counter terrorist procedures with central government resulting in a series of notifications and activations; this will not affect the scene management at this stage.

A police Gold Commander is appointed to manage the strategic level. Full incident management is now ongoing and developing via the TCC and the SCC, which is opening. A strategic decision is made to withdraw the fire service, due to the increased risk posed by this new information, and let the vehicle burn. The local authority is involved considering a rest centre for those being evacuated and that is ongoing. It is clear that the scene will be cordoned for some time to secure evidence. The garage owner and surrounding businesses will need to consider their BCM issues: Have they got any?

A short time later the vehicle explodes causing massive damage to the town centre. No casualties are reported.

We will stop the example there...

The incident now has the full management structure in place which was implemented as required, as the situation escalated. There would have been no need to go straight to full STO or GSB on the initial incident. This example highlights how a normal incident can be managed using STO or GSB and invoking the separate management levels as needed. Although this is a simple example, it is intended to illustrate how STO or GSB can be a very flexible management tool and how seamless it should and can be. The processes demonstrate how STO or GSB can be fully integrated into daily activity and should be proportional to the situation.

In this example, co-ordination would lead to a sub-national element and a meeting of COBR in view of the terrorist implications. Refer to Figure 5.11 to see how this incident could expand to the highest level of co-ordination.

Summary

You should now understand:

- The full co-ordination structure.
- How the police instigate co-ordination by using the Strategic, Tactical and Operational management system. Bear in mind that Gold, Silver and Bronze is still in widespread use but refers to the same structure. Again it is also emphasised how important it is not to confuse the nationally agreed multi-agency response structures with internal crisis management procedures.
- How the sub-national and national structures support the local response.
- The importance of the single agency incident room' in support of the police managed multi-agency co-ordination centres of Strategic, Tactical and Operational (Forward Command Post).
- The importance of good information sharing, record keeping and managing crisis meetings.
- How to manage control centres to obtain the most efficient use of both resources and personnel.

KEY POINT

Control facilities describe a generic facility to administer and provide support to commanders and managers. Co-ordination facilities are there to support the multi-agency response as described in UK emergency response guidance.

Conclusion

We have seen how the police are responsible for co-ordination. If that co-ordination is not effective the whole response can be compromised. The starting point for effective co-ordination begins, or should begin early, and will set the pace or 'battle rhythm' for the whole response.

Training and exercising will ensure those skills are acquired and retained by those responsible for emergency response. In the remaining Chapters we will look at how we can achieve an exercise programme that will deliver those skills.

Log sheet errors

1. No blocking out or erasures—what was written?
2. Missing references—difficult locating the original
3. Lines left empty—could insert words later
4. Loggist not ruling off when finished
5. Initialling needed for all alterations.

Exercise Design

Having the knowledge to choose the *right* exercise is so important for the overall success of the exercise and achieving the aim and objectives. Making the right choice will ensure that the plans are properly evaluated and tested. As a result it is hoped that lessons are learnt and fed back into the planning processes, so setting up a continuous cycle of improvement.

Exercising is a key part of the emergency planning cycle (see Figure 6.1). The exercise will reveal any shortcomings in the plan which will lead to a review, which in turn will lead to amending the plan and then training staff in the revised arrangements. We then evaluate the plan again and the process

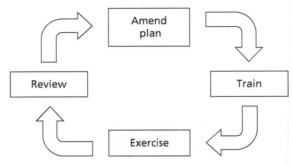

Figure 6.1 Emergency Planning Cycle

continues. As we mentioned in an earlier Chapter, the plan should be a living dynamic piece of work, constantly evolving and improving. Choosing the wrong exercise type can compromise that planning cycle and in fact can devalue the exercise as a whole resulting in people who are involved becoming reluctant to take part in future exercises because they feel the exercise was contrived, unrealistic or of no benefit. The right exercise will maximise the learning potential and also produce an exercise that is interesting, enjoyable and cost-effective, and more importantly reflect a true test of the plan in delivering an effective response when it is used.

General Principles

An exercise should not in itself detract from the agreed aim and objectives by being unnecessarily complicated. If the participants spend most of their time trying to understand, or interpret the 'rules' of the exercise, or are absorbed by the technological 'play station' wizardry they are not concentrating on the objectives and it is a bad exercise. The exercise elements should be 'invisible', in other words the exercise should only facilitate the activity and not become the activity itself.

The golden rule is to keep it as simple as possible to achieve the exercise objectives.

> **KEY POINT**
>
> Do not over-rehearse exercises—it devalues the outcomes.

An exercise should be a true and honest evaluation, a snapshot on the day. It is of no use to over plan an exercise to such an extent that it is devalued by rehearsing the players, leaking exercise information or briefing players on the scenario. It then can become a 'choreographed play'. There is ample evidence that many large scale exercises are blatantly practised beforehand to such an extent that they are openly created in two parts: Exercise Watermole 'Prepare' and Exercise Watermole—as an example. This may be a temptation when the exercise is required for validation reasons for regulators, for example, or to showcase resources but it is counterproductive and the rehearsed elements will be watched for and spotted by a good exercise assessor.

Practising an exercise also creates a dangerous over-confidence and misplaced reassurance. The most effective exercise is the no notice exercise where participants have to react as if for real with no prior warning or information—like the real thing! However, this is often unrealistic and in some cases with live exercise play can be positively dangerous, not only for participants but bystanders too. So some control has to be included and participants prepared to some degree.

However, one major pitfall surrounding exercising is blurring the difference between exercising and training—using the exercise as a training event.

Training

Exercising is not a training event in itself. An exercise is intended to evaluate training, processes and procedures. It should not be used to test participants or be a substitute for properly structured training. An exercise will of course be a learning experience but training and exercising are structured very differently. Exercising can however be configured to extend training into testing individuals but that has to be made clear and assessments prepared and participants sufficiently briefed. The danger in using exercising for personnel evaluation is that a flawed plan, poorly chosen exercise or a badly constructed exercise can create real confusion and uncertainty which is no fault of the person being assessed and therefore renders the personal evaluation suspect and unreliable. Under no circumstances should an individual be subject to 'covert' personal assessment by way of exercising.

Under normal circumstances most people are continually assessed in the workplace through appraisal schemes set against performance targets either set by the organisations or National Occupational Standards—for which there are now Civil Contingencies standards. A major incident, a crisis or a disaster are few and far between and therefore it is hard to assess someone's performance in that situation. In terms of assessment a 'simulation' can therefore be a very useful means of placing or immersing a person in a pressured situation, which is safe, to test specific skills and abilities under controlled conditions. That is assessment.

For training purposes, properly structured training is required which will involve a number of methods to allow the learner to assimilate, absorb and understand the subject and task. Those methods could include straightforward information, reflection, discussion, personal discovery, application of know-ledge and understanding in an environment against scenarios which are spe-cifically designed to build on the structured learning—not to test a plan or evaluate ability.

In summary:

- **Exercises** test and evaluate procedures, systems and processes. Exercising may identify and point to training deficiencies.
- **Simulations** test dynamic ability, knowledge and skills under controlled conditions under pressures set against set criteria to establish a grade or performance.
- **Training** is about learning and understanding.

In general, training and exercising should be kept apart, the only exception being within a seminar-type exercise which we will discuss later.

At this point it is worth mentioning the importance of training although it is something that will be referred to throughout this book because it is so central to what we all do in the workplace. Unfortunately, training for many organisations is seen as a 'luxury' item. It is usually the first to be affected by budget cuts. For an organisation the implications of failing to plan—individual incompetence due to lack of training; an accident due to negligence; ignoring potential deliberate sabotage or terrorist attacks that lead to injury or death—will inevitably lead to serious consequences for that organisation: consequences that they are unlikely to recover from.

In part, training and developing staff is a statutory duty for many employ-ers. The Management of Health and Safety at Work Regulations 1999 place duties on employers to have competent staff in place to respond to and miti-gate threats and hazards that have been risk assessed. Part of that risk assess-ment should include a factor for staff knowledge, skills and competence in their emergency response tasks. It is not about getting staff formal qualifica-tions—although that would be beneficial—it is about being able to demon-strate that key staff are made aware of plans and emergency procedures, how to protect themselves and those they have responsibility for, and have had their training tested or exercised.

Another crucial factor is having personnel who are competent, confident and trained, not only in the sense of protecting themselves and others from personal injury but in terms of managing a crisis within their organisation and support-ing partners, for example as a Category 1 or 2 responder within the CCA. Having properly trained staff will protect an organisation both internally and externally making them more resilient and better able to manage and survive emergencies.

Training is not a luxury item—it is essential and will be one of the first issues inquired into by regulators, legal enforcement agencies and insurers following any incident or dangerous occurrence.

Exercising goes hand-in-hand with training. The only way of evaluating your procedures and identifying training needs is by exercising—but choosing the right exercise is vital.

The first consideration in exercising is what the requirement is—what makes us exercise? This will inform the choice of scenario.

The Basic Scenario

Deciding to hold an exercise can be driven by a number of different factors. For example, an EPO may be faced with a need to evaluate emergency response arrangements in preparation for a forthcoming event or operation. They may also be directed by a risk assessment such as that provided by the CRR or within the organisation as part of a policy for exercising plans against a given scenario or BCM issue. It could also be because a similar event has recently occurred, perhaps elsewhere, and there is a need to evaluate existing arrangements in case it happens again in your area or organisation! It could be a requirement by law if one is required to exercise to satisfy a regulator or it could simply be that it falls within a testing cycle for the plans as an organisational policy of good practice.

On the other hand there could be a need to exercise a particular plan or part of a plan which is generic and a scenario has to be created to fit. For example, testing Rest Centres, the scenario can be very flexible. It could be anything from a flood to a toxic cloud. So the exercise may be driven by preparing for a real event, anticipating a hazard or threat following risk assessment or testing an existing plan.

Scenario design—general considerations

But whatever the reason to hold the exercise the scenario chosen is key to its success. There are some basic general principles to consider from the outset. When considering a scenario it is important to keep it simple and realistic. A complicated scenario will overwhelm a group and they can easily lose sight of the objectives. An unrealistic scenario will 'turn off' a group of exercise participants. Overloading an exercise with too much information is also a great temptation in order to squeeze out as much learning as possible but what can seem reasonable in the planning stage can overwhelm an exercise. For example, when developing a flooding scenario circumstances can be aggravated by incidents such as blocked roads and rail routes perhaps leading to stranded passengers or a chemical site threatened by rising waters affecting the industrial processes. This seems reasonable. However, having a plane crash, a major rail accident or a terrorist attack at the same time will reduce the exercise to almost a farce. Again, realistic and simple will enable the key participants to remain engaged and focused on the objectives.

Another consideration is the context of your scenario. Are the settings and people involved appropriate? Ensure that the scenario does not create alarm or concern. For example, do not choose a specific community or minority group as the perpetrator or cause of the event. Everything must be done to avoid insulting, isolating or demonising a section of community. After all, exercising should be primarily a unifying and learning experience for all, remembering that an informed and cohesive community will react better in crisis than a divided one. If the scenario involves criminal activity such as terrorism, be sympathetic and considerate before choosing who will be responsible for the act! Do not reinforce stereotypes.

Choosing unrealistic or inflated scenarios can alarm local communities who have to live with the hazard. The aim of that type of exercise is to inform, educate and as far as possible reassure the community. For example, by choosing a local chemical site to use as a subject of an exercise may alarm local residents who may start thinking that there must be a good reason why there is an exercise: *'Is it really that dangerous?'* There is no difficulty with that type of scenario as long as it is managed with a sound information and media strategy which can in fact reassure that community that a proactive and responsible approach is being adopted for community safety. It is so easy to overlook these points in the scenario development process but it could cause problems later on for the EPO. A little thought early on can save many difficulties and issuing apologies.

Also, some transport companies will be sensitive to using pictures of their trains, planes or ferries in case it gives the impression that they are not safe. Industry too can be sensitive, and for good reason: creating scenarios which in reality would not or could never happen can send the wrong message about their organisation and its safety procedures.

The scenario must also include some simple and obvious information. But again choose this information carefully because it can change the whole dynamic of an exercise. For example:

- Time/date—may influence resources availability e.g. Bank Holiday, early morning, etc.
- Weather conditions, temperature, wind speed, visibility and wind direction can affect the whole exercise in terms of rescue.
- Traffic conditions—can inhibit and constrain response activities.
- Those involved, e.g. young or elderly, foreign nationals, infirm, etc.

These simple considerations if used correctly can have a profound effect on the response elements of an exercise even before the scenario is developed.

During the scenario development consider what will add to the realism. Think about photographs, pre-prepared news inputs in audio or visual, mapping, edited film footage from real events and computer generated effects.

But only add material if it will add real value and not distract or confuse those taking part.

We will look in more detail later about developing a scenario with a worked example.

TASK 6.1

Can you think of at least five examples where the inappropriate choice of an exercise scenario could cause you difficulties?

Aims and Objectives

Whatever the reason for exercising, once that decision is made there will need to be a careful examination and consideration of the aim and objectives of the exercise. The aim and objectives will be the driving force to develop the scenario. In making the right choice of exercise format there is a need to decide exactly what it is that has to be achieved. Examine the plan being evaluated, or look at the basic scenario being considered and identify exactly what it is that needs to be evaluated. That will be the 'aim'. There will only be one aim. The aim should be quite broad, almost strategic in terms of its scope. Aims should be short, simple statements avoiding 'ands' and consisting of one sentence.

Some examples, the aim could be:.

1. To test the existing companies major incident procedures (this could be a COMAH or REPPIR site—see later).

2. To test the media handling arrangements following a major incident.

3. To test the emergency plan for an aircraft emergency at any town airport.

4. To test emergency arrangements for a terrorist chemical attack in a town centre.

The aim describes your overall goal. This will be underpinned by a series of 'objectives'. The objectives can in fact be viewed as tactical in scope as the aim is strategic. The objectives will break the aim down into activities during the exercise which together will achieve your aim. In simple terms it will look like the diagram in Figure 6.2. This is a simple single organisational-type exercise where there is a single agreed aim supported by several objectives.

It can also represent an organisation's contribution to a larger multi-agency exercise or a component part in support of a multi-agency exercise. In other words, what your organisation brings to the table as your first proposal, as to your desired outcomes from the exercise.

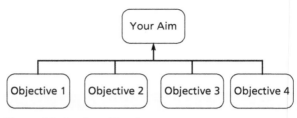

Figure 6.2 Setting objectives

Where several organisations or departments are contemplating an exercise a single overall aim should be agreed, as given in the examples listed. This gives the exercise focus and a unity.

Each organisation or department will then consider or modify its individual objectives so that it complements the overall aim and can be supplemented by a series of their own objectives as in Figure 6.3. The objectives will drive the exercise and they must be compatible with the objectives of the other participants. This is important because it would be of no use to an organisation to choose an objective that is unachievable because another agency or department will not, or could not, support that objective. For example, one objective in an exercise for the local authority may be to examine their strategic decision making at an SCC. The police however, do not have that as an objective, preferring to achieve that by a notional or virtual SCC as they are concentrating on tactical decision making aspects of the exercise. Clearly without police support the local authority objective cannot be met—so a negotiated compromise may be required.

Therefore the process will start with a 'proposed' aim suggested by the lead organisation that is running the exercise and each support organisation or department will look to examine that proposed aim and set their own objectives to meet that aim. This is done by consensus and possibly by some compromise but the benefits of compromise far outweigh the negative aspects when there is an opportunity to interact across other organisations or departments. Figure 6.3 shows how the process works with the ultimate end result being an agreed overall 'Aim' underpinned with a series of agreed and compatible 'Objectives'. In essence the proposed aim is discussed between organisations or departments and a consensus is reached. Each participant will then propose their own objectives and they are discussed to ensure they are compatible across all participants and are supported and integrate fully. The end result is one aim supported by a range of objectives which then go on to form the blueprint for the scenario.

TASK 6.2

Category 1 responders have a duty under the CCA to exercise. What is the duty on Category 2 responders?

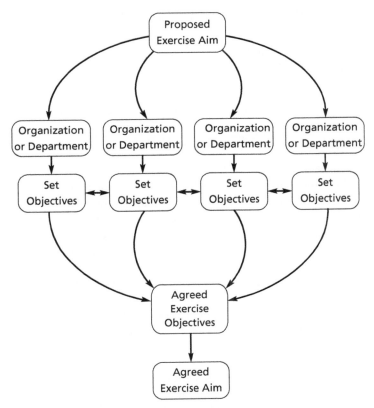

Figure 6.3 Multi-agency aim and objectives

TASK 6.3

From your current or a previous workplace environment think of an emergency or crisis scenario you would like to test, for example, a fire, a major IT failure or building collapse caused by a gas leak. Set the Aim and support the aim by listing at least five objectives.

Let us take a look at the process by considering an example—Taking the 'aim' in example 3 listed earlier, the agreed final multi-agency aim is:

'To test the emergency plan for an aircraft emergency at any town airport'.

The agreed multi-agency objectives for each participating organisation will be different but will all complement each other and dovetail.

The Fire and Rescue Service objectives might be:

(a) To assess the initial activation, notifications, mobilisation and co-ordination of the emergency response.

(b) To examine the liaison interface with all the blue light services at the airport.

(c) To test the adequacy of the on-site Emergency Control Centre (ECC) at the airport.

(d) To manage a co-ordinated media response in liaison with the police.

(e) To assess the liaison arrangements and joint working practices with the airport Fire Service.

(f) To test the upgraded breathing apparatus.

Most of the Fire and Rescue Service objectives just listed could not be achieved without other services agreeing to complement them with their own objectives, in particular where there is a multi-agency element. The only independent objective that is solely their objective is (f). Co-ordinating all the objectives for a large multi-agency exercise, to make them fit, is a task for an exercise planning team which can be achieved through discussion with all those taking part. It is not difficult but is a case of negotiating and shaping the objectives until a coherent set emerge that can be agreed and signed off.

Ideally the aim and objectives should dictate and drive the type of exercise that takes place. After all, they are the agreed priority objectives designed to fully evaluate the plan. However, there is a practical relationship between the aim and objectives and the type of exercise that can in fact be realised. In the example just given, some exercise objectives may not be possible to be achieved unless there is a live element in the exercise which may not be possible. There may be constraints on time, resources or finances so the ultimate decision will rest with the planning team as to what type of exercise can realistically be achieved, which we will now explore.

Exercise Types

Having agreed the aim and objectives, what exercise choices are there?
Exercises will broadly fall into five categories:

- The seminar or workshop exercise
- The table or desk top exercise
- The control post exercise
- The live exercise
- The modular exercise

The seminar or workshop exercise

A seminar or workshop exercise is essentially a meeting in two parts. The first part will be used to introduce a new or revised plan and the second part will be to test understanding and knowledge. The emphasis will be on problem identification and solutions rather than decision making. It will also be primarily designed to focus on one aspect of the plan which will have been identified and agreed by the exercise planner(s). This exercise deliberately introduces a structured training element which will include a personal evaluation method. For example, at the end of the seminar a multiple choice question paper or quiz, taken individually or in teams, based upon the plan can be introduced.

Although the plan will have undergone quality assurance (QA) in the writing stage this exercise can also highlight any issues within the plan that may need revision, prior to re-circulation and can indeed form part of the QA process.

This type of exercise can accommodate large numbers of people, is low cost and requires a small amount of planning. It can realistically be completed in half a day—depending on the size of the plan and what elements are being considered. It can either be an internal event for key players within the organisation only or in addition can involve external support agencies. If the latter is chosen it is useful to use them as a panel of experts. They can contribute to the exercise by giving a short overview of their role and assisting with questions from the group. For example, if a university is testing the emergency response plan to an internal threat such as a major fire in halls of residence, they may invite the emergency services and local authority to the exercise to offer advice and information as the scenario develops, for example in fire evacuation procedures and possibly re-housing of students.

This type of exercise can be managed and facilitated by one person.

TASK 6.4

Exercising and training should be considered as two separate activities: compare and contrast the potential learning outcomes from each activity to reinforce the distinction.

The table or desk top exercise

This is probably the most common exercise type in the emergency planning world and for very good reason. It is cost-effective, involves decision making and good interaction between participants. It is a safe learning environment but can create realistic pressures with the right scenarios. The usual format involves syndicate groups made up of eight to 10 people of up to eight syndicates. Any more can make the exercise difficult to manage. The groups can be made up of multi-disciplinary—a range of departments, multi-agency—a range of agencies or a single issue group who focus on only one aspect of the plan, for example a senior management or strategic group, tactical decision making or operational issues. The combinations of agencies and disciplines are vast and an appropriate combination will be easily found.

This format can cover a large amount of topics based upon a given scenario. The scenario is developed in stages by 'paper feeds' (or display screen) requiring each syndicate to address a series of problems, perhaps three to four. Depending on the format of the exercise, all syndicates will address the same problems or will address a specific aspect. Choosing the syndicate make-up or combination is important for achieving the aims and objectives.

The most common type is the 'multi-agency' table. This is made up of people from different agencies at similar management level. Similar tables can be made up to contain other management levels with additional multi-agency specialists, for example the media or HAZMAT there to address those specialist areas within the context of the scenario. The tables behave as a unit and are effectively self-contained dealing with all the issues as a team. It is almost as though each syndicate is competing with the others. This is not such a bad thing as it creates a team spirit and a factor that many facilitators make use of to drive the exercise. This format is good because it exposes the group to a wide range of issues from the practical operational issues to strategic thinking. It also gives each participant good insight into each other's roles, including limitations of the others within the group, and is a superb networking opportunity. This is also a useful format to consider the impact of 'Groupthink' and other team building dynamics. How does each group arrive at consensus and how do group dynamics affect decision making? This is an interesting issue for the facilitator.

Another format is 'single agency'. For example each table could be all company, police, fire, local authority, etc. This format would require physical interaction between tables by 'forcing' players to seek advice and information from the other tables. Although this sounds useful, in practice single agency tables can become isolated and reluctant to interact unless the facilitator ensures this happens. The onus is on the facilitator to make this work.

Another format is 'management level' only. In this format it is multi-agency or cross-department but the tables are divided up into management levels. One or more tables will address operational issues, another tactical and another strategic. Again it sounds quite useful to focus on decision making and developing skills at that appropriate level. Interaction between tables is essential for this to work. There has to be a continuous dialogue between tables to keep the exercise running smoothly. The facilitators and presenters play a key role in managing this type of exercise.

There are other formats and variations on the main three. The one chosen should deliver the best fit for the aim and objectives.

Each syndicate will be required to give feedback followed by general facilitated discussion. Added realism can be added by film, audio, mapping and photographs. Many such exercises are punctuated by short presentations from 'experts' in particular aspects of the emergency response, for example the police, fire and rescue service, business continuity manager, etc. or indeed an invited specialist speaker. These exercises usually have a panel of experts to offer advice and support and each syndicate is facilitated to ensure the group remains focused and all participants have an opportunity to take part.

TOP TIP

Do not be tempted to treat exercises as an examination or personal test—make sure the participants have all the relevant guidance at least available if they ask for it.

We will discuss running this type of exercise in more detail later but one point is very important to mention at this stage. In table top exercises many organisers treat the exercise as almost an examination. In other words the players are left to think through the issues without any reference to established plans or guidance. The exercise is not an examination. The participants should have available to them all the necessary reference material that they would normally have access to in the real event including maps and all reference works. However, an interesting twist is the holding back of plans and reference material unless it is asked for. The facilitator can then hand over the relevant document or plan if requested. The facilitator may also consider giving hints to players if they are not asking for the right material—a training issue for later perhaps!

In general it is counterproductive to restrict plans and reference material to exercise participants.

At least one day should be allowed for these exercises.

TASK 6.5

Although most table top or desk top exercises are actually carried out at tables and desks—can you think of an environment where the principles of table top would work without tables?

The control post exercise

This type of exercise is primarily focused on communication, decision making and information sharing, all critical aspects of any plan. It also tests the adequacy of the facilities used to manage the incident. The 'control post' refers to the locations such as co-ordination or control centres where incident management actually takes place. In effect, it is a live exercise but without any operational activity. There is nothing to see on the ground. All the activity is confined to co-ordination or control centres.

Each co-ordination or control centre becomes 'live' on declaration of an event. Participants can be introduced in real time to test response times or pre-positioned at the start time. The exercise is driven from an Exercise Control room and managed and monitored by an exercise team including umpires located at each co-ordination or control centre working to a separate communications network. Although the exercise is initiated by the given scenario, because there is no real activity on the ground the exercise is 'driven' from Exercise Control by a 'script' of 'exercise drivers or inputs' and fed into the co-ordination or control centres at pre-determined times or at the request of the umpires. The exercise drivers are simply telephone messages, fax or e-mail messages from participants role playing a wide range of interested individuals or organisations, for example members of the public, civic leaders, other organisations, etc. creating problems or questions that require a response. These can range from questions from the media, local politicians and members of the public to government ministers. There are also 'controlled players' which we will discuss later who role play and drive the exercise forward. The exercise can become very real to the players and get very heated!

These exercises will usually be full day exercises.

The live exercise

Live exercises are clearly the most accurate and realistic method of testing any emergency arrangements and probably the easiest to understand in that it is the operational activity that is tested. In some cases live exercises are the only viable option to test emergency arrangements, for example, evacuation procedures, media interviews/conferences, casualty handling, decontamination procedures, scene management, body recovery, etc. They can be configured to exercise a small part of a plan right up to a full scale major live play exercise involving a whole organisation and hundreds of participants. They can also be combined to form part of a control post or a table top exercise. The combined control post and operational live play represents the most ambitious exercise as it completely replicates the real emergency but in many ways is more complex to manage. The reason for this is that not only do real events have to be managed but sitting above that is an exercise management layer which would not exist in reality, which in turn has to be managed.

Clearly, live exercises by their very nature are costly in terms of the use of resources and the consequential impact on day-to-day business by extracting those resources for an exercise. They can also be hazardous and create potential public concern, all of which has to be managed. With that in mind it is important to have a high degree of confidence that the participants are trained and prepared. But that does not mean rehearsing as we have already discussed. If participants are not prepared, then consideration of a table top exercise may be more appropriate. Running a full live exercise with ill-prepared staff can be a risky undertaking in terms of wasted time and resources. Planning too has to be comprehensive and it can require several months to plan. But the potential learning from a live play exercise is enormous and in those terms can be value for money provided the planning and execution of the exercise is effective with a comprehensive debrief process to extract that learning that is fed back into the planning process.

The key to a successful exercise is ensuring that the exercise itself does not become the goal. The exercise should enable the activities to proceed without becoming an obstacle. Exercise management operates in the background. Ambiguity and confusion as to what is real or notional (pretend) play will frustrate participants and in all exercises all the participants need to be fully briefed as to the exercise format and rules.

TOP TIP

When testing call out lists do not tell anyone when it will be or preface the call by saying it is a test—save that for the end of the call.

Communication/alert/call out exercise

Allied to and often preceding a control post or live exercise is a communications, alert or call out exercise. Trying to combine both in a realistic test can be too problematic. If the alerts fail or response fails or is delayed the control post or live exercise can be seriously compromised and a lot of effort and money wasted.

This kind of exercise simply evaluates and tests the alert communications. That is, are you telling the right people? Are they in turn telling the right people? Are they on the right telephone numbers? Have you got the right contact details? Can they turn out? Communications networks tend to work in cascade. For example, your operator tells four key people or organisations and each one of those tells a further three and they in turn tell another half dozen and so on. It is easy to see if one number is wrong or not accurate that the effect can be significant. A large proportion of the emergency response can be compromised if contact details are incorrect.

An advantage of this exercise is that one can confirm that the real emergency numbers do work and during the exercise one can substitute some of the real numbers to reduce pressure on day-to-day activities and reduce the potential for false alarms. 'Controlled players' (see later) can also be introduced to make and field these calls so the usual telephone/communications operator or control room staff are not tied up so preventing day-to-day activity continuing.

False alarms during exercises can have serious consequences. It is not unheard of for hospitals to be put on emergency alert or the media to run a story as though it was real. This reinforces the need to prefix all exercise communications with the exercise name and make it clear it is an exercise and not real. Therefore in any live exercise or control post exercise proper and adequate measures must be taken to avoid false alarms. This is an issue often watched for by umpires who will intervene to stop this. Creating concern and potential panic in the community is probably the worst case scenario coming from an exercise. Again, proper measures, notification and advertising must be considered. The media element of the exercise planning team should address this.

Having said that, there are occasions when one wants a very realistic test of communications, alerts and call outs. A 'No-notice' test will give the most accurate picture of how effective the communications links are. If calling people out with no notice they will be unprepared and will give a spontaneous and honest response on their ability to turn out. But when contacting people on call out lists they should not be told initially it is a test. If they know it is a test they will be inclined to be over-optimistic and confirm that they can respond. If they think it is for real it may come as a surprise how many people are unable to turn out. But obviously they should be told at some point that a test is being run, preferably after they have been asked the question!

No notice communication exercises will also quickly highlight any wrong or inaccurate numbers held in the plan.

A compromise to a pure no notice test is to give notice that it will happen within a certain period of time or dates, perhaps a day or within a week commencing. Giving notice of a communications, alert or call out exercise clearly reduces potential false alarms but it also creates an artificial result. If a person is notified of a communications test they will prepare for it by making sure that they or someone else is on that phone at the right time and prepared to say the right things. Not really an accurate test, which can lead to a false sense of security!

TASK 6.6

List three reasons why it is desirable to separate call out and notifications testing from a live or control post exercise.

Modular exercising

Increasingly, organisations are choosing to exercise their larger plans in a modular fashion. It simply means assessing the exercise requirements and deciding which aspects of the plan are best suited to various forms of exercising, as described earlier and 'bolting' them together. For example, a communications exercise and a control post exercise or a live exercise up to a point and then remaining aspects by table top. The advantage is that they can:

- be spread over time;
- be smaller in scale;
- be more focused on target groups;
- be more cost-effective

Inevitably, modular exercising requires more planning, administration and co-ordination to ensure that the separate elements are tied together and form a seamless transition between each aspect of the relevant exercise format. It also means that elements of an exercise can be staggered over time or certain elements can be tested more frequently than others. For example, the communications exercise would probably need more testing than say the decision making elements because they are more likely to change.

Simulation Exercises

Computer simulation driven exercises are a highly specialised method of exercising and for many software developers a potentially very lucrative enterprise. They seem to be gaining in popularity. Clearly they are out of reach of most organisations to own outright due to the high costs of hardware and software needed to operate the system, including specialist operators or facilitators required to set up the equipment or train in-house staff to operate the systems. They have to be brought in or participants have to attend a specialist centre, which is not always convenient. It is also questionable what added value such systems add to basic exercise formats. Essentially they are there to add realism by immersion into the scenario, but even the most sophisticated simulations can easily become a 'computer game' or novelty and detract from the actual exercise objectives as the participants become engrossed in the entertainment value of the simulation or trying to understand how the system works. In many cases the software and hardware will not be familiar to the player and may not be available in the real event. There will always be a large element of familiarisation with the software and hardware prior to a computer based simulation exercise.

Simulation is useful however in training and testing individuals against performance measures which can be written into the scenario. It is important to realise—as we have previously mentioned—an exercise should not be a test or assessment of individual capability of performance. Of course exercising is a learning experience and can identify learning needs but where individuals are subjected to assessment during an exercise it fails to be an exercise and becomes an 'assessment' requiring very precise inputs set against performance standards of behaviours, knowledge and skills which need to be observed and measured by professional assessors and trainers. The focus in this case is not on a plan but an individual.

To carry out effective and meaningful exercises computer simulations are not essential but can be usefully configured to aid realism and assist in visualisation.

Visualisation

Visualisation reinforces a message. People more easily assimilate information presented in graphic form or pictures, or indeed in solid objects. The use of mapping, scene photographs, site plans, models on tables/road layouts and simulated media including audio and visual inputs during an exercise are of great benefit and value to create an atmosphere of realism—in effect creating the right environment and atmosphere. The difference between this and computer generated simulation is that there is a point at which the simulation becomes the focus of interest whereas the exercise and its aims and objectives must remain paramount.

It has been observed that pilots flying highly sophisticated 'fly by wire' aircraft have experienced difficulty in recognising basic abnormal flying characteristics within the aircraft due to trying to interpret the 'data' provided by the display. They appear to be focused on trying to understand the display and the data as opposed to feeling the aircraft and are distracted.

TASK 6.7

Having considered both simulation and visualisation in exercising can you articulate the differences between the two in a way that creates a clear distinction?

Making a Choice

Returning to our earlier example—let's remind ourselves of the objectives for our airport exercise.

(a) To assess the initial activation, notifications, mobilisation and co-ordination of the emergency response.

(b) To examine the liaison interface with all the blue light services at the airport.

(c) To test the adequacy of the Emergency Control Centre (ECC) at the airport.

(d) To manage a co-ordinated media response in liaison with the police.

(e) To assess the liaison arrangements and joint working practices with the airport Fire Service.

(f) To test the upgraded breathing apparatus.

This is not a new or revised plan, so a seminar exercise is not appropriate, and as it has a number of objectives, a seminar exercise would not work. The intention is to choose the simplest format or combination of formats to achieve our objectives in the most economic way. Now we will consider each exercise objective in turn to see what exercise format best suits.

Objective (a)

This objective can be broken down into two parts, activation and notifications followed by mobilisation and co-ordination. Activation and notification elements would be best tested by a communications exercise. This could be done as a separate exercise in advance. Mobilisation and co-ordination could be achieved by a live test or table top or control post exercise. The easiest option is table top. Each syndicate could be asked the question: what are the initial mobilisation and co-ordination arrangements in the plan? By discussion and then explaining this, any anomalies and ambiguities will be exposed.

Objective (b)

This could also be achieved by a live test or table top or control post. But again the easiest option is table top. With multi-agency support these areas can be examined and explored in great detail, supported by a panel of experts.

Objective (c)

This would require a control post exercise to actually test the facility. However, a small scale control post exercise would achieve this objective using the scenario and inputs and creating a modular exercise.

Objective (d)

This could be achieved by a live test or table top exercise. But with a multi-agency group this could be achieved at a table top exercise, especially if supported by a group of invited professional media.

Objective (e)

This could be achieved by a live test or table top or control post exercises. Again the easiest option would be by table top. Having all the participants in one room discussing their respective roles and responsibilities will scrutinise that interface.

Objective (f)

This could only be achieved by a live play element as it requires the use of real equipment and operational observation.

Final considerations

The difficulty with this exercise is dealing with objective (a) and (c). A modular approach is required to meet all of these objectives or indeed the planning team may revisit the objectives and reject them if necessary should resources and time not allow an extended modular approach. But assuming there is a requirement to meet all objectives, in this case the best option would be to carry out a table top for objectives part of (a), (b), (d) and (e); (c) would require a control post exercise and the remaining part of (a) would be a communications exercise. Objective (f), being a live play only, may be rejected as a component of the multi-agency exercise and referred back for a single agency internal exercise. This illustrates the development of agreed compatible exercise objectives.

The exercise programme would look like this:

- **Exercise Module 1**—Communications exercise. Objective (a) Activation and Notification. Carried out in advance of the main exercise and used as part of the introduction to inform the table top exercise.

- **Exercise Module 2**—Table top exercise. Objective (a) Mobilisation and co-ordination and the remaining objectives of (b), (d) and (e).

- **Exercise Module 3**—Small scale control post exercise. Objective (c) Carried out after the table top and using the information in table top injects to create driver inputs.

This example, although quite complicated, is only intended to illustrate the process of configuring exercise formats to meet aims and objectives. It also introduces the idea of modular exercising. The terminology used will be explained in more detail in Chapter 7.

KEY POINTS TO REMEMBER IN CHOOSING AN EXERCISE FORMAT

Seminar

- Good for introducing new and revised plans

- Low cost
- Focuses on problem solving
- Single presenter
- Minimal planning
- Can accommodate large numbers
- Structured for training
- Mainly for internal use
- Achievable in half a day

Table top

- Can test a wide range of parts within a plan
- Cost-effective
- Excellent interaction potential
- Explores decision making
- Tests management functions
- Can be realistic
- Good for multi-agency or multi-disciplinary
- Significant planning required
- Requires facilitation and presenter
- Requires a full day
- Full debrief required

Control post

- Will test the critical communications, decision and information sharing
- Will test control facilities, such as Tactical or Strategic Co-ordination Centres
- Very realistic experience for participants
- Extensive long term planning required
- Planning team necessary
- Requires Exercise Control/management
- Separate communications network required
- Debrief required
- Will impact upon 'normal' business
- Will incur significant costs
- May invoke cost recovery from blue light services

Live

- The ultimate test of operational systems and procedures
- Can be configured to test small or large parts of a plan

- Can be combined with table top and control post exercises
- Extensive long term planning required
- Will impact upon 'normal' business
- Requires health and safety management
- Can be very costly to run
- Requires an exercise management team
- Extensive debriefing required.
- Can promote confidence in your organisation amongst communities
- May invoke cost recovery from blue light services

Remember—apart from the training element in the seminar exercise, exercises are NOT examinations. Players should have access to all plans and anything they would have access to normally day to day. It is not a test of memory for the players.

Whichever exercise format is chosen, with a systematic approach a successful exercise is easily achievable.

General Costs

In an age of financial accountability 'cost' is a primary driver in exercise management. Exercising will incur costs either directly or indirectly. We will discuss 'cost recovery' next but there will have to be consideration potentially for paying for professional speakers, venues, catering, props, writing materials, visual and audio aids, etc. However, cost can be kept to a minimum as many of these costs can be met from internal resources and sharing amongst agencies. It is essential though that costs are identified early and factored in and most importantly to identify who will pay. Consider funding and sharing costs, in particular through the LRF. It is hard to envisage a significant exercise not including some support or input from the LRF.

KEY POINT

Factor in costs early in the exercise process and identify who will pay—get it in writing.

Cost Recovery

Two main pieces of legislation created the right for blue light organisations to recover costs incurred in taking part in exercises to test plans created under that legislation. They are the Control of Major Accident Hazards Regulations 1999 (COMAH) and the Radiation Preparedness and Public Information Regulations 2001 (REPPIR). The introduction of the legislation created some difficulty for the emergency services in that there was no nationally agreed pricing structure or methodology to apply those 'charges'. 'Charges' is placed in quotation marks because it is cost recovery, not charging for services. It is explained as cost neutral as the money recovered goes back into emergency service operational budgets. This lack of agreed methodology resulted in vast anomalies across the UK. Some emergency services cost recovered and others did not. Some 'charged' tens of thousands of pounds and others very little or not at all. In addition, the 'broker' tasked with negotiating and managing cost recovery was the local authority, but many local authorities did not take on this role.

Some attempts have been made to resolve the disparity but there still remain significant differences in approaches to cost recovery. Indeed, some LRFs have extended the cost recovery principle to all commercial organisations. The rationale for this is based upon equity and even-handedness. If an organisation is in business to make a profit and is required to exercise for either regulatory reasons or just good management, why should the taxpayer subsidise that through the emergency services? Indeed, some organisations who pay cost recovery actively promote their contributions as putting back into emergency service budgets money that can go to support core activities such as tackling crime or reducing fires, a commendable attitude.

On the other hand businesses support the community in other ways and through taxes, and after all, it gives the emergency services valuable opportunities to practise. Whatever the view, cost recovery is a fact that has to be factored in and budgeted for if it applies.

TASK 6.8

Research the two pieces of legislation mentioned in the text concerning cost recovery and in no more than 500 words summarise the process.

If a company is subject to cost recovery or an emergency service is considering how to apply it, how does any organisation know what they are paying for or if they are being asked to pay too much? How does any organisation know if the emergency services are unwittingly specifying too many staff and passing the cost on? Perhaps a bit cynical, but it reflects opinion. It is difficult to know what should be paid or asked for unless a specialist consultant is engaged to review and assess the invoice. But consulting with peers, similar organisations in other areas or consulting with the local authority should assist in making these decisions. After all it is the local authority who should be co-ordinating the application of the COMAH and REPPIR regulations on cost recovery.

Important issues to consider are how and by what rationale organisations levy the costs. How transparent is the process? How well is it broken down and itemised?

Training benefit is a key term that can be used in this process. If being 'charged' cost recovery an organisation should be presented with how training benefit is calculated. Training benefit is the positive learning experience that the emergency services will gain from taking part in an exercise. Some services will apportion a percentage to this based upon the participants' previous experience and training. This is in recognition that opportunities will arise where certain aspects of a particular exercise role may hold elements of training benefits for some participants and the exercise will be a useful vehicle to develop that participant, without hindering the exercise. Clearly there are roles that the emergency services carry out every day, and doing it again in an exercise will not advance their skills or training. In particular, where the emergency services are repeatedly asked to take part in many exercises per year. But there is acknowledgement that some emergency staff will benefit from the experience and that should be accounted for. An example of a sample police training benefit matrix is illustrated in Figure 6.4.

For each participant a general assessment is carried out based upon previous experience and relevant training. In this case four areas are evaluated; each area will carry a 25% allowance against training benefit. For example if a participant ticks three criteria that will attract a 75% levy this results in a 25% discount, i.e. 100% – 75% = 25%. In other words they have experience in three areas and none in the fourth, so 25% of their input will provide a degree of learning and development. This is not a definitive or officially endorsed process but represents a model to consider as a rationale or methodology to add some objectivity to the training benefit evaluation process. Without some rational process the figure can become purely subjective and difficult to audit.

There is no doubt that the emergency services will endeavour to achieve a balanced approach to ensure an efficient and effective exercise response, delivered by skilled and knowledgeable personnel. This is particularly important for the overall success of any exercise, for the police in particular who play such a key role in the overall co-ordination, communication and management of all emergency situations. An efficient emergency service will from the outset of any planned exercise be open, transparent and flexible in the selection of key personnel and the likely costs that that may incur.

KEY POINT

Inserting 'trainees' into an exercise will devalue it for other participants, as the trainees will not be able to offer sufficient skill or knowledge to provide a valid test of the processes—although attracting maximum training benefit in cost recovery.

Role/Name	Key Skill Area	Previous Experience			%
Rank/Grade for costing purposes	Each area carries equal weighting making up 100% benefit for no relevant competencies	YES (tick)	NO (tick)	Full Costs	Office Use Only
Gold Commander Name.......... Rank	1. Performed Gold Commander for major Incident 2. Chaired Multi-agency strategic meetings 3. Participated in civil nuclear exercise 4. Attended nuclear incident management training/seminars				
Staff Officer to Gold Commander Name.......... Rank	1. Performed Staff Officer to Gold Commander 2. Participated in any other Gold Control function 3. Participated in civil nuclear exercise 4. Attended nuclear incident management training				
Senior Gold Co-ordinator Name.......... Rank	1. Performed the role of Senior Gold Co-ordinator 2. Participated in any other Gold Control function 3. Participated in civil nuclear exercise 4. Attended nuclear incident management training				

Figure 6.4 Sample training benefit matrix for the police

Summary

You should now understand:

- The need to use exercising as a management tool.
- Exercise aim and objectives and be able to recognise and formulate them.
- How to choose and mix and match exercise types to create the ideal exercise.
- The principle of basic cost recovery and the benefits it brings in promoting emergency response.

Conclusion

Exercising is a vital management tool in today's business and public service environment, whether it be emergency response or managing a business continuity issue. That initial analysis as to the form and type of exercise is crucial. Choosing the right exercise will deliver cost-effective and beneficial rewards for any organisation and lead to a planning cycle which is built on continuous improvement and development.

Understanding cost recovery is again a relatively new concept still bedding in across both private and public sectors. It is a significant issue for many, and in particular the smaller organisation, so choosing the right exercise directly affects the costs incurred.

Having considered what exercise types are available we will now look at how the exercise is managed.

Exercise Management

Overview

In this Chapter, you will learn:

- Who's who in exercise management?
- Using the input script
- Staffing schedules
- Controlled play and free play exercises
- Exercise Control
- Exercise communications network overlay
- Time line
- Compressing time
- Exercise order or programme
- Players' information pack
- Debrief schedule

Who's Who in Exercise Management?

Now that the exercise aim, objectives and type of exercise are understood it is time to consider how the exercise will be managed. This falls into two parts. Firstly, this Chapter will concentrate on the key personnel that will be involved in planning the exercise and taking part; and secondly the exercise structure and how that is developed to deliver the aim and objectives.

Exercise Director

Planning the exercise itself will be described in more detail in Chapter 8, but for clarity, it should be understood that the Exercise Director should be agreed and confirmed at the first exercise planning meeting. The director will have overall responsibility for the exercise and can terminate and significantly alter the exercise as required. The Exercise Director tends to be a person involved in the policy or strategic decision making within the organisation—usually someone who has 'sponsored' and supported the exercise. This is a key appointment and a role that requires training, qualifications and experience; this is endorsed by the CCA. Although the Exercise Director need not chair the planning meetings, which is often a task delegated to an exercise manager, the director must be closely involved with the exercise throughout the planning process and consulted when necessary. Unless otherwise agreed whoever initiates the exercise will provide the chairperson at the planning meetings. At the first planning meeting, when all participating organisations or departments are assembled, a core planning team will be agreed. These may involve other agencies too. At this point, if not already evident there will be a need to agree who will be the overall Exercise Director.

In addition to the director, the following is a list of those who may be operating within an exercise:

- Manager(s)
- Players
- Controlled players
- Umpires
- Assessors
- Observers
- Observer chaperones
- Facilitators
- Assistants
- Inputters
- Health and Safety Officers

We will take a closer look at each of them in turn.

Exercise Managers

Exercise Managers are usually drawn from the planning team and will manage discreet aspects of the exercise, for example:

- Exercise Control, Strategic Co-ordination Centre (SCC), Tactical Co-ordination Centre (TCC), etc.
- Observers chaperone (for high level/VIP observers)
- Exercise facilitator or presenter for table tops
- Individual organisational activity of a single agency, e.g. the company, police service, fire service, etc.

They will be designated as directing staff, working at all times to the Exercise Director, acting as liaison between the umpires and assessors. Where numbers of exercise management staff may be limited, they can also have a role as exercise umpires and assessors.

Exercise players

Exercise participants—as the name suggests, these people actually take part and have a role within the exercise. They should have a role or potential role within the plan or plans being used. They are not scripted, coached or rehearsed in the exercise scenario at all, apart from the exercise format and exercise rules. They should be briefed just before the exercise starts and have had a players' information pack outlining all necessary information.

Exercise controlled players

These players are introduced into the exercise with a role to play but are scripted, coached or rehearsed in parts of the exercise scenario. They may be for example, casualties, suspects, witnesses, members of the public or exercise inputters. They may also role play senior managers and commanders to direct players in free play exercises (see later). For example, you can introduce a controlled player to act as a Gold Commander to take all Gold decisions without having a full Strategic Co-ordination Centre. They can be assisted by a handful of controlled players from other organisations instead of scores of real players—as long as that facility, i.e. SCC, or the strategic decision aspect is not being tested.

Exercise umpires

Exercise umpires are the eyes and ears of exercise management. For that reason they must be easily identified by wearing a suitable tabard. They will communicate directly with exercise managers and the director through Exercise Control, if there is one, or face to face. Their job is to operate in the background watching and listening to exercise play to ensure the exercise is on track. They can be approached by players to clear up any ambiguity in exercise play and umpires can confirm that a request has been actioned or completed. 'Notional' or 'virtual' (see later) play is a matter for the umpire to manage. Certain requests from players will have to be dealt with as notional because to carry out the request or action would be unrealistic and may involve the activation of real resources or facilities that are not taking part. The notional elements within the exercise will be agreed and worked through in the planning stage. Umpires can also communicate with players to clarify level of understanding and rationale for actions if acting as exercise assessors but will usually confine their comments to players in response to questions about exercise play or to intervene to change exercise play at the request of Exercise Control or for safety reasons. Please note in this context being an 'assessor' is not about assessing any individual, it is about assessing exercise play and adherence to the exercise inputs and the overall plan under test (see later).

Notional or virtual exercise play

What do we mean by notional in this scenario? As an example assume that the planning team have recently tested the Control Post aspects, perhaps in a modular fashion, as we have already looked at, and are now concentrating on the operational and tactical elements. However, there will still be a need for a Communications Centre, SCC or Gold Control and MBC to ensure the exercise runs. This can be achieved by having controlled players acting as Communications Centre staff, Gold Commander and MBC Manager. They will have an assistant each to make notes and take phone calls and can be positioned in Exercise Control. The notional 'Communications Centre' will manage the initial operational response until the TCC goes live. In reality, the day-to-day Communications Centre(s) will manage the incident until the management structure is in place. The notional Gold Commander and MBC Manager will each field and reply to questions or requests put to them by other live centres, principally by TCC. The SCC can consist of controlled players from other organisations and/or departments each acting as their Gold or MBC advisor. In this way it is possible to achieve a Gold and MBC element with a handful of controlled players and not scores of people as would be the case in running a full SCC or MBC.

Exercise assessors

The Exercise assessors role can be combined with the umpire role, but on complex or large scale exercises separate and independent assessors may be brought in. This is a matter for the planning team and the Exercise Director. Exercise assessors are sometimes used to ensure a more objective assessment of the exercise is carried out and that the exercise had not been 'rehearsed' or 'choreographed' to obtain a good result for the benefit of others such as regulators! Exercise umpires, if assessing their own organisation in a multi-agency environment, may be inclined to be a little too subjective. In any event both the umpires and assessors will have a crucial role to play in the debrief process. Assessors must be easily identifiable. Assessors can communicate with players to clarify level of understanding and rationale for actions.

Exercise observers/chaperones

Exercise observers must have a legitimate role to play in an exercise. They should not simply be there for a 'day out' and a 'free lunch'. Observers must add value to the exercise by providing feedback in written questionnaires prepared by the planning team or exceptionally, be invited for another purpose—usually to add support and/or to demonstrate to them the effectiveness of exercising. This can extend to local community leaders, politicians, VIPs or other senior managers to 'sell' the benefits of exercising. Inviting senior managers may positively change opinions on the usefulness of exercising and free up resources for future exercises.

Inviting the real media may provide useful publicity too and subsequently provide reassurance to the public. However, the converse may be true if the debrief or live report is negative or badly reported, which could alarm the public and create 'bad' press for the organisations taking part. Therefore, the decision to invite the media is one for the planning team and Exercise Director to consider with advice from the media themselves or PR professionals. Most large organisations will have a media manager who will assist with this decision as they will have a better understanding of the local press opinions and general views.

Observers must be closely chaperoned and not left to wander. They should be separated into small groups and managed at all times. Restricting observers to specific areas is useful to prevent their interference with the exercise. This can be achieved by having designated observers' observation areas. They must also have a thorough briefing to ensure that they fully understand the exercise as their ability to ask questions may be restricted. Observers must not communicate with players as it can be too distracting and may confuse the players and influence the exercise play. Observers must also be easily identifiable and wear conspicuous badges. It is not unheard of for rogue observers or uninvited press to access exercise sites!

Facilitators

Facilitators are usually drawn from the planning team and act as umpires in a table top exercise format. If not drawn from the planning team they will require a comprehensive briefing as to their role as an action from the planning meeting. Not only will they require a good knowledge of the plan being evaluated but a good understanding of the exercise and objectives in order to 'steer' discussions and exercise play in the right direction. They are there to guide and assist only. They should not be drawn into being a group leader or answering questions directly. Facilitating is a skill and fitting the right facilitator to the right group is often overlooked by exercise planners. For example, on a table of senior executives or chief officers putting a young inexperienced EPO with them may create some difficulty for that EPO in trying to 'manage' such a highly experienced group and can be quite intimidating, the result being that exercise discussion can be stifled and inhibited.

TOP TIP

Although plans should be provided to players a useful tip for facilitators in table top exercises is to hold back additional and ancillary documents and plans, which are mentioned in the provided plans, in a briefcase. If they are asked for by the players the facilitator can produce them, but only if asked for!

Exercise assistants

Quite simply they are not playing in the exercise but are nominated to a task to ensure the smooth running of the exercise. These can be:

- player liaison in the holding area/room (see later);
- distribution of refreshments and catering;
- general transport for observers;
- observer chaperone assistant;
- telecommunications support;
- IT support;
- security.

Exercise driver inputters

Driver inputters are controlled players in Exercise Control. They will be seated at a desk with a telephone and the driving script within which, in chronological order, will be the inputs prepared by each participating organisation to introduce information into exercise play. It is useful to have each organisation designated a colour as the single script will be used by all. This will allow other inputters to be aware of what is going on around them and going into the exercise at any given time. The inputter will usually be from the organisation with general responsibility for that type of input. For example, company inputs from a company manager; health related may be by the ambulance service, Health Protection or NHS staff; public safety interest issues from the police, etc. In that way they will have enough knowledge to sound credible and be able to ask and respond to pertinent questions, if asked. A sample driving script extract can be seen in Chapter 8, Figure 8.2. This relates to a chemical tanker spill producing a toxic plume. The exercise code word is 'Mayflower'.

Exercise Health and Safety Officer

In any live play exercise there will be a need to appoint designated Health and Safety Officers to monitor any potentially hazardous activity. This will be risk assessed by the planning team and the appropriate risk treatments applied. On a given signal, which will be described in all exercise documents and at all briefings (which could be a whistle or air horn), the exercise will halt immediately.

The exercise will only recommence again on a given signal.

Live exercising presents many hazards, some obvious, some hidden. A mechanism must exist to intervene immediately to prevent injury or discomfort.

Using the Input Script

Please note that each inputter will have at least one phone number. The inputter must give this number to the receiver of the call and the inputter must tell the receiver what number to call them back on and who to ask for. For example, the inputter might say: '*This is Mr. Jones from the local authority [message]…can you ring me back on 0202897645 and ask for Mr. Jones.*' This will ensure that the inputter will know who is ringing them back as they may be 'acting' several parts. It is useful for each inputter to have a notepad or prepared sheet to record what was said on each call so they can respond to call backs as accurately as possible. Clearly, they are pretending to be several people! This becomes more important as the inputs mount up. It is also useful to chase up calls that have not been returned as this increases pressure for the players as it would in real life. This is actually quite a fun exercise as the inputters can role play vulnerable, angry, upset, pompous or concerned people.

They should also note the nature of the calls and where they are going. For example, some issues will not be strategic but go to the SCC, and others will be strategic and go to the TCC. Umpires will watch for this to assess if the information is managed and routed to the right location for an answer. This is important as the question and response must be managed at the most appropriate level. It is no good at the SCC dealing with purely operational issues and visa versa. The inputs must be configured to reflect the type of question and at what level it is aimed. Within the driving script the input question or statement can be marked with an (S), (T) or (O) to indicate if the general nature of the question is aimed at strategic, tactical or operational level. Will Strategic pass a tactical message down or does Operational pass a strategic message up? This ability to manage and process information will be key in any debrief process.

Staffing Schedules

Common to all exercises will be a requirement to set out an exercise staff and player schedule. On a larger exercise this could involve up to 100 people so a means of identifying roles, locations and function will be essential. Where costs are involved it will be an audit of the hours worked and the rate applied. It will include everyone involved, for example the exercise players and everyone on the exercise management team. A simple spreadsheet will accommodate this and will include information such as:

1. Exercise Site.
2. Name.
3. Position—where they will be positioned during the exercise.
4. Function—Player, Controlled Player, Management, Support, etc.
5. Role—their task. For example, communications operator.
6. Hours—engaged in role. Time from to time to including total hours.
7. Hourly rate—include this column but leave blank unless you are submitting it for cost recovery purposes. Then include total cost.
8. Training benefit analysis—a percentage reduction for cost recovery purposes.

Only include columns 6, 7 and 8 where you are actively pursuing cost recovery.

A typical schedule would look like Figure 7.1. This example is a schedule for a major control post exercise. Although it is centred on police facilities the format is applicable across any organisation. It is a useful document to keep track of any personnel changes or amendments.

A schedule such as that in Figure 7.1 should be used to list all those who would be taking part in the exercise. It is a convenient way of keeping track of those involved and for noting any changes.

Controlled Play and Free Play Exercises

Controlled play exercises are based upon a strictly managed script with set times for events to occur. Controlled play exercises effectively guarantee that all the objectives will at least be addressed. However, controlled play exercises tend to restrict the freedom of players and some spontaneity is lost in running with ideas and testing the flexibility of the plan. Can the plan deal with the unexpected events if it is so heavily scripted and controlled?

Free play exercises in which the basic scenario is given to players and their actions determine future events are very exciting and stimulating for players.

1. Exercise Site	2. Position	3. Function	4. Role	5. Hours	6. Rate £	7. Training benefit %
Police HQ	Communications Room	Duty Officer	CP			
		Communications Officer	P			
	Entrance Door	Security	A			
	SCC & MBC	General Staffing – IT Support	A			
		Transport Services	A			
Silver Control	Main Police Station	Silver Commander	P			
		Silver Co ordinator	P			
		Silver Staff Officer	P			
		Communications Operator	P			
Bronze Control	Local Police Station	Bronze Commander Tasking	P			
		Logistics	P			
		Communications	P			
FCP		Liaison Officer	CP			

Key: P = Player CP = Controlled Player A = Assistant DS = Directing Staff

Figure 7.1 Staffing Schedules

1. Exercise Site	2. Position	3. Function	4. Role	5. Hours	6. Rate £	7. Training benefit %
Exercise Control	Conference Suite	Exercise Director	DS			N/A
		Police Exercise Manager	DS			N/A
		Exercise inputs	CP			
		Exercise inputs	CP			
		Exercise logistics	A			
Exercise Umpires	SCC	Umpire	DS			N/A
	Communications Centre	Umpire	DS			N/A
	Main Police Station Silver	Umpire	DS			N/A
	Main Police Station Silver	Umpire	DS			N/A
	Local PS Bronze	Umpire	DS			N/A
	MBC	Umpire	DS			N/A
Exercise Assessors						
	SCC	Assessor	DS			N/A
	MBC	Assessor	DS			N/A
Company Site	ECC	Police Liaison Officer	CP			

Figure 7.1 Staffing Schedules (*cont.*)

1. Exercise Site	2. Position	3. Function	4. Role	5. Hours	6. Rate £	7. Training benefit %
SCC	Police Gold Command	Room Gold Command	P			
		Staff Officer	P			
		Senior Gold Co-ordinator	P			
		Gold Support Officer	P			
		Communications	P			
		Loggist	P			
		Clerical	P			
	Police - Gold Media Room	Media Officer	CP			
	Multi-Agency Room	Room Manager	P			
		Information Manager	P			
		Call Taker/ Liaison Officer	P			
		Clerk/Runner	P			
		Clerk/Runner	P			
	Reception/Booking in	Reception/Help Desk	P			
	Reception/Booking in	Reception/Help Desk	P			

Figure 7.1 Staffing Schedules (*cont.*)

1. Exercise Site	2. Position	3. Function	4. Role	5. Hours	6. Rate £	7. Training benefit %
MBC	Conference Centre	Media Gold Command	P			
		Media Manager	P			
		MCC Manager	P			
		Press Officer	P			
		Press Officer	P			
		Clerical	P			
		Clerical	P			
	MCC	Media Officer	CP			
	Multi-Agency Room	Room Manager	P			
		Information Manager	P			
		Call Taker/Liaison Officer	P			
		Clerk/Runner	P			
		Clerk/Runner	P			
	Reception/Booking in	Reception/Help Desk	P			
	Reception/Booking in	Reception/Help Desk	P			

Figure 7.1 Staffing Schedules (*cont.*)

For example, 'a 400 kg bomb has exploded in the town centre on a busy Saturday afternoon...what would your service or organisation do?' Very little additional information is provided and the issues and questions are managed dynamically as they arise. The main disadvantage with this type of exercise is that it requires very careful umpiring because the umpires will be constantly managing the play by having to answer queries from players as to exact detail and what is and is not to be taken as play.

Exercises such as these can also use controlled players at the end of a phone. This type of exercise will require many more controlled players to keep the exercise on track and will also need to have to hand a vast array of background information to answer any queries from players. For example, can I get sufficient Red Cross volunteers here within 2 hours? In a free play exercise, consideration should be given to having a supplementary Exercise Control Group (ECG), a 'dynamic think tank' of experts set apart who can answer any questions from the players via the umpires. In this case the players have a directory of contacts to ring for advice and information.

Never underestimate how involved players can get in an exercise...it can become their reality! For example, is the request from a player notional or real? They may ask 'Do we assume the hospital has been notified or do we have to do that?'

Probably the most serious flaw with free play exercises is losing control of it and actually missing parts of the plan that really need to be tested or evaluated.

Essentially, running with an exercise, which has broad and flexible parameters, such as in a free play exercise, requires considerable experience and practice by the exercise management team supported by a team of knowledgeable and thoroughly briefed personnel. The rewards can be very beneficial. However, run badly it can become a disaster, with little chance to recover or steer it back on course. Players too can become very frustrated if the exercise flow slows because the 'dynamic think tank' dries up.

With controlled play, the outcome can be more predictable in terms 'what it is we are looking to achieve' and in that respect may offer a more reliable exercise format.

Exercise Control

Exercise Control is the engine room that drives an exercise and for control post and live exercises probably presents the most challenging aspect of exercise preparation and management. It is located separately from any exercise site. It is at Exercise Control that the exercise will be managed, monitored and driven. The nominated Exercise Director will sit in Exercise Control together with the exercise manager(s). Exercise Control will also house the exercise driver inputters, the people who will input the messages by telephone, fax,

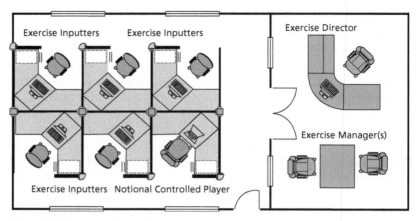

Figure 7.2 Exercise Control

e-mail or even text message for each service or department from a prepared and timed script. Exercise Control will operate on a separate communications network to the exercise itself (see later). Exercise Control can be viewed as a management and communications layer that sits above the exercise. The umpires act as the field operatives for Exercise Control who have regular and direct communication with Exercise Control at all times. They are the eyes and ears of Exercise Control. Figure 7.2 illustrates a typical Exercise Control.

Exercise Communications Network Overlay

Figure 7.3 illustrates the exercise communications layer, which is put in place to manage the exercise through Exercise Control and out to the umpires acting at each of the live sites. The dotted lines indicate exercise management communication only. The other solid lines are the exercise communication lines—note how they are separate.

TASK 7.1

There are two communications networks in a control post and live exercise. Explain why that is necessary.

In this example, there are two active operational sites 1 and 2, a forward media briefing point, a Tactical Co-ordination Centre (TCC) (Silver), a Strategic Co-ordination Centre (SCC) Gold and a centralised Media Briefing Centre (MBC).

The exercise communications network operates independently of the actual communications links, if in fact they are being tested in the exercise.

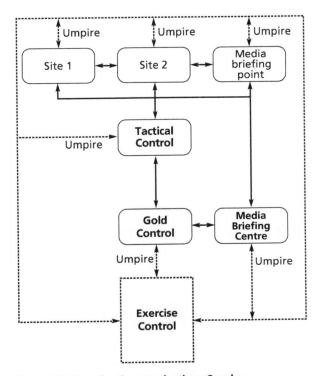

Figure 7.3 Exercise Communications Overlay

It is therefore important that all the telephone and radio call signs are held in Exercise Control so that the exercise managers can contact the exercise umpires at all times.

TASK 7.2

In your workplace, identify a location suitable for an Exercise Control? Draw a sketch and position the key players within that room.

Time Line

A time line (see Figure 7.4) is a very useful way to 'visualise' an exercise particularly where multiple sites are involved and how activities relate and interact. Activities laid against each other in this way it is easy to see what is happening where and when. This process also lends itself to precise co-ordination as to when each facility is active or not active. We will look again at time lines in planning the exercise.

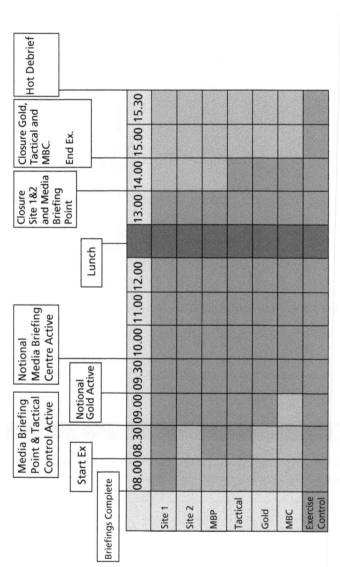

Figure 7.4 Exercise time line

In Figure 7.4 it will be noted that the dark shaded area indicates live active sites or facilities, the light shaded sites that are not active. It is useful to post this chart in the Exercise Control in a prominent position.

Compressing Time

Compressing time is a very effective way of moving an exercise on, particularly for table top exercises. In real time it would take many hours to set up certain facilities, access certain resources or for things to actually happen, so compressing time is the only realistic way to achieve this. This is where a detailed time line will clarify the timings. The time factor is also so important to introduce pressure and drive decision making. Careful use of time can enhance an exercise greatly. Introducing exercise inputs as, 'T' time of incident and then 'T' + 1, 'T' + 6 etc. can bring into play identified exercise objectives which in real time could not be achieved. For example, an SCC could take 2–3 hours to become active in reality or an emergency mortuary management which in reality would take 12–24 hours to set up. These issues can then be introduced and be discussed with an exercise input given as e.g. T + 12. 'Injects' are usually described as: 'it is now 0930 hrs', the next input may be... 'it is now 1345 hrs' and the next '1746 hrs', etc. so time moves on in chunks or 'leap frogs' ahead to enable the required facilities or situations to develop.

TASK 7.3

Consider a scenario over an extended period and create a time line using 'T' at points at which significant events could take place.

Having created the exercise format(s) and agreed all the component parts into a coherent co-ordinated process it is now necessary to prepare a document, which sets out in clear and concise terms the whole process. This is called the 'exercise order or programme'.

Exercise Order or Programme

This document describes the entire exercise and will develop as the planning process proceeds. It is the definitive exercise programme outlining the management structure and is used by the Exercise Director, Exercise Manager(s), planning team, facilitators, umpires, assessors and observers. It is usually made up as follows:

Cover

- Exercise name/time/date/venue(s)/logos (various participating organisations)

Foreword

Senior manager signatory including:

- General reason for exercise
- Support and importance of exercising
- Encouraging those to get involved
- Enjoy the day

Timetable for the day

- For seminar and table top exercises include times of sessions and breaks during the day or course of the seminar.
- For control post or live the start time and estimated finish time only.

Introduction

- Specific reason for exercise
- The planning team—who are they?
- CV for Exercise management staff and presenters

This is a good section to highlight the profile of those taking responsibility for these important roles and adds to the credibility of the exercise.

Aim and objectives

- Include all those submitted to the planning team by all participating organisations and departments

Exercise management

- Format—type of exercise
- Managers—their role
- Umpires—their role
- Assessors—their role

- How the exercise will be run—briefings
- Vocabulary—code words
  - Exercise...Startex. Begin exercise
  - Exercise...Hold. Suspend exercise
  - Exercise...Resume. Resume exercise after hold.
  - Exercise...Abort. Emergency termination.
  - Exercise...Endex. End exercise.

TASK 7.4

The exercise vocabulary is not fixed. Can you think of a vocabulary that could be applied to a live exercise scenario? Think of all the activity that will occur and try to think of code words to publish with an exercise order.

Communications

- This is probably the most important section. Without good and effective communication during control post and live exercises the exercise will fail.
- Dedicated radio channels for the exercise play and Exercise Control should be separate. All telephone numbers in use in the exercise should be in a directory as part of the players' briefing pack. All telephone numbers both land line and mobile/radio call signs should be displayed upon a board in Exercise Control.
- All exercise communication should be prefixed with the exercise name to prevent any confusion if the message reaches the 'real' world.
- All non-participating communication centres and switchboards should be advised in advance of any exercise to avoid any false alarms.

Exercise inputs

- For table top exercises the questions that will be asked of the syndicates and suggested model answers to assist the facilitators, presenters and observers prepared.
- For control post and live exercises do not include the driver inputs but a simple section to describe the process only. Inputs are for Exercise Control staff only and would in fact be too bulky as they are large documents.

Debrief process

- All exercises should be debriefed. Clearly, the more complex the exercise the more thorough the debrief. What kind of debrief will it be, where and at what time? A feedback 'pro forma' can be included in the exercise order or programme for use bythose in possession of the document. It is useful to have a common pro forma as it will provide a common feedback structure and so ease the administration of the debrief report.

Glossary

- It is useful to have a comprehensive glossary of terms. Although there is generally a common language for exercising there are some anomalies across organisations and industries.
- Many observers will not understand many of the terms used.

Players' Information Pack (PIP)

A players' information pack can be as simple as a briefing sheet sent by e-mail. It can also be more comprehensive including identification tabard, identification badge, directions to venues, etc.

Every player must receive a minimum of information, which must include:

- Exercise name
- Day and date
- Exercise duration
- Report time/briefing time
- Reporting to whom
- Exercise start time
- Dress type—particularly if outdoors!
- Their location
- Their precise job description—be explicit that it is or is not a personal test
- The exercise rules
- Refreshment arrangements
- Use of mobile phone information
- What to do if sick
- A debrief form
- Health and safety information
- Glossary of terms

TASK 7.5

Looking at the list of details just given—can you list in order of priority the most important to the player and the least?

It may seem strange but preparing the debrief exercise schedule during the planning stage is vital. The exercise performance outcomes or measures need a set format to be able to assimilate all the data and identify areas of improvement. This can only be prepared as part of the original planning set against the objectives.

Debrief Schedule

The debrief is the most important link between exercising and realising positive change in working practices in emergency planning. Recording information for debriefing purposes must have structure and clarity otherwise the debrief will become unfocused and ambiguous. It may also result in lessons being missed or an organisation avoiding responsibility for implementing change. Throughout the exercise process all participants should be working to address specific areas of the plan and the designated objectives which should be grouped together into a 'Debrief Schedule' under 'activity areas', see Figure 7.5. Therefore, during the planning process a debrief schedule document should be produced which reflects the 'activity areas' under which the debrief will be focused, these are general areas of activity and based around the objectives, the exercise feedback sheet can be configured around these activities, for example:

Activity Area	Sub-Issue	Areas for improvement	Positive comments	Organization commenting
Activation	• Alert • Decision to activate • Etc	There was confusion as to the interpretation of the incoming alert information	Once the correct information was received a very quick management decision was made.	Police / Fire / Ambulance
Notification	• Telephone • Call out • Etc	The telephone contacts were out of date. The call out list was also out of date.		Police
Set-up of facilities	• Reception • Briefing • Etc			
Information sharing	• Message systems • Etc			
Decision making	• Meetings • Etc			

Figure 7.5 Debrief schedule

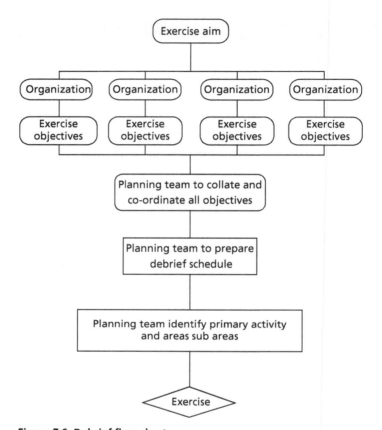

Figure 7.6 Debrief flow chart

- Information exchange
- Team working
- Alert notifications
- Set up of Co-ordination or Control Centre(s)
- Interpretation of information
- Communication
- Information sharing
- Decision making
- Media management, etc.

The exercise activities that will form the debrief process are agreed in the planning process. So, looking at the agreed aim and objectives, decide how they can be categorised into 'activity areas' as shown in the list for example. Create the activity areas to suit the exercise. The activity areas will be sub-divided into sub-issues. For example, if one of the objectives is the 'set up of the emergency facility' (an activity area) consider what the parking was like. What was reception like? Were attendees properly briefed on arrival?

The debrief team, which will be set up as a sister group to the planning team, will divide up the feedback or evaluation forms from the exercise into the activity areas and assign sub-issues. This will keep the debrief focused and give it structure. It will also make allocating and identifying actions much easier. An example of a partially completed debrief schedule is shown in Figure 7.5.

You can see from the short extract in Figure 7.5 that a picture will soon emerge of common areas for concern or any good points as the debrief team begin to populate the schedule following the exercise and transfer the information from the evaluation data. Nevertheless, more about that in Chapter 10—debriefing. This debrief schedule will then create the action tracking table document which we will look at later.

The debrief flow chart shown in Figure 7.6 gives an overview of the debrief process from initial aim to action tracking.

Summary

You should now understand:

- The basic principles of exercise management.
- The role of key personnel used in an exercise.
- How the exercise structure is shaped to manage an exercise.
- The concept of exercise inputs.
- The role of umpires.
- Preparing for the debrief.
- The manipulation of exercise time and the use of timelines to clarify the progress of the exercise.
- The provision of a players information pack to assist everyone to get most from the exercise.

Conclusion

Sometimes perceived as a complicated topic, exercise management is straight-forward if approached in a methodical and systematic fashion. Developing an understanding of the roles and how they interact is vital for a successful exercise. Following the basic principles outlined in this Chapter will produce an exercise that will test and evaluate plans to the full and create a learning environment that is not only very informative but fun too!

In Chapter 8 you will continue to develop the process of planning the exercise and applying the principles of scenario development

8

Planning and Organising the Exercise

Overview

In this Chapter you will cover:

- Basic preparation
- Planning meetings
- Developing the scenario—Exercise 'Mayflower'
- Driver inputs
- Preparing resource boards
- Seminar exercise
- Table top checklist
- Control post exercise checklist
- Live exercise checklist

Having gained an understanding of the exercise management process and the key people that are involved, the detailed exercise planning process can begin. The general term 'exercise management' covers both the 'planning'of the exercise and 'managing' the exercise on the day. The exercise planning process is in effect a project management activity. All the elements of effective project management can be seen in this planning process and those with a project management background will appreciate the skills required.

TOP TIP

Use a project management approach to exercise planning and development.

In this Chapter we will be consolidating the knowledge gained so far and looking in more depth at the practicalities of planning an exercise. To do that a worked example will be used to bring the processes to life in a logical manner. The easiest approach to planning the exercise is by considering what each of the four formats already described will require. But there are some basic planning preparations to consider for any type of exercise.

Basic Preparation

There are some common preparations and considerations in all exercises.

- Senior management support—The EPO should inform the highest ranking manager of their intentions. Obtain their endorsement and a commitment to participate, even if it is just to open the exercise.

- Notify people early—The EPO should identify all those who should be invitedto the first planning meeting, both internal and external. Do not underestimate the time needed to secure participants' attendance. Several months' notice will be needed to get it into busy diaries and to ensure their absence during the exercise can be covered if your chosen participant cannot attend. Once they agree to take part make sure the emphasis is on them to find a replacement should they have to back out. It does no harm to use the senior management endorsement as a means of reinforcing the request.

TOP TIP

Always put the responsibility on the participant to find a replacement if they back out.

- Involve the LRF—If other agencies are involved ensure that the relevant LRF planning group is notified. This will usually mean the LRF secretary; this is crucial to obtain the support of any external agencies early in the planning process.

- Book early!—Reserve the necessary rooms and facilities well in advance including any catering that may be needed.

- Financial support—Secure any finance that may be required or at least inform those who manage finance within the organisation or approach the LRF. Find out if the LRF supports cost recovery in which case the blue light services and local authority may charge a fee to take part.

- Reserves—Ensure there are stand-ins or reserves for key exercise presenters, facilitators and managers—see Top Tip earlier.

- Start drafting key documents—Begin to consider a draft 'Exercise Order' and 'Players Information' pack. Start with a draft overall aim and your own objectives—this will form the basis and your contribution to the joint multi-agency objectives if external agencies are involved or for other departments in your own organisation.

- Contingencies or threats—Plan for and include contingencies for a situation that the exercise, as planned, is adversely affected. There may be a need to consider postponing it, downsizing or changing a venue quickly. It could be affected by real events such as sickness, bad weather or a real crisis. The consequential costs incurred in abandoning an exercise could be very significant. The more resource intensive the more detailed the contingencies need to be. If cost recovery is involved ensure that the issue of cancellation is discussed and documented. Accept that the emergency services will always participate on condition that there are no real events that require operational response. Some organisations try to deploy staff on overtime to prevent such cancellations taking place, in particular where there is a major training benefit for them.

Planning Meetings

Beginning the planning stage

As already alluded to in Chapter 7 a lead individual will take overall charge of exercise administration. The lead individual will be a person from the organisation who is effectively 'sponsoring' the exercise; the organisation which has initiated the exercise. This is not the Exercise Director. This task usually falls to a lead person from that initiating organisation. The responsibility usually falls to the EPO or contingency planning or business continuity manager role within an organisation. They will also invariably be an exercise manager too.

Begin to consider who will make up the planning team. All those who have a part within the plan must be invited initially. The core planning team will eventually become smaller but not to invite a key stakeholder could create tension, arguably with some justification. At this stage it is quite arbitrary but err on the side of inviting too many to the first planning meeting and then agree a core planning team.

The core planning team

The lead person will be responsible for:

- ensuring an Exercise Director is appointed;

- scheduling the exercise planning meetings;
- preparing the agendas;
- monitoring planning actions;
- collating aim and objectives;
- collating driver inputs and arranging the script preparation;
- co-ordinating the preparation and production of the 'Exercise Order' or 'Programme';
- co-ordinating the preparation and production of the 'Players Pack'.

The initial invitation to attend the planning meeting should be in good time and wide ranging. At the first planning meeting the core planning team will be selected and agreed. In that way key stakeholders within the plan will have a say in who attends the meetings or by what means they can be kept informed if they choose not to attend, perhaps being copied into e-mails or periodic updates. In this way they can contribute at any time.

Depending on the scale and complexity of the exercise the planning team may meet many times and the whole team will certainly have a key role to play in the exercise.

One of the first tasks of the planning meeting will be to begin the initial exercise planning processes. The example that follows illustrates how that can be achieved in six steps.

Developing the Scenario—Exercise Mayflower

We have already looked at the basic issues to consider in deciding on a scenario and how aims and objectives are constructed. More specifically, how does it work in practice? This simple practical example will illustrate the whole process—called exercise 'Mayflower'. The process can be summed up in the illustration shown in Figure 8.1.

It is a six stage process that will result in the production of precise and relevant exercise drivers and inputs to address all of the exercise objectives. This process is relevant for table top, control post or live exercises.

To set the scene—'Bridgestone' is a fictious small rural village within which sits the ACME chemical company. The ACME chemical company is not designated as particularly hazardous (not designated under the Control Of Major Accident Hazards Regulations), but does store and receive hazardous chemicals from time to time.

Stage 1—What is the reason for this exercise?

This exercise has been agreed because there is a concern expressed by local residents of Bridgestone Village. The emergency services and other emergency

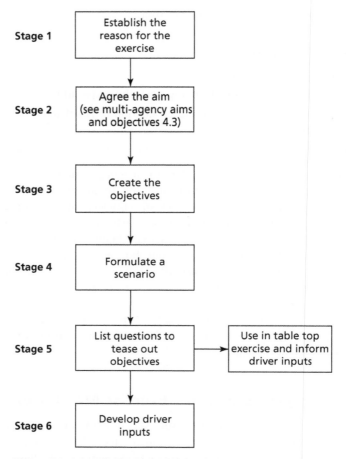

Figure 8.1 Scenario development stages

responders including the company wish to evaluate their emergency arrangements, evaluate the plan and reassure the community at the same time.

Stage 2—Aim

'To test emergency response arrangement for a chemical tanker incident in Bridgestone Village'.

Stage 3—Objectives

These are the combined objectives of all those involved in planning stage and are required to meet the aim.

1. To evaluate the ACME company response to an incident involving one of their tankers.

2. To examine the emergency response and joint working arrangements of the emergency services.

3. To consider the implications of a widespread impact of a toxic chemical spill and possible deposition on agricultural land.

4. To examine the warning and informing arrangements to protect the public.

5. To examine the management issues in dealing with evacuation over an extended period for local residents.

6. To test the crisis management arrangements of the company.

7. To provide reassurance to local residents.

Using a table top format of multi-agency tables—made up of the police, fire, ambulance, local authority, the ACME chemical company, Environment Agency and the Health Protection Agency and the relevant health professionals locally—take one objective and decide what circumstances will explore that objective and then do the same for each objective. At this stage it may seem a little disjointed bolting all the circumstances together. However, what will happen eventually is a situation or scenario will begin to emerge that will build into a coherent and realistic situation that will address each objective.

For example:

- To meet objective 1 we need a tanker crash involving ACME.

- To meet objective 2 we need a major incident involving all blue lights.

- To meet objective 3 we need spreading toxic plume.

- To meet objective 4 we need large numbers of people that need to be warned and kept informed.

- To meet objective 5 we need large numbers of people displaced from their homes.

- To meet objective 6 we need the company to be subjected to scrutiny in terms of their culpability, reputation, business continuity, sustainability in the wake of such an event and PR going forward—in short, their resilience.

- To meet objective 7—this is a public relations exercise following the event with potentially key community leaders attending the exercise as observers. After the exercise consideration may be given to holding a community meeting or using follow up questionnaires to assess the success in reassuring the community.

Stage 4—Scenario

Drawing together the points made so far we could consider the following scenario:

'It is 0930 hours on 6 April 2014, Bank Holiday Friday. The weather is fine and the road is dry. The wind is a light north westerly. The ACME chemical company tanker is intending to make a delivery to their chemical plant located in the High Street, Bridgestone Village. The tanker veers for no obvious reason as it approaches the gate and collides with a bus and car. The bus is carrying 35 elderly pensioners on a day trip and the car contains two people.

> A map provided would show that the chemical incident is located in a small village of about 20 shops and near a large school and housing estate. The wind direction indicates that the toxic plume will blow over the estate.

Three elderly people remain trapped, as are the drivers of the tanker, bus and car. The car passenger has escaped and called the emergency services.

People in the vicinity are choking and having difficulty breathing. Local residents have been warning of the potential of such an incident for years and the press are already ringing the police.'

This is the basic scenario and introduction.

Now consider what paper feeds or inputs will drive this exercise or how this will affect any driving inputs for a Control Post or Live exercise.

Stage 5—Questions

To tease out the issues/objectives consider asking the following questions of the syndicates.

1. Having been made aware of this incident what would *your* organisation's initial response be?
2. What Command and Control arrangements would be put in place?
3. How would the casualties be managed in the initial stages?
4. How would local people be made aware of the incident and advised how to protect themselves?
5. What impact would this toxic substance have on surrounding farm land and livestock?
6. How would an evacuation be effected, or would it be necessary?
7. How would the media be managed?
8. What kind of investigation may follow such an incident?
9. What action would the company take at this time?

There may be more questions that could be added to address specific local issues but we have moved from aim to objective to scenario to questions—it is a logical sequence. Even if it is a not a table top exercise still prepare the questions. They will clarify the outcomes of the exercise and they will be invaluable in preparing driver inputs for a Control Post or Live Exercise. Therefore the final stage would be to develop the driver inputs if the intention is to run a Control Post or Live exercise.

Stage 6—Driver inputs

Figure 8.2 illustrates an extract from a driver script from the incident in the example. It is useful when producing such scripts to introduce colour, for example: using blue colour script is input by the Police, red by Fire, brown by Local Authority and so on. Preparing the script is a major task for the planning team as it is a follow on process from agreeing the aim and objectives. Each organisation or department will submit their inputs to the planning team having agreed the overall objectives and the master script will be compiled from those submissions. It is worth keeping these scripts after the exercise as they can, with some modification, be used again and again.

These driver inputs will be used by controlled players (inputters) from Exercise Control. Careful and detailed briefing will be required to assist and prepare the inputters. As we have seen in Chapter 7, the ability to manage several conversations and enquiries, playing several different people and remain in character is daunting but can be very rewarding and fun.

TASK 8.1

Continue the list of inputs and create another 15.

Preparing Resource Boards

Whichever exercise is chosen, be it live, control post or table top, a key factor in the developing scenario will be resourcing. This is an aspect so often overlooked. Exercises seem to have infinite resources, unlimited staff working continuous hours without days off! The reality, as everyone knows, is that depending on the time of day resources can vary enormously. So for each exercise a decision will have to be made as to the level of resourcing to allow. There is an option of course to run with unlimited resourcing, if for example there is a need to concentrate exclusively on one aspect of the plan where resourcing is not an issue but it will create a false dynamic leading to a false sense of security.

Using 'actual' resource numbers can be a very sobering experience for senior managers when they see how fast they are swallowed up and additional resourcing is required urgently. Creating inputs that explore how additional resourcing

	Input by	Input Time	From	To	Where	Text – Prefix each message with the words 'Exercise Mayfl ower'
1	Fire	08.54	Mrs Green 3 High St. 020 45345	Fire	Police Tactical Control	My husband is a fire-fi ghter and I understand he has collapsed at an incident in Bridgestone Village. What can you tell me?
2	Ambulance	08.47	Dr Patel Surgery 12 Low St. 020 45341	HPA	Police Strategic Control	I have a couple of patients who are complaining of chest tightness. Can this be as a result of the chemical spill?
3	Police	09.00	Mr Graham Global Products Ind. Estate 020 34467	Police Liaison	Company Emergency Control Centre	We are next door to the ACME site: can you advise if we should evacuate our building?
4	Company	09.05	Mr Brown 7 Small St. 020 45346	Company ACME	Company Emergency Control Centre	I can see a yellow plume of gas coming from the ACME factory. Is it safe to go out?
5	Company	09.10	Mrs Evans 33 Garden Street 020 34567	Company ACME	Police Strategic Control Centre	My husband was working in the ACME factory this morning. My friend tells me he has been injured. Is that true?
6	Police	09.15	Daily Mercury 020 34567	Police	Police Strategic	Can you tell me the time of the next press briefing?
7	Local Authority	09.20	Red Cross 020 12346	Local Authority	Police Strategic Control Centre	Are you evacuating and if so where is the rest centre?
8	Fire	09.30	Mr Simmons FBU 020 45345	Fire	Police Strategic Control Centre	I understand this site is highly toxic. Can I be reassured that our members are fully protected?

Figure 8.2 Input driver script

can be obtained, from where, from whom and how long it will take will focus the mind of many managers. If using resource boards, which are essentially staffing and resource schedules introduce them at the beginning of the exercise to each of the organisations taking part. Resource schedules can be arranged in the planning stage for each organisation. They can be displayed on dry wipe boards in a live exercise, control post or table top exercises. They can also be handed to facilitators or umpires in paper form to manage on behalf of the players.

To get a feel for the level of resourcing available for any given exercise at a particular time and date approach the HR department or those who prepare the duties or staffing levels. Then consider the available hardware such as vehicles and specialist support equipment. A list can then be prepared of what level of resourcing could reasonably be expected.

TASK 8.2

If possible—for any given time and date—your choice—ascertain what level of resourcing is available to deal with an incident. Approach your organisation and find out how you can get that information.

We will now consider the planning issues related to the four main types of exercise. The following lists could be used to prepare agendas for the meetings and/or prepare information to players.

Seminar Exercise

Send out invitations to all those taking part at least four weeks in advance, with the following information:

1. Introduction to the exercise to include the reason and 'buy-in' support for senior management.
2. Time, date and location of exercise including parking arrangements.
3. Dress code (if any—possibly uniform or non-uniform).
4. Catering arrangements.
5. Advise participants of the limited use of mobile phones.
6. The schedule for the day (they will know when mobiles can be used).
7. Set out the aim of the exercise.
8. Inform participants that there will be a test at the end of the exercise.
9. Inform them that they are responsible for finding a replacement if necessary.
10. Prepare the questions for the test paper based upon your aim and emergency plan content.
11. Inform the participants which plan is being used (this will give an opportunity to pre-read if they wish—some will, many won't!).

12. Plan how you intend to present the plan. The plan format suggested earlier lends itself to a systematic presentation. In other words take each section in order using the contents page as a guide.

A word on dress code—an exercise is a professional activity attended by experts and senior managers who will give their time and support and will expect a degree of professionalism from the participants, in particular where the uniformed services are involved. If participants turn up in tee shirts, shorts, dirty training shoes, etc. it reflects poorly not only on the participant but the organisation they represent—try saying smart but casual and don't be frightened to say no trainers or football shirts!

Include separate invitations to those external agencies that will make up the 'expert' panel.

TASK 8.3

Can you suggest reasons why using a test paper or quiz will be a useful activity in a seminar exercise?

Table Top Checklist

It will be necessary to allow at least 3–4 months' planning time for a table top exercise. The time between meetings allows for actions to be completed in good time. It is important that actions are actively followed. Setting out a provisional schedule of planning meetings will be useful even if it is amended as the process proceeds. The following schedule is suggested as a minimum, more planning meetings may be necessary depending on the completion of actions.

First planning meeting

- Invite representatives of all participating organisations and internal departments who have a role within the plan.
- Obtain their contact details at the first meeting and circulate to everyone present or before the end of the meeting if possible.
- Confirm who the lead organisation or department is for the exercise.
- Confirm who is exercise director/sponsor.
- Confirm who is the lead person.
- Discuss a date for the exercise.
- Outline a scenario—discuss.
- Discuss the exercise 'aim'.
- Ask for 'objectives' to be forwarded to the exercise lead prior to the next meeting.

- Agree an exercise name.
- Agree the core planning team.
- Discuss a policy on exercise observers—see section on Observers.
- Discuss Exercise Director, Exercise Facilitator(s). Two main facilitators/presenters and one facilitator per table.
- Discuss who will 'compere' or 'host' the exercise.
- Discuss policy on exercise assessor(s).
- Agree table top format.
- Discuss venue—will you need microphones?
- Discuss media involvement to promote and report the exercise.
- Discuss exercise logistics—badges and administration.
- Discuss any costs and agree where those costs lie.
- Agree/confirm the schedule of planning meetings.
- Create an action tracking list and whose action it is.

Second planning meeting (two–three weeks later)

- Confirm exercise aim.
- Update exercise objectives.
- Decide on resource boards.
- Confirm the scenario.
- Agree/confirm the presenters and facilitators.
- Agree venue.
- Agree the table top format—syndicate make-up/presentations by guest speakers/expert panel.
- Draft the exercise inputs.
- Agree what additional material is required, e.g. photos, maps, audio/visual inputs.
- Discuss exercise inputs and agree 'model' answers.
- Present draft 'Exercise Order'.
- Check action list for outstanding actions and add new ones as required.

Third planning meeting (two–three weeks later)

- Assemble all exercise management team for briefing. Including main facilitators, syndicate facilitators and presenters (if available). Also include the facility manager to confirm catering and reception arrangements.
- Visit/check venue/seating and audio/visual.

- Agree exercise inputs and agree 'model' answers.
- Agree exercise order and players briefing pack.
- Prepare the debrief document schedule or headings based upon the objectives.
- Run through any additional material—flip charts, photos, maps etc.
- Agree what plans will be made available to the players.
- Schedule the first debrief meeting.

Control Post Exercise Checklist

Remember that a project management approach can be very useful in large complex exercises. Allow 6–9 months' planning time for this exercise. Setting out a provisional schedule of planning meetings will be useful even if it is amended as the process proceeds. The points in this section will assist in preparing a planning meeting agenda.

The following schedule/actions are suggested as a minimum.

First planning meeting

- Invite representatives of all participating organisations and internal departments who have a role within the plan.
- Obtain their contact details and circulate at the first meeting to everyone present.
- Invite all those who have an exercise support role such as catering staff, telecommunications, facilities managers, HR managers, etc. for each of the locations being used.
- Confirm who the lead organisation is for the exercise.
- Agree who is the designated Exercise Director.
- Confirm who is the lead person.
- Discuss a date for the exercise.
- Outline a scenario.
- Agree the exercise 'aim'.
- Ask for 'objectives' to be forwarded prior to the next meeting.
- Discuss media objectives both real and exercise.
- Agree an exercise name.
- Agree the core planning team.
- Discuss a policy on exercise observers—see Observers.

- Discuss policy on exercise assessor(s).
- Discuss which sites/co-ordination or control centres will be active.
- Discuss where the site will be for Exercise Control.
- Agree exercise logistics—badges and administration.
- Discuss any costs and agree where those costs lie.
- Discuss any cost recovery issues and agree how this will be administered.
- Agree/confirm the schedule of planning meetings.
- Arrange to have the exercise videoed and/or photographs taken.
- Create an action tracking list and whose action it is.

Second planning meeting (4–6 weeks later)

- Confirm exercise aim.
- Update exercise objectives.
- Decide on resource boards.
- Confirm the scenario.
- Confirm Exercise Director.
- Agree/confirm exercise managers and umpires.
- Agree site for Exercise Control.
- Agree exercise communications.
- Draft/collate the exercise inputs.
- Agree what additional material is required, e.g. photos, maps, audio/visual inputs.
- Present draft 'Exercise Document' (or exercise order).
- Check action list for outstanding actions and add new ones.

Third planning meeting (4–6 weeks later)

- Update scenario if required.
- Confirm exercise objectives.
- Confirm exercise inputs.
- Confirm active/live sites.
- Present updated Exercise Order.
- Update on observers and their management.
- Confirm umpires and exercise managers (and assessors if operating).
- Confirm communications network for both exercise and exercise management.

- Collate all relevant telephone phone numbers for both exercise play and exercise management.
- Prepare the debrief schedule and activity areas based upon the objectives.
- Agree Exercise Order and players briefing pack.
- Agree how players will be introduced into exercise—pre-positioned, called in as required by umpires or in real time.
- Confirm media arrangements and any Media Briefing Centre (MBC).

Fourth planning meeting (4–6 weeks later)

- Assemble all exercise management team for briefing based upon exercise order. Include Director, exercise managers, umpires and assessors.
- Visit and check live venue(s) including MBC.
- Visit and check Exercise Control.
- Sign off Exercise Order and players briefing pack for printing.
- Run through additional material.
- Agree what plans will be made available to players.
- Check communications directory.
- Fix dates to brief driver inputters.
- Schedule the first debrief meeting.
- Identify/draft debrief activities schedule.

Fifth planning meeting (4–6 weeks later or just before the exercise)

- Brief senior exercise players.
- Brief any controlled players.
- Brief exercise support staff and assistants.
- Final briefing of Exercise Management Team.
- Revisit all co-ordination or control centres—final inspection.

TASK 8.4

Can you suggest why taking video and photographing an exercise can be beneficial?

Live Exercise Checklist

Live exercising is the most realistic form of exercising. Some aspects of emergency response can only be accurately tested or evaluated by live exercising. Depending upon the nature of the exercise it can be quite modest in scale and can exercise only a small part of the overall plan. In fact it can form a chapter of a larger exercise including components from table top and control post as we have seen.

The primary issue for concern in planning for a live exercise is the safety of all those involved. Where there is a site or multiple sites, including the use of props such as buildings, trains, vehicles, shipping or aircraft extensive risk assessment is needed. Close observation of all activity sites is vital and clearly understood rules of disengagement should a real incident occur. Dedicated health and safety officers *must* be deployed at all times to supervise activities. They can interrupt exercise play by a given signal, usually a whistle or air horn—the meaning of which will appear in all exercise documents and will form part of any briefings.

For a major live play exercise allow 6–12 months' planning time. The points in this section will assist in preparing a planning meeting agenda.

The following schedule/actions are suggested.

First planning meeting

- Invite representatives of all participating organisations and internal departments who have a role within the plan.
- Obtain their contact details and circulate during the meeting if possible.
- Invite all those who have an exercise support role such as catering staff, telecommunications, facilities managers, HR managers, potential site owners, etc.
- Discuss the exercise 'aim'.
- Ask for relevant 'objectives' to be forwarded prior to the next meeting.
- Confirm who the lead organisation is for the exercise.
- Confirm who the lead person will be.
- Discuss any cost recovery issues and agree how this will be administered.
- Discuss and confirm the need to live exercise. Combined exercising options?
- Discuss the proposed location of the exercise site or sites.
- Discuss the use of notional live sites—where controlled players are used. See Chapter 9.

- Discuss which sites/co-ordination or control centres will be active.
- Discuss where the site will be for Exercise Control.
- Discuss the use of resource boards (real or notional resources).
- Consider time of year and likely weather conditions.
- Consider what additional props may be needed e.g. dummy casualties, wreckage, artificial smoke, etc.
- Consider a public awareness strategy to prevent concern and panic.
- Agree a media policy to observe and report the exercise. How are you going to promote the exercise?
- Discuss media objectives both real and exercise.
- Discuss a date for the exercise.
- Outline a scenario.
- Agree an exercise name.
- Agree the core planning team.
- Discuss a policy on exercise observers—see Observers.
- Agree Exercise Director, exercise umpires.
- Discuss a policy on exercise assessor(s).
- Agree exercise logistics—badges and administration.
- Will you need onsite toilets?
- Discuss any costs and agree where those costs lie.
- Agree/confirm the schedule of planning meetings.
- Try to arrange for an exercise to be videoed and/or photographs taken.
- Create an action tracking list and decide whose action it is.

Second planning meeting (4–6 weeks later)

- Confirm Exercise Director.
- Confirm the scenario.
- Confirm exercise aim.
- Update exercise objectives.
- Decide on resource boards.
- Consider any proposed site and arrange for site visits.
- Discuss a contingency in case the weather is not suitable for the exercise—what else can you do?
- Discuss additional props needed for the exercise.

- Agree what additional material is required, e.g. photos, maps, audio/visual inputs.
- Agree site for Exercise Control.
- Agree/confirm exercise managers and umpires.
- Draft/collate the exercise inputs.
- Present draft 'Exercise Order' (or exercise programme).
- Check action list for outstanding actions and add new ones.

Third planning meeting (4–6 weeks later)

- Update scenario if required.
- Confirm exercise objectives.
- Confirm exercise inputs.
- Confirm active/live sites.
- Confirm site locations.
- Confirm all props are available and booked/sourced.
- Present updated Exercise Order.
- Update on observers and their management.
- Confirm umpires and exercise managers(and assessors, if operating).
- Confirm communications network for both exercise and exercise management.
- Collate all relevant telephone phone numbers for both exercise play and exercise management.
- Prepare the debrief schedule and activity areas based upon the objectives.
- Agree Exercise Order and players' briefing pack.
- Agree how players will be introduced into exercise—pre-positioned, called in as required by umpires or in real time.
- Confirm media arrangements and any Media Briefing Centre (MBC).

Fourth/fifth planning meeting (4–6 weeks later)

Note: A fifth meeting may be needed to be able to visit all sites depending on their distribution.

- Assemble all exercise management team for briefing based upon exercise order. Include Director, exercise manager, umpires, assessors.
- Visit and check live co-ordination or control centre(s) including MBC.

- Visit and check Exercise Control.
- Visit exercise site(s).
- Sign off Exercise Order and players' briefing pack for printing.
- Run through additional material.
- Agree what plans will be made available to players.
- Check communications directory.
- Fix dates to brief driver inputters.
- Confirm exercise evaluation forms.
- Agree the debrief team.
- Schedule the first debrief meeting.
- Agree debrief activity schedule.

Sixth planning meeting (4–6 weeks later or just before the exercise)

- Brief senior exercise players.
- Brief any controlled players.
- Brief exercise support staff and assistants.
- Final briefing of Exercise Management Team.
- Distribute all exercise documents.
- Revisit all sites—final inspection.

TASK 8.5

During live exercises a public information strategy is important—can you suggest why that is?

Summary

You will now understand:

- The basic preparations to make for exercise planning meetings and the advantage of the project management approach.
- The key issues that need to be addressed in planning for an exercise meeting for any type of exercise and be able to prepare a comprehensive agenda.

Conclusion

This Chapter has concentrated on preparing checklists to assist in creating a logical planning process to the exercise. Preparing agendas is an important part of the meeting process. It will keep the planning process and discussion on track and together with completing actions associated with those meetings the overall planning should be problem free. Approached in a systematic way, preparing for an exercise is a straightforward activity.

Chapter 9 will consider how to actually run the exercise on the day including the final preparations and ensuring it all goes smoothly.

How to Run the Exercise

Overview

In this Chapter, you will cover the following:

- The seminar exercise
- Table top exercise
- Control post exercise
- Live exercise

Having now looked at the main types of exercises, the key participants, scenario development and planning the exercise, we can now turn to actually running the exercise on the day. We will look at this from the perspective of the exercise manager and/or main presenter, who may have also chaired or jointly chaired the planning meetings. We will assume that it is the EPO.

This Chapter is intended to provide a sample programme for each type of exercise we have already described. Use the programmes given as a template to develop your own more detailed programmes.

The Seminar Exercise

We will start with the **seminar exercise**.

The day before or earlier that day, the EPO will arrive at the venue, which will have been pre-booked in advance, and checked that refreshments have been ordered. The room layout will be in the form of group tables of 8–10 people. It is a good idea if the groups are mixed up into senior and junior staff with a mix of expertise to assist in sharing information.

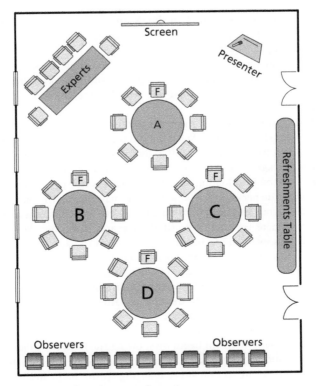

Figure 9.1 Exercise room layout

The room is laid out in 'cabaret style', as illustrated in Figure 9.1. This is ideal for interaction and forming teams. The IT should be checked for example, the PowerPoint projector and that the presentation is working correctly. Ensure that the multiple choice questions (about 30 questions) and answers are prepared and there are sufficient copies for all. A hardcopy plan should be placed on each table with notepaper and pens. Label each table A, B, C, etc. It is always useful to have a flip chart or dry wipe board to hand for spontaneous use.

The exercise programme may look something like this.

Instructions for the EPO

0930 Reception
Set up a reception desk and issue badges. Try to make the first name prominent on the badge so other participants can easily read it. A seating plan should be displayed, prepared by you earlier. Again, ensure you create a good mix of experience and skills. Registration is important to record those who have attended for record purposes and

for health and safety reasons should an evacuation be required. Try to get e-mail addresses at registration. Coffee/tea should be provided.

0945 Opening

A senior manager should do this if possible. You should have approached and secured their attendance during the planning process. It is a good idea to prepare a draft of what you would like them to say!

0950 Introduction

At this point, you thank the person offering the opening remarks and everyone for attending. You will then introduce yourself with a little personal background. It is often useful to go into some depth about your background. Why? Your credibility will affect how participants receive the information you deliver. This is not to say you should overdo the personal introduction as it may also tip the participants against you. But the right balance is needed. Just deliver the main key areas where you can demonstrate relevant experience. You should then ask everyone to introduce themselves to each other on their tables, not to the whole seminar. Allow about 5–10 minutes for this. If there is an expert panel, ask them to introduce themselves.

Cover health and safety and domestic arrangements.

Explain the format for the day and explain the purpose of the test or quiz at the end of the seminar.

1000 Presentation of the Plan

Your presentation will begin by showing the hard copy plan to the group and the importance of the session. Work through the plan sequentially in section order referring to the main headings and drawing out the most important areas. Constantly ask for thoughts and their observations. Make sure you address all the areas that will appear in the test later.

If you have assembled an 'expert' panel, frequently refer to them for comment.

1100 Coffee—breaks are important, not only as a comfort break but to allow interaction between participants and to share their comments and observations among themselves.

1115 Resume—as above

1230 Finish/Lunch

1330 Quiz

Offer a quick resume of the critical areas of the plan. Explain the purpose of the quiz. The emphasis is on it being fun. Refer to it as a quiz and each table can form a team. This will promote discussion. Offer a token prize for the winning team.

1430 Finish the quiz and collect the question papers. Break for coffee.

1445 Answers to the quiz

Resume and go through the paper giving the correct answers. Do not be too hasty to move on if there is a query on any question. Take this opportunity to clarify, leave no doubt. In fact, there may be occasions where some very useful and valid suggestions are made to amend the plan. Take these points on board and thank them for their comments. This engenders ownership. If you have an 'expert' panel, ask for final comments from them.

1530 Conclusion

Conclude the session. Announce the winning team. And ask for any final comments. Hand out a simple feedback sheet and ask them to complete. Ensure that you encourage them to make contact with you if they have any further questions—give them your details.

1600 Finish exercise

TASK 9.1

Create an evaluation sheet that is suitable for this type of exercise.

Table Top Exercise

In this example, we will have multi-agency syndicates as 'units' of equal knowledge and expertise.

It is a good idea to visit the venue the day before and check out the audio and visuals. Contact any presenters to confirm their attendance. It is also a good idea to have some back-up audio visual (AV) in case of failures. Also, make sure the catering is scheduled and reception arrangements are in place. Check that badges are ready and the tables have the necessary documents, such as plans, maps, photos, notepaper and pens, with A1 flip charts. Label each table A, B, C, D, E, etc. as in Figure 9.1. The table layout is the same as for the seminar exercise. If the venue is a hotel or conference centre meet the facilities manager and discuss final points.

In this exercise it is assumed that the EPO has managed to enlist four presenters to give four 15-minute inputs on subjects relevant to the plan.

The exercise programme may look like this.

Instructions for the EPO

0800 Final Checks

Arrange to meet the exercise planning staff at the venue for a last-minute briefing. Check out the AV and that all presentations are loaded on the computer and displaying correctly. Check out the microphones if the venue is large. Ensure reception is ready to receive participants.

0900 Reception

A seating plan should be displayed in a prominent position. This will be prepared before the day ensuring you have the right mix of people in the syndicates to suit the format you have chosen for this exercise.

Registration is important to record those who have attended and for health and safety reasons should an evacuation be required. Try to get e-mail addresses of those present by handing out an attendance list if you do not have that information at registration.

Coffee/tea should be provided.

0930 Opening

A senior manager should do this if possible. You should have approached and secured their attendance during the planning process. As in the seminar exercise it is a good idea to prepare a draft of what you would like them to say!

0935 Introduction

At this point you thank the person offering the opening remarks and everyone for attending. You will then introduce yourself with a little background (see seminar exercise earlier) and ask players to introduce themselves to their tables.

Then introduce the other principal facilitator and each facilitator on the tables. Introduce the expert panel—a short CV provided by them will assist you. These short CVs can be pre-positioned on each table.

Cover health and safety and domestic arrangements.

Explain that the exercise is about testing systems, processes and procedures and is not an examination. Encourage all to get involved and enjoy the day.

The exercise will now be explained, for example:

- It is a syndicate based table top exercise
- Each syndicate is made up of... *explain the makeup of the groups, and are facilitated to assist your discussion*
- *'A scenario will be outlined and you will be asked to consider a number of issues arising from the incident as described. These will be in the form of a number of written questions or paper feeds, as they are sometimes called. You will be given a set time to do this and one syndicate will be asked to give the primary feedback. Feel free to use the flip charts to outline your response. Please nominate a spokesperson to do this. We will then open the issues up for general discussion,'* (With regard to nominated spokespersons—often participants may feel a little shy about talking in front of so many people or senior managers. Sometimes it is useful to brief facilitators to encourage the 'host' organisation to volunteer the spokesperson if there are no other volunteers.)

'Please feel free to ask the advice of the expert panel at any time and use the plans on the tables which will deal with this incident.'

'I will now outline the current circumstances'...as prepared by the planning team. This will be the general situation with all attendant details leading up to the incident. There is an example of an introduction and questions in the Chapter dealing with scenario development.

• Read the current circumstances and refer to any video, photos, maps already prepared for the purpose.

1000 Hand out the questions, first input, usually 3–4 questions and start the clock, say 30 minutes.

Near the end of time, it is a good idea to inform which group will be giving feedback. You will select which group gives feedback so this can be shared out evenly and you may identify a particular team that would be expected to give good feedback. Do not ask for volunteers to feedback—as there will be uneasy laughter and a reluctance to do so. Count them down from 10 minutes.

1030 Ask the nominated syndicate to give feedback and facilitate the response ensuring that maximum information is extracted. Be positive and encouraging throughout. Your Exercise Order should have prompts to assist you in terms of the 'model' answer.

Open it up to the whole group and ask for contributions from the expert panel. Facilitate the following discussion.

1050 Conclude Feedback

(At this point you can introduce a presenter to cover a relevant topic—15 minutes)

1105 Second input. Develop the scenario.

1135 Second feedback session.

1200 Second presenter (15 minutes)

1215 Third Input. Further develop the scenario.

1245 Third Feedback Session.

1300 Conclude Third Feedback session.

1300 **Lunch**

1345 Re-start with third presenter.

1400 Final Fourth Input.

1430 Fourth feedback session.

1500 **Coffee**

1515 Final presenter.

1530 De-brief/lessons learned. At this point you will refer to your facilitators to summarise the learning points from each syndicate. These should be on a flip chart and collected later. These will be collated and form the de-brief report. This should be forwarded to all those participating and where necessary fed back into the plan. Leave evaluation sheets on each table for players to complete.

1600 Conclusion and closing comments. This should be delivered by a senior manager.

1615 **Disperse.**

TASK 9.2

Create an evaluation sheet that is suitable for this type of exercise.

Control Post Exercise

In preparing for a control post exercise the live co-ordination or control centres, including the media briefing centre (MBC), if being used, should be available for use at least the day before the exercise and subject of a visit by all the planning team, including the director, umpires and assessors.

Formal briefings should have been held in the preceding few days for all the planning team members and those involved in the exercise management, for example, security, catering, facilities managers, etc. Arrangements for observers will be confirmed as they will need a briefing away from exercise activity and then to be brought to the venue(s). Exercise Control should be visited and scrutinised to ensure the exercise driving scripts are there and telephone numbers are posted on the walls or on each desk. If there is a time line that should also be displayed.

Depending how it has been decided to introduce players, either pre-positioned at the start of the exercise or their attendance is controlled from a 'holding' area, is a matter for the planning team. A holding area is useful if the attending players would have had to travel long distances to the co-ordination or control centre. A holding area means that they can travel the night before and be introduced in a gradual fashion to simulate a more realistic staged response and that enables briefing arrangements to be tested by the exercise players on their arrival. The players can be notified and brought forward to the co-ordination or control centre as they are requested by the players by an umpire contacting the holding room and requesting their attendance.

A staged response will also reduce the 'log jam' of attendees at the control centre reception for booking them in. But if a holding area is agreed it should be visited to ensure that players, as they are directed to the holding area have a comfortable spacious room with refreshments. In the holding room arrangements must be in place for the players to have contact within the respective co-ordination or control centres as they would have in reality by either land line or mobile phone. To this end all telephone numbers must be posted in the holding room as they appear in the exercise order. The holding area will need to have at least two exercise assistants to deal with the reception of players and escorting them to the co-ordination or control centre(s).

Any controlled players will receive a separate 'edited' briefing and it is permissible to brief senior management staff taking part in the exercise on the general conduct of the exercise only, in particular the role of umpires, assessors and observers.

Ensure that all key management staff playing in the exercise in co-ordination or control centres in particular are wearing tabards displaying their role. This is important for players who may be attending the centre for the first time and unfamiliar with the roles.

In this example we will assume that there are five live co-ordination or control centres and a media briefing centre operating:

1. Company Site Emergency Control—located at site.
2. Multi-agency Police Strategic Co-ordination Centre (Gold Control).
3. Multi-agency Police Tactical Co-ordination Centre (Silver Control).
4. Multi-agency Police Operational Co-ordination Centre (Bronze Control).
5. Local Authority Emergency Room—located at LA premises.
6. Multi-agency Media Briefing Centre—located at police premises.

Figure 9.2 illustrates the communication links between the centres and Exercise Control. Exercise Control with communication links with all active centres and the players holding area. The dotted lines show the interaction between the active sites.

The exercise day may look like this. What follows are the instruction for the EPO who is exercise manager in Exercise Control.

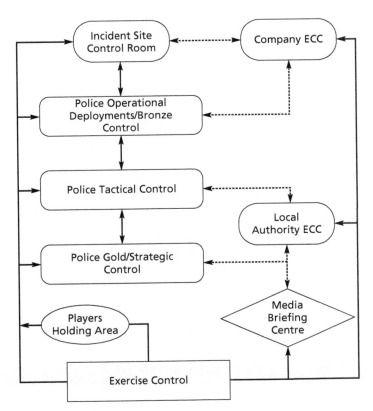

Figure 9.2 Control post exercise module

0700 Arrive at Exercise Control. Contact each umpire/assessor in turn and confirm that they are in position at each live site.

0730 Assemble Exercise Control staff and exercise director and brief the exercise inputters.

0800 Contact all umpires to confirm that their senior management players have been briefed on the conduct of the exercise.

Contact 'Observer Liaison' to ensure observers are in position.

Contact player liaison assistants at the holding area(s), if one is being used.

0830 Startex—Exercise start. Contact each umpire to declare the exercise is running at each co-ordination or control centre.

- Ensure exercise inputs are on time
- Keep regular contact with all umpires and exercise assistants
- Deal with any questions and/or refer to the Exercise Director for decision
- The exercise will proceed and create its own momentum. As lunch time approaches ensure that agreed refreshments arrangements are implemented.
- The exercise will terminate on the instructions of the Exercise Director. This can be at the request of any regulators who are assessing the exercise for regulatory purposes but the ultimate decision rests with the director to ensure that every reasonable opportunity has been used to achieve all the objectives of the exercise.

1630 Assuming the exercise has been terminated, a Hot DeBrief (see Chapter 10) will be called in a site of suitable size. It should be open to all those who wish to attend. If it is an exercise required by regulators they will lead or share the debrief with the lead organisation. A Hot Debrief will only take very brief details of perhaps three positive points and three areas for improvement. These will be recorded for use at the formal or cold debrief. (Further information relating to debriefs will follow in Chapter 10.)

1700 Hot Debrief to take place. The closing remarks would normally be jointly shared but led by the Exercise Director followed by other senior managers or indeed any high profile observers.

Following the exercise there will be a considerable amount of clean up and returning co-ordination or control centres to normality. Feedback will have been provided from several sources and we will look in Chapter 10 at how to approach the debrief process to ensure that every piece of useful information is used to improve structures, procedures and processes including evaluating training.

TASK 9.3

Create an evaluation sheet that is suitable for this type of exercise.

Live Exercise

This exercise will probably be the most challenging logistically with several days of preparation being required.

If the exercise has potential to impact upon the public, for example if they can see any exercise activity there will be a need to pre-warn residents or passers-by, by either placing advertisements in newspapers, addressing community groups or neighbourhood groups. In restricted locations leaflet drops can be useful and taking the opportunity to reassure the public too. This is important for fixed chemical or nuclear sites subject to special regulations and public information obligations. Another useful means to advise the public is to display a sign making it clear what is happening.

For example, see Figure 9.3 as an example for displaying a very large sign or banner covering all areas if running an exercise in a railway siding which can be seen from other trains, the road or adjacent properties.

A direct information line should be clearly visible for genuine public interest which should be routed into exercise control. This will also prevent the public dialling emergency numbers and informing the press and setting 'hares running'. It is money well spent as the sign or signs can be re-used.

In this example of a live exercise we assume to have:

1. Two live sites A & B
2. One Tactical Co-ordination Centre (Silver)
3. One Forward Media Briefing Point
4. One notional Strategic Co-ordination Centre (Gold)
5. One notional Communications Centre
6. One notional Media Briefing Centre

Figure 9.4 illustrates the communications links connecting the exercise centres and Exercise Control. The dotted line indicates exercise control communications. The solid lines actual exercise interaction; note that exercise control is monitoring as well as 'feeding' the exercise with notional input.

ANYTOWN RESILIENCE FORUM / WWW.ALRF.COM

EMERGENCY EXERCISE IN PROGRESS

Figure 9.3 A conspicuous sign to inform and promote exercising

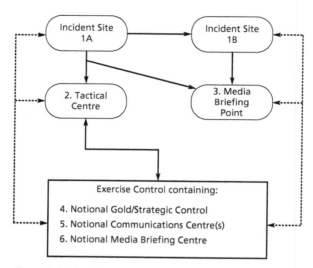

Figure 9.4 Live exercise module

Site visits

The sites at which the exercise will take place have to be visited in the final three days before the exercise and any safety measures put in place. This may take the form of cordons, lighting, directions and first aid arrangements. During the planning phase the site(s) will have been surveyed and a full health and safety risk assessment carried out. During the exercise each site will have a health and safety officer on duty ready to stop the exercise if necessary. The health and safety officer will wear high visibility clothing and use a whistle or air horn to attract attention in the event of an incident requiring the exercise to be stopped or attract attention to an unsafe practice. Ensure that there will be places to brief players and assemble resources as holding areas prior to deployment. Consideration may have to be given to providing shelter in case of bad weather. Consider the Marshalling Area principle as a potential briefing/holding area as we have already seen earlier.

During the final preparations a communications check is vital for both exercise purposes and Exercise Control. Both the Tactical Co-ordination Centre and the Forward Media Briefing Point will need to be visited to ensure everything is ready to begin the exercise.

The day before or shortly before the exercise the full planning team, including the director, umpires, managers, controlled players, assessors and health and safety officer should visit the site(s) to become familiar with the layout and/or terrain. It is at this time that banners or signs will be positioned alerting the public to the exercise. Previous notifications to the public by newspaper or leaflet drops would have been completed days in advance.

On the day of the exercise all players will be assembled in the various locations and will be briefed by the umpires which will be in two parts:

1. Exercise rules, exercise programme and health and safety.

2. An update or situation report to that point for them and what their next duty or task will be—a real time briefing in other words. Point out that they may need to make their own notes to recall the detail—as it would be for real.

This briefing is very important because it will have implications for the health and safety of all players and how the exercise will be stopped if an incident occurs which compromises safety. It will also give players the parameters within which the exercise is run. In other words, what is acceptable behaviour and practice and where to get advice and information from, e.g. the umpires.

During all parts of the exercise try to have it video recorded for future use and training purposes. Still photographs are also very useful for reports and media use at a later stage.

It is assumed in this exercise all players are in position at 'Startex' and no real time attendance is being tested. That is not to say that all personnel are literally standing out in the open waiting to start. Initial response resources are held back in holding positions and called forward as required and directed by Exercise Control via the umpires. There is no need to have police cars, fire engines and ambulances or company vehicles screaming through the streets with 'blues& twos' or orange lights flashing, indeed it would be unnecessary, unjustifiable and perhaps unlawful.

At 'Startex' response resources will be sent to the scene by umpires as directed by Exercise Control in a controlled manner. Activity will begin at the scene as outlined in the exercise order. In reality, it would take a Tactical Co-ordination Centre (Silver) perhaps one hour to set up and begin managing the incident. Therefore, Tactical Co-ordination Centre (Silver) will only be allowed to begin activity by Exercise Control at T + 1 hour. This is where a time line, see Chapter 7, Figure 7.4, would be very useful to 'visualise' the stages. Exercise Control will manage the incident as the notional police Communications Centre until the Tactical Co-ordination Centre is live and Exercise Controlwill hand over to them.

The day would look like this. These are instructions for the EPO:

0700 Exercise Control is open and contact is established with all umpires, assessors and health and safety officers. Inputters are in place to provide the agreed inputs. Confirmation is sought that all sites are ready. In particular, if the weather is suitable—do you need to implement your contingency?

0730 Umpires will assemble their players and carry out the two-part briefing. Tea and coffee is a good idea at this time!

0800 Startex—initial response is activated and directed to the site(s).

> Inputs commence as agreed in the planning stage, e.g. request to open Tactical Co-ordination Centre.
>
> 0900 Tactical Co-ordination Centre and Forward Media Briefing point are open and both are operating.
>
> - Inputs and live play will continue under strict supervision of the health and safety officers at the sites and the exercise will develop its own momentum. Be aware of players in the open being expose to adverse weather—both cold and too much sun.
> - Keep regular contact with all umpires and exercise assistants. Ensure catering is provided at regular intervals.
> - Deal with any questions and/or refer to the Exercise Director for decision.
> - The exercise will terminate on the instructions of the Exercise Director. This can be at the request of any regulators who are assessing the exercise for regulatory purposes but the ultimate decision rests with the director to ensure that every reasonable opportunity has been used to achieve all the objectives of the exercise.
>
> 1500 Assuming the exercise has been terminated. A Hot Debrief (see Debriefing—Chapter 10) will be called at a site of suitable size. It should be open to all those who wish to attend. If it is an exercise required by regulators they will lead or share the debrief with the lead organisation. A Hot Debrief will only take very brief details of perhaps three positive points and three areas for improvement. These will be recorded for use at the formal or cold debrief.
>
> 1600 Hot Debrief to take place. The closing remarks would normally be jointly shared but led by the Exercise Director followed by other senior managers or indeed any high profile observers.

The time line is a useful tool to keep track of activity. A very simple one is shown in Chapter 7, Figure 7.4, with the dark-shaded areas indicating live active sites or facilities and the light-shaded areas indicating sites that are not active.

Following a live exercise there is considerable clean up and return to 'normality'. At this stage all the feedback will be collated in preparation for the forthcoming debriefs. The planning team will have planned a meeting to co-ordinate the collection and analysis of this information. In addition, and often overlooked following a large exercise is to ensure that letters of thanks are sent to all those who took leading roles or who made significant contribution, for example those who provided props, venues, etc. In addition, a corporate message should go out for two reasons. Firstly, to thank everyone for taking part and secondly to reassure everyone that the debrief is imminent and contributions will be welcomed and fed back into the planning process.

Video and photographs should have been taken and they can be edited into a short film for debrief, training and public relations issues.

If the 'real' press were invited to witness the exercise a member of the planning team, preferably a media person should liaise with the relevant editors to agree the copy prior to going to print or broadcast. This will ensure that key public safety messages are delivered in a rational and measured way. There is a temptation for the media to 'hype-up' or sensationalise the event with dramatic headlines. This may sell papers but also alarm the public!

Summary

You will now understand:

- How each form of exercise is set up, controlled and managed.
- The creation of feedback sheets and be aware how important it is to collate and gather that information.
- The importance of using graphical communications networks to add clarity to often complex arrangementsand use of time lines to add structure.

Conclusion

We have looked at running four types of exercise. Although it may seem daunting on paper, the actual events are very rewarding and enjoyable. After planning for and completing the first exercises it will become very clear what needs to be done and although the examples given here only represent one format for each type of exercise there is a whole range to be achieved by mixing and matching the various types.

In Chapter 10 we will take a close look at debriefing. This is the culmination of the whole planning process and the one that will reap the benefits of exercising for any organisation.

10

Debriefing

Overview

In this final Chapter you will cover:

- Effective debriefing
- Debrief types
- Debriefing an exercise
- What is entailed in each form of debrief?
- Running the exercise debrief
- Debriefing a real event
- Completing the debrief report
- Implementing findings
- Overall action monitoring
- Spreading the word

In this final Chapter we will look at the process of debriefing. Although this Chapter is primarily examining the exercise debrief process it will be useful to compare, and in some areas to contrast the process involved in debriefing a real event.

Why do we need to debrief if everything went well? A phrase still heard today. Perhaps it did, but that is unlikely. The debrief is about improvement and continuous development. What went well is just as important as what did not go so well.

The debrief can also be seen as affecting two critical areas. Firstly, the Health and Safety at Work Act 1974 imposes a duty on employers to have in place systems, procedures and processes underpinned by risk assessment offering safe work practices and environments. The debrief is an ideal way of assessing those factors and changing or improving them if required. Secondly, the debrief will evaluate plans. But debriefing must be managed correctly to be of any real benefit which is not always as simple as it may first appear. Naturally people and organisations as a whole shy away from anything that may be critical of them, both on a personal level and an organisational level, which may have implications in terms of liability and reputation.

These concerns must be overcome and the role of the EPO is to present, facilitate and manage the debrief to maximise its undoubted benefit. A good, open, honest and progressive approach to self-analysis is a sign of a mature and healthy organisation and the debrief is the demonstration of that maturity.

As we have already discussed, corporate manslaughter is now a reality in modern management and managers with a directing influence on matters where lives could be lost may be held accountable for their actions. Debriefing is the first stage in realising positive change and improvement within an organisation's emergency arrangements and demonstrating a commitment to duty of care. Being able to show a robust training, exercise and review programme for plans can help negate any accusations that an organisation is complacent with regard to health and safety and emergency arrangements. How an organisation implements lessons learned is the key element in demonstrating that commitment. That is why debriefing is so important.

The right tone and atmosphere must be set from the start of a debrief process. A debrief can quickly degrade into accusations and blame for apparent failures. This must be avoided at all costs. Participants must feel free and confident to speak out and contribute spontaneously, the chair has an important role to play here. The purpose of the debrief should be:

- To review processes, procedures, structures, and not individuals apart from identifying potential training needs generally. It is not an opportunity to point the finger.
- To identify good practice and areas for future development.
- To promote an open and honest discussion.
- Not to compromise any ongoing investigation and acknowledge an individual's wish to decline to comment if that will compromise or incriminate them in any investigation.

This final point is important, this has been addressed earlier to some extent but the desire to have a debrief following a real incident, in particular where fatalities are involved may present difficulties for those charged with the investigation of that incident. Issues disclosed within a debrief may compromise an investigation. For that reason any decision to proceed with a debrief in such circumstances must be discussed with those carrying out that investigation, which may include the police, the coroner, Crown Prosecution Service (CPS) or the Health and Safety Executive and any observations or guidelines given by them followed to the letter. However, this situation does not prevent a debrief taking place but just means care needs to be taken. Delaying a debrief for anything up to two years pending the outcome of a complex criminal trial would be nonsense and leave opportunities for the same thing to happen again because lessons were not learned and passed on to improve. Clearly, the need to prevent a reoccurrence is paramount.

For exercising, after months of planning and following the exercise itself there is an understandable tendency to think that the debrief and review is just a formality. In fact, it is the debrief and more importantly, the subsequent process that will see the implementation of lessons learned from the exercise and is the most important part of the whole exercise process.

The implementation of lessons learned must be based upon a robust, tenacious and auditable process. The planning team for the exercise or the debrief team for a real event will oversee this process and responsibility must be made clear who will carry the process through to conclusion.

In the event of a real incident, there will be some form of inquiry. It can take the form of anything from:

- Single agency/company internal departmental debrief and inquiry with insurers
- A multi-agency debrief at which everyone's actions are examined
- A coroner's inquest
- A public inquiry
- A Health and Safety Executive investigation
- A police investigation

In some cases there will be a combination of more than one. How do we ensure we get the most benefit from an exercise or following a real event?

TASK 10.1

Research the process and conditions to allow a public inquiry to proceed.

Effective Debriefing

Debriefing is often undertaken by people who, because of the very nature of their position within an organisation it is assumed will know what to do, similar in many ways to assuming that the Chief Executive Officer (CEO) will be great in front of a TV camera...not always so.

Without an effective chair a debrief can easily become confused, disjointed and confrontational. Debriefing is not difficult but does require someone who has good communication and facilitation skills, a good and experienced chairperson for example. Detailed knowledge of the precise nature of the exercise or incident is not in itself necessary and in some cases can be a positive disadvantage. The chair should be seen as objective and independent and it is therefore useful for the debrief chairperson to be able to declare that at the debrief. Under no circumstances can a player or a person involved in a real event facilitate the debrief. With the best will in the world they will be biased in favour of their own performance and perceptions.

Choosing a debrief chair is a task for the planning team or debrief team. Whoever takes the role of debrief chair or facilitator they must have the support of the planning team or debrief team in the form of providing them with the necessary information, evaluation reports, recommendations and the final draft debrief reports to allow them to quality assure the document before it is published.

What kind of debrief format should be used? Some observations now from the outset about 'structured debriefing'—structured debriefing is a term relating to a form of debriefing popular with some organisations. It has gained popularity essentially in the absence of a real alternative methodology, such as that described in this book. It is not intended here to explain in detail structured debriefing which has some positive benefits but it does have inherent limitations. For example, the number of participants can be very limiting. This is because of the seating configuration and a requirement for participants to leave their seats to place sticky post-it notes on a board. In addition, structured debriefing only takes the debrief process to the identification of the issues and not through to action allocation and post-incident implementation. The process does discourage group problem solving or decision-making. The advantages often cited for using structured debriefing are often issues that an effective facilitator or chairperson can deal with. For example, allowing those who are less assertive to take a full and active part, a good facilitator will be aware of that and address it. In essence, structured debriefing is useful for small groups with limited scope for carrying the debrief process to conclusion. In some cases a combination of structured debriefing and more formal debriefing can be achieved to take advantage of the structured concept.

Alternatively, following the advice in this book provides a flexible framework approach to exercise and real incident debriefing. This system allows for large numbers of people to attend and to reach conclusions and implement actions. In reality the nature and scale of debriefs today often involves large numbers of people being driven by a strong imperative to issue actions to organisations to implement auditable change.

An exercise or indeed a real incident could have several debriefs. A debrief is not required for a seminar based exercise. The objective and outcomes of a seminar exercise are different to a table top, control post, live exercise or real incident. Let's now look at the types of debrief that are available.

TASK 10.2

Outline a number of examples where it would be undesirable to have the debrief chair as someone who took part in the exercise or incident and explore the reasons.

Debrief Types

There are a number of debrief formats which each have a place in the overall debrief process. They are:

- Hot
- Single Agency
- Internal
- Multi-agency
- Formal
- Cold

We will now consider each one and how they build into a co-ordinated debrief process.

Debriefing an Exercise

Getting the information? Following the exercise the first task is to collect and collate all the feedback. The following activities and people will have provided most of the material.

- Hot debrief (notes taken at the time)
- Umpires (reports)
- Assessors (reports)
- Regulators (if present)
- Managers (reports)
- Players (through evaluation sheets)
- Observers (through feedback sheets)
- Health and Safety Officers (Live exercise observations)

The format of the feedback will come in a variety of ways from evaluation sheets, written reports, message forms, logs, minutes, screen shots, photos of status boards and observations. All that information will have to be analysed, categorised, interpreted and set out in a form that is easily understood.

This is where the debrief schedule will help you as described earlier in Chapter 8.

What is Entailed in Each Form of Debrief?

Hot debrief

It occurs immediately after the exercise (or incident) to capture key issues. It is more informal and flexible than a formal or cold debrief, as we shall see, in that a reporting debrief schedule as illustrated earlier will not be necessary. The hot debrief should be opened by and facilitated by the Exercise Director and any additional opening remarks from attending regulators or high profile observers taken. This hot debrief will be chaired by the Exercise Director and supported by any regulators.

At the hot debrief everyone involved in the exercise should have an opportunity to provide feedback. This is often extremely useful as it is fresh in the mind and usually brings out the key or 'hot' issues. Having a note taker present is essential to capture this information.

The purpose of the debrief process should be outlined and those present encouraged to offer their views. Umpires and assessors should be ready to provide at least three areas of improvement and three positive points and they should be called upon by the director to start the feedback and evaluation at the start of the debrief. Those facilitating or chairing debriefs must try to avoid using negative language—such as bad points, criticisms or blame. Using such words can ignite a negative and defensive reaction. Using words like, areas for improvement, more efficient methods, enhanced the procedure, develop the system, etc., keeping the language positive and optimistic will encourage more constructive contributions.

At the hot debrief reinforce the need to complete the evaluation sheets provided to everyone and have them returned to a nominated person within the planning team. Use stamped addressed envelopes if necessary and have plenty of evaluation sheets available to hand out. In addition, issue an e-mail address clearly displayed for anyone to make contact with the planning or debrief team. Evaluation sheets and e-mails are also useful as some players may be a little reluctant to openly express their views in a hot debrief situation, particularly if it involves another member of staff—remember 'Groupthink'.

In concluding the hot debrief outline the process of collating feedback and the production of the final report.

Single agency/company/internal (formal or cold) debrief

These are restricted to single agency or company personnel. They are carried out by organisations and companies to identify issues which are peculiar to themselves in terms of internal processes and to co-ordinate issues to be taken forward to any multi-agency, external or cold debrief. These debriefs are normally chaired by their own agency or company personnel who were not players in the exercise. An exercise manager for that organisation or company can act as debrief chair. If, however, it is an internal exercise only, an independent chair would be more appropriate from another branch or department. These internal debriefs are useful opportunities to 'iron-out' any issues before presenting to the more formal multi-agency or external debrief. Organisations may feel more comfortable discussing internal issues in a closed environment.

In a multi-agency exercise each participating organisation should hold their own internal debrief. Not to do so is a missed opportunity.

It is also important to consider using a debrief schedule as illustrated earlier, for an internal debrief too but configure it to address the issues relevant to the company or organisation based upon their objectives.

Invite everyone who took part in the exercise to the internal debrief. This is important to demonstrate appreciation for their contribution and an opportunity to personally thank everyone. It is also about building confidence in the organisation in the debrief process. However, in reality there may appear to be a distinct lack of enthusiasm for this phase of the post-exercise process. It can often appear tedious and boring as all the exciting and interesting stuff is over! It is important, though, to encourage everyone to attend. It is better to be open and inclusive rather than restrict access only to those who genuinely have an interest or an 'issue'. Having as many people at the debrief as possible will perhaps open up new areas or viewpoints previously not considered. Active encouragement is the key—again ensuring senior management support to allow participants to attend and support the debrief process.

This debrief is also an ideal opportunity to nominate representatives to attend any multi-agency debriefs that are scheduled. The internal reporting and implementation of actions once identified should follow the model outlined in Figure 10.2 later.

Multi-agency (formal or cold) debrief

The multi-agency (formal or cold) debrief is the culmination of the debrief process in which all participating organisations meet to discuss the learning outcomes of the exercise.

Multi-agency exercises, because of the sheer numbers of participants, can be very big indeed. A degree of selection and negotiating may be required to keep the numbers manageable but not to the detriment of ensuring the key people are there.

Multi-agency debriefs are usually a number of months following the exercise and it is therefore useful to recap before the debrief begins. If a video has been taken, which is essential during a live exercise, this can be shown as an introduction. A properly edited version of the exercise video is an asset for future training and briefing too. These debriefs are also an ideal means of consolidating relations and building a rapport with colleagues and partners because this will pay real dividends in a real event where most people are known to each other.

During this debrief the debrief schedule is vital as a reference and for giving the debrief structure and direction.

Running the Exercise Debrief

A short meeting will be required of the debrief team/planning team to agree the format and running order for the debrief. This will be an action on the final meeting of the planning team.

Ensure that the entire exercise planning team is available, in particular the debrief team together with the umpires and the assessors. Any debrief facilitators who dealt with single agency debriefs should also be there, in most cases they will be part of the exercise planning team anyway. The Exercise Director should also be there and representatives from all participating organisations.

The nominated chair will open the debrief and introduce the director (if not chairing) and key personnel, usually the exercise managers, umpires and assessors. A recap of the exercise should take place as it may have been several months since the exercise. As already mentioned if a video has been taken this is a good opportunity to use it and refresh memories.

The debrief chair will then draw attention to the debrief schedule (see Chapter 7, Figure 7.5) and address the first activity area. This will have been populated by the debrief team based upon all the feedback and evaluation received. General discussion will follow and an action may be identified to address the issues raised. That is then recorded by the 'Action Recorder' on the 'Action Tracking' document (see Figure 10.2 later).

Participants at the debrief should be warned as to any potential restricted classification of any draft debrief report until it is finally published and even then a final classification may be assigned to it—remember the Government Protective Marking Scheme (GPMS). This could be as a result of issues which are commercially sensitive or official secrets issues.

The chair should ask all those present who have held internal debriefs if there are issues that should be raised and declare them, almost like any other business.

The prepared debrief schedule/activity chapter document will be available to all those present. Two note takers will be required. One to record what was said in the form of minutes and the other to write down any actions that come out of the discussions. This person is called the 'Action Recorder'. Actions can come thick and fast and the minute taker could be overwhelmed and possibly miss a vital word or phrase. In addition, the 'Action Recorder' can give a summary at the end of the debrief or real time updates during the debrief as to what actions have been agreed. The chair would find it quite difficult to do any of this having been concentrating on the discussion.

The Action Recorder records the precise nature of the action, who it is allocated to and a proposed time scale. This action-tracking schedule will form the basis for the implementation of lessons learned from the exercise.

To recap, key persons present:

- Exercise Director (chair)
- All planning staff
- Umpires
- Assessors
- Regulators (if any)
- Selected players—representatives
- Invited observer(s)
- Minute taker
- Action recorder

Key documents:

- All evaluation sheets
- Logs/minutes of meetings (SCG/TCG)
- Messages used (SCG/TCG)
- Debrief schedule/Activity Chapters (see Chapter 7, Figure 7.5)
- Action tracking (see Figure 10.2 later)

TASK 10.3

Can you think of ways in which the debrief chair can put participants at ease and ensure everyone has a say?

The debrief will continue using the debrief schedule as a guide and eventually all the issues relating to the objectives will be covered. At that point, the 'Action Tracking' document will contain all the actions raised and who will be responsible for leading on each.

The debrief chair will then ask the 'Action Recorder' to read out all the actions. Participants will then be invited to comment and agree the details. If not, participants should declare any issue they have. When everyone agrees then the 'Action Tracking' document will be accepted.

The chair will conclude the meeting by reminding the participants how the process will move to the final report. A suggested process may look like this:

- A draft debrief report will be produced by the lead organisation or department with an action summary and circulated within two (2) weeks of the debrief to all participating organisations or departments for observations. Circulation will normally be by e-mail.
- Participating organisations or departments should take no longer than one (1) week to lodge observations on the draft with the lead organisation or department.
- This report will be forwarded to the chairperson of the debrief for final approval prior to circulation.
- The report will be forwarded on behalf of the chairperson of the debrief to the lead organisation or department.
- The lead organisation or department will be responsible for distribution of the report.
- Individual organisations or departments will only implement and monitor their own actions.

A typical multi-agency debrief table layout is illustrated in Figure 10.1.

Debriefing a Real Event

Whereas in an exercise the information will be collected and collated as part of the exercise management process, following a real event that information will be captured and recovered by a debrief team designated by the overall incident manager and/or police strategic commander. For inquiry and debrief purposes it is vital to recover all data from all sources as it is not only good practice but will be demanded by legislatives bodies such as the HSE, Coroner, etc. Issues to consider are:

- Prevent the disposal or destruction of any documents, e-mails, message forms, meeting tapes, logbooks or computer disks/drives. Print to hard copy if necessary.
- Ensure everyone is made aware of that requirement and locate those who may have that information.
- Request the information and require 'negative' returns and who gave you the information.
- Deal with any legal privilege issues—take legal advice if necessary.

A debrief team will be appointed to oversee and arrange the recovery of relevant material as just outlined and they will begin to arrange the debrief. In many respects this mirrors the exercise situation where in-house 'hot' debriefs and 'internal' debriefs are followed by a multi-agency debrief. However, a debrief schedule will not be in place to guide the process but an

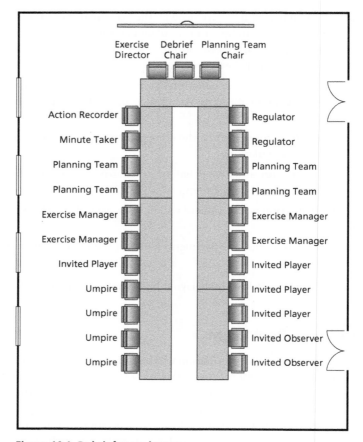

Figure 10.1 Debrief room layout

'Action Tracking' document should be prepared to record the actions from the debrief.

Therefore, it is suggested that a template be created to act as a reminder or aide memoire for the chairperson to use. The following list of issues or template adopts a generic approach to the most common features of the beginning of an incident and its subsequent development. The template is intended to be modified and adapted to suit individual needs.

Managing a real incident debrief

The chairperson, following a general introduction of the incident and the proposed conduct of the debrief, which should include a cautionary note on issues of incrimination and sub-judice, would lead by providing a review or overview of the incident and using any film footage or pictures that are available. This sets the context and reminds those present of the events and allows them to re-focus on the events.

If the event led to fatalities, it may be appropriate to consider a request for a moment to reflect on those who died and their families. This is not a minute's silence, but a few moments. There is no better or poignant reminder of why debriefing is so important.

In this example, it is following an incident where the police led the co-ordination, but the areas covered are as relevant to any organisation in their design. Each formal real incident debrief should have a guide based upon the issues emerging from the incident and this guide should be produced by the debrief team. An example:

---

1. **General overview of incident**

   Chairperson.

2. **Initial notification**
   a) How did we all find out? Was it timely?
   b) Did we tell who needed to know?
   c) Were there 'information only' messages to agencies?
   d) Did any agency stand down another?

3. **Mobilisation**
   a) Were plans utilised?
   b) Actions by agencies?
   c) Was there specialist input or support required?
   d) Was there a need for additional support?

4. **Liaison**
   a) Basic liaison structures put in place? Did it work?
   b) Did we start talking to each other?
   c) Did police commander (Silver) attend the scene and liaise effectively? Was a Forward Command Post (FCP) used?
   d) Was there adequate communication ongoing?

5. **Police Co-ordination—was it**
   a) Clear?
   b) Pro-active?
   c) Decisive?
   d) Inclusive?

6. **Police Co-ordination**
   a) Was formal co-ordination involved—TCC and SCC?
   b) Were they supported by agencies?
   c) Were control room processes easy to use for agencies e.g. messaging, actions and briefings?

7. **Media/Public relations issues**

   a) Media interest—local/national
   b) Media management
   c) Response agencies media co-ordination
   d) Media Briefing Centres

8. **Resourcing**

   a) Enough personnel
   b) Sufficient equipment
   c) IT back-up

9. **Welfare**

   a) Personnel
   b) Health and Safety

10. **Business continuity**

    a) Able to maintain core services
    b) Impact on core business

11. **Areas for improvement—to be taken forward.**

    a) Each agency
    b) Actions—to whom?
    c) AOB

12. **Summary**

    By Chair/Action Recorder taker

13. **Closing**

    By Chair

This list is not exhaustive but is introduced to illustrate a means of adding structure and progression within a debrief yet providing the flexibility that is needed. The closure of this debrief will follow in a similar way to the exercise debrief by describing the process to the final report and the implementing of actions.

TASK 10.4

Outline the key differences between the conduct of an exercise debrief and a real incident debrief.

Completing the Debrief Report

Once the debrief is complete the 'Action Tracking' table document will be populated by the planning team. See Figure 10.2.

The debrief report will be created in draft form and may be set out like this:

No.	Activity Area	No.	Sub Issues	Positive Points	Areas for Improvement	Action Point	To whom 'Owner'	Monitoring Organisation	Completion/ Review Date
1.		1a							
		1b							
		1c							
2.		2a							
		2b							
3.		3a							
		3b							
		3c							
→									

EXERCISE ...............................ORGANISATION/COMPANY ....

Figure 10.2 Action tracking document

1. Foreword—A suitable foreword by the exercise director
2. Distribution list
3. Contents
4. Exercise overview—summary
5. Key Issues arising—top five issues
6. Action tracking table
7. Action tracking process

It is important to keep the document concise, as a complex weighty document will be quite off-putting and less likely to be read.

Implementing findings

This is the final and most critical part of the exercise cycle and the most likely part to fail. Why will it fail? If there is no mandatory or moral imperative to implement lessons learned, for example, following an investigation, inquiry, HSE conviction, media pressure, victim or family pressure it is unlikely that there will be the appetite or drive to take action if the organisation or company is not engaged or committed to learning. This is particularly true where changes or improvements involve spending money. But it can be false economy not to spend this extra money when weighed against the impact an adverse event may have on businesses or any organisation. Some managers may choose to 'risk manage' by not implementing findings but such decisions can come back to haunt.

How do you manage the action tracking to conclusion? A flow chart has been created to illustrate the process. This is inclusive from the beginning of the exercise to the implementation of action—see Figure 10.3.

Overall Action Monitoring

Once the action(s) has been allocated it should be the responsibility of each organisation to ensure the implementation of that action takes place. They become the 'owner' of the action. If it transpires that this has not been done in a reasonable time, the organisation may be held accountable for their failure to do so. It must be remembered that all the debrief material could be disclosed in future inquiries and failure to implement outstanding actions could be construed as potentially negligent.

Therefore, during the debrief meeting consideration should be given to a lead organisation taking the role of overall 'Action Co-ordinator'. The 'Action Co-ordinator' may be designated by the lead organisation that initiated the exercise or led by the co-ordinated response in the real incident. Being the co-ordinator simply means that someone will monitor the action progress relating to that incident from each organisation. This does not mean they have the responsibility or any authority to implement the actions but merely to monitor progress. The 'Action Co-ordinator' may in fact report progress to the Chair or indeed to an official body such as the LRF or relevant sub-group. The LRF may be in a position to highlight critical issues that affect resilience generally in the locality and drive the actions forward or indeed draw attention to an organisation or company that is lacking.

For actions relevant to an individual organisation, a named individual or post holder should be allocated this task as 'Action Administrator' internally. If the exercise is wholly internal the 'Action Administrator' will be

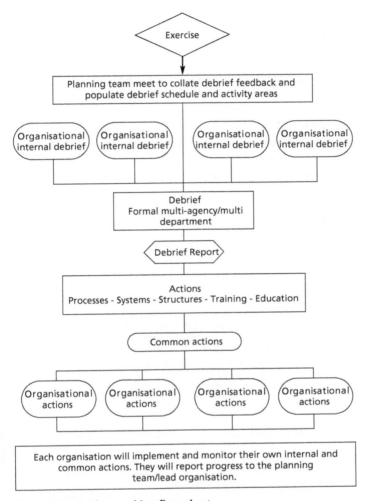

Figure 10.3 Action tracking flow chart

solely responsible to action monitoring. The person who is responsible for the action will be the action 'Owner'. The administrator will contact each owner in turn by e-mail or in writing specifying the action. A completion date should be set along with review dates.

In summary, the monitoring process for a multi-agency exercise or real event will be overseen by a lead Action Co-ordinator, usually from the lead organisation. Then within each participating organisation, an internal Action Administrator will be appointed to follow each action with each action Owner and report back to the Action Co-ordinator. The role of the administrators is shown in Figure 10.4.

These arrangements must be strictly adhered to:

- Give the owner responsibility and measurable accountability.
- Change attitudes and organisational culture as to the importance to organisational learning.

If there is multi-agency action tracking a composite action tracking document will be used by the lead organisation which will specify where the actions lie and who is monitoring. It must be remembered that the multi-agency action tracking document held by the Action Co-ordinator is there to give a general overview of progress—even reporting to the LRF. Individual organisational action tracking by the Action Administrator is the original document and evidence that actions are progressed and completed, and indeed could be cited in inquiries and investigations.

Spreading the word

There will be a need to disseminate any lessons learned within the organisation to ensure that the improvements are fully integrated into plans. How can this be done effectively?

Figure 10.4 Keeping track of actions

- Arrange a seminar exercise when the plan is revised.
- Hold short, half-hour–1 hour, briefings for key staff.
- Post a global e-mail on the system with key points.
- Create an interesting article for an in-house magazine or a poster for rest rooms and canteens.
- Put an article in the local newspaper.
- Arrange to have a short summary taken to key management meetings by a line manager or volunteer to do a short presentation on the exercise—this is where the video will score.
- Arrange to give presentations to interest groups which will energise management when feedback filters through to them.

Whichever method is used to implement the lessons learned it is, without doubt, time and effort well spent. Not fully debriefing is like going into a shop with your hard-earned cash, carefully selecting what you want, paying for it and then leaving the shop without it! An EPO can plan, train and exercise continually but it becomes meaningless unless lessons are implemented and the emergency planning cycle continues, increasing efficiency, developing people and the organisation.

In short debriefing develops resilience across organisations, both public and private in emergency and crisis management, and business continuity management.

Summary

You will now understand:

- The importance of debriefing.
- The differences between an exercise debrief and a real incident debrief.
- The key elements to effective debriefing.
- How to collate information from a variety of exercises.
- How to organise and run a debrief.
- How to track and monitor actions to conclusion.

Conclusion

This Chapter has given insights and practical advice to successfully organise and run a debrief. In addition, it is hoped that the importance of action tracking and implementation has been recognised.

Index